FIRST TIME UP

FIRST TIME UP

An Insider's Guide for New Composition Instructors

BROCK DETHIER

UTAH STATE UNIVERSITY PRESS
Logan, Utah 84322

Utah State University Press
Logan, UT 84322–7800
Copyright 2005 Utah State University Press

The poem "Adjunct" was first published in *Composition Studies,* Spring 1997, and reprinted in *In Praise of Pedagogy,* ed. Wendy Bishop and David Starkey (Portland ME: Calendar Islands, 2000).

Appendix D "In Defense of Subjective Grading," was first published in *North Carolina English Teacher* XXX: 4, Summer 1983.

"The Arrowmaker," a traditional Kiowa story, was retold by N. Scott Momaday and published in *The Way to Rainy Mountain,* © 1969 N. Scott Momaday. University of New Mexico Press. Reprinted by permission.

"Motivation Through Metaphor," by Charles Woodard, was first published in *AWP Newsletter* 17:3, 1985. Reprinted by permission.

Figure 9, Indicators of TA Development, was adapted from Sprague, J., & Nyquist, J. D. (1991), A developmental perspective on the TA role. In J. D. Nyquist, R. D. Abbott, D. H. Wulff, & J. Sprague (Eds.), *Preparing the Professoriate of Tomorrow to Teach: Selected Readings in TA Training* (pp. 295–312). Dubuque, IA: Kendall/Hunt. Used by permission.

Cover design by Barbara Yale-Read

Library of Congress Cataloging-in-Publication Data

Dethier, Brock.
  First time up : an insider's guide for new composition instructors / Brock Dethier.
    p. cm.
  Includes bibliographical references and index.
  ISBN 0-87421-620-6 (pbk. : alk. paper)
  1. English language–Rhetoric–Study and teaching. 2. Report writing–Study and teaching (Higher) I. Title.
  PE1404.D394 2005
  808'.042'0711–dc22
                                   2005021840

To MELODY
who animates my life

CONTENTS

ACKNOWLEDGMENTS

This book distills much of what I've learned about teaching writing since I first graded a student paper thirty years ago. A thorough acknowledgments page would include every student and colleague I've worked with during that time. Without the memory required to create such a list, I will mention only those people directly involved in bringing this book to print.

As she has done often during our thirty-four years together, my wife Melody Graulich provided the initial idea and the firm push for this project. My colleagues in the FHE writing group helped me improve the initial proposal and the most difficult chapter. Tom Newkirk and John Ernest at the University of New Hampshire, Bruce Ballenger and Michelle Payne at Boise State University, and Lynn Meeks at Utah State University shared ideas with me and put me in touch with new graduate students—Alisha Geary, Steve Harrison, Julie Johns, Leslie Lewis, Emma Mecham, Tim Orme, Mandy Page, Rebecca Perkins, Jim Webber—whose insights and fears helped me update my own thoughts. My Spring 2004 Teaching Writing class at USU added to my list of new teachers' concerns.

Rachel Rich interviewed students and combed the Web for me. Susan Andersen co-authored the academic integrity packet, which became Appendix E. Marina Hall, Tim Slocum, and Denice Turner helped keep my wheels on the tracks, while my kids, Corey and Larkin, coped with the old man off in his study again. I owe particular gratitude to Shanan Ballam, who filled in for me when I was on research leave and again when I was sick in 2004; Andrea Barnes, who took over my family duties when I was in the hospital and saved me from a misdiagnosis; Lynn Meeks, who shouldered without complaint the administrative burdens I had to unload; and Sheila McNamee, who explained the distinction between constructionist and constructivist while driving me to radiation treatments.

I hope that the wisdom of Donald Murray infuses this book; the spirit of Murray guides everything I do in a writing classroom, and I'm far from alone in my loyalty to that spirit and to the belief that writing should be fun.

I am grateful to Utah State University and its College of Humanities, Arts, and Social Sciences for a New Faculty Research Grant that supported my work on this project, and to the English department for a research leave that gave me the time to complete it. And thanks to the Northern Rockies Consortium for Higher Education, which sponsored the creation of the ethics packet with its 2003 Instructional Improvement prize.

A nod to someone in the publishing house is, I suppose, obligatory, but I owe particular and unique thanks to Michael Spooner of USU Press. At a writing group meeting where everyone else saw weaknesses in my proposal, Michael saw a book. Here it is.

INTRODUCTION

This book is for people about to teach college composition for the first time ever . . . or for the first time at a particular school . . . or for the first time with the greater independence generally given to adjuncts. It doesn't assume anything about readers or their knowledge of composition— except that they have an interest in teaching well and with enjoyment.

Based on thirty years of teaching composition and a decade of teaching and supervising composition instructors, this book responds both to concerns of my own that I had when I first began to teach and to those of teachers just entering graduate school now. It builds on ideas about improving students' and teachers' attitudes that I have been exploring throughout my career. It attempts to ease new teachers through their first year, providing advice, resources, and insights to help them overcome their fears and make painless and fun what can be a tense time.

This is not a career guide. My *Composition Instructor's Survival Guide*, Wilhoit's *The Allyn & Bacon Teaching Assistant's Handbook*, Haswell & Lu's *Comp Tales*, and anthologies like Corbett, Myers, and Tate's *The Writing Teacher's Sourcebook* or Roen's *Strategies for Teaching First-Year Composition* can provide readers with a more comprehensive sense of the concerns of experienced composition teachers. The issues I discuss do, however, have relevance to everyone in the composition community. Even someone who has taught twenty "first classes" will find something new and amusing to try in my "First Day" chapter, fresh ideas about resources in Chapter 3, and, in Chapter 11, a more positive way to view the skills that writing teachers practice.

The book reflects the limitations of my experience as well as its depths. I do not attempt to give advice about severe behavioral problems, "basic" writers, English Language Learners, learning disabilities, team teaching, online or high-tech courses, or working with ethnic, racial, or cultural minorities. I simply haven't dealt with those issues enough to establish authority about them; you'd be better off consulting experts in those fields rather than reading something secondhand from me.

Having abandoned the idea of making this book a complete guide to teaching composition, I concentrated on making it a slim volume, a companion, not a rule book, intended to fortify, not overwhelm. Because I assumed many busy readers would start with the index rather than the first chapter, you'll find some repetition of ideas from chapter to chapter. I wanted, for instance, to have something about plagiarism both in the syllabus section of Chapter 2 and in "Nightmares," Chapter 9.

The organization of the book imagines a new teacher thinking about a course a few weeks before the first class. I begin with some cheerleading about the job itself, an examination of the barriers that keep us from enjoying it as much as we should, and some suggestions for planning ahead to reduce the stress of the job. After chapters on preparation and on resources, I offer suggestions for making the first day an engaging introduction to the heart of the course.

Once we're sailing through that first week, I slow down to consider the many difficulties of grading, the relevance of theory to our daily activities, the contradictory demands of teaching composition, and ways to protect against the nightmares of the profession. Finally, I look outside the classroom and beyond the end of the year, highlighting the career-building value of what we do, confronting some of the issues that will become more important as the first-year nerves calm.

Although much of this book focuses on the negative, on facing down the worries and nightmares that may bedevil a first-year composition teacher, I expect that most readers will soon be hooked on the positive aspects of the job, and that by the momentous first day, readers will develop enough self-assurance to fully enjoy the experience. I love walking down the halls when the first classes of the semester are letting out, teasing last week's novices with the line, "First time up?" The new teachers are coming out of their classrooms surrounded by students, talking manicly, beaming, and as I pass, they whisper things like, "That was cool!," "They did what I asked!" and "They like me!"

My goal is to help readers enter the classroom well-prepared, confident, humble, and grinning.

1
WHY YOU'VE MADE THE RIGHT CHOICE

It is time to give away the secret: teaching writing is fun.
Donald M. Murray, *A Writer Teaches Writing*

I know, it's pretty cheesy to start a book with a line stolen from someone else's opener. You may think I'm just being lazy, but that isn't my only motivation. As a new composition teacher, you need to get used to borrowing, whether from veterans like me, founding fathers like Murray, or your officemate whose class ends just before yours begins. If you think you're going to do everything your own way, not follow anyone's footsteps, you'll blow fuses before you turn in your first set of grades. Teaching composition is, and as far as I can tell always has been, a cooperative venture: comp teachers share ideas across the hall, across the country, across generations. Give credit when you can, but always remember, in a very real sense, you are not alone.

Murray's quote may have pissed you off when you first read it. You may be nauseous from fear, frantic with last-minute preparations, panicked about everything you don't know. Murray's words may sound like sadistic gloating.

But they're true. Think about it. Although you may be new to the department, you probably already know, or know of, people who finished their graduate study years ago but stick around, teaching a course or two as an adjunct when they can. Most of them eventually move on—it's a rare department that will let adjuncts stay indefinitely. Some find "real" jobs that pay real money. Some go back to school. Some take the plunge to full-time writing. But they don't quit teaching comp because they're bored. People stick to it, come back to it from much better-paying jobs, because it's fascinating. And fun.

Administrators, students, and the job itself may create headaches and make it difficult for you to enjoy yourself. But that's why you bought this book. I wrote it to reduce the barriers and hassles and mysteries of the job, to help you get to the "fun" part as quickly as possible.

WHAT'S FUN ABOUT IT?

Getting the teaching rush. Adrenaline's a powerful drug with impressive effects. You may be sick, worn out, irritated, distracted, but when you walk into your classroom, even years after you've conquered your novice butterflies, you'll get a burst of energy that will carry you through. It may be hours before you remember, "Oh yeah, I barely slept last night." Unless you're unusual, you won't be nervous after a few months (or maybe years) of teaching, but you'll still get "up" for every class.

Being your own boss. In most places, you get to teach what you want. As Steven L. VanderStaay puts it, "Teachers are professionals in the sense that they are not so much told how to do their job as appointed to decide for themselves how best to do it" (96). You'll rarely teach more than twelve hours each week, and you'll control your other work hours: you'll determine when to grade papers, prepare for class, or have conferences, so you can ski or play Grand Theft Auto during the day and work until 2 a.m. if you want. Even if the writing program gives you a book or a syllabus and administrators observe you frequently, to a large extent, you'll be on your own. And that freedom gives you the opportunity to enjoy many other sources of fun, including:

Being creative. If you're a creative writer, you may worry that you have to shelve your creativity while you teach your expository writing classes. But teaching a good comp course requires as much creativity as writing a short story, and few activities produce more and better writing. Writing teachers *should* write as much as they have time for, in front of students and on their own, both to sharpen their own skills and to make fresh and personal the frustrations and triumphs that their students are experiencing. Teachers who have never thought of themselves as "creative" soon find themselves coming up with clever, original ideas for almost every class. How can you interest your students in punctuation? How can you help a young writer develop an anecdote into an essay?

Answering such questions daily can make even your subconscious creative. In the midst of working on this book, I had a teaching anxiety dream (yes, even veterans get them). This one had all the elements: I had forgotten the class—an American lit survey; I couldn't get to my office; I couldn't find the classroom; students jammed the halls; I hadn't ordered the books. But even in the nightmare, I thought like a creative teacher—I figured we'd read James Fenimore Cooper's *The Pioneers* first, and I'd explain to my class that I hadn't ordered the book because it was so readily available in so many editions that I decided to let them save money and buy an old copy wherever they could.

Peeking into other lives. Yes, writing teachers are voyeurs. Benevolent voyeurs. We witness the inner workings of minds at one of the great transitional moments of life. We watch as writers discover that their parents' divorce actually improved their lives, that the religion they grew up with doesn't work for them any more, that the gun control debate has two rational sides, that they really *are* as smart as "kids" half their age. We're bystanders, and sometimes coaches, as students plan their futures and make sense of the lives they've led.

And what fascinating lives to peer into! Do you remember what you were like at eighteen, nineteen, twenty? Or when you went back to school after years at home or on the job? It's a time of rapid, radical change, and comp teachers get to sit in the bleachers, cheer, and sometimes affect this tumultuous race toward maturity. If you're a people watcher, there's no better vantage point.

Learning. If you've gotten this far in the educational system, you probably enjoy learning, not because you get to become some kind of "better person" in the abstract, but because you enjoy doing things you've never done and being places you've never been. You may think that, because you're a teacher, your learning will be limited to pedagogy, but with an enthusiastic student guide, you can imagine yourself as an archaeologist, a computer programmer, an Olympic skier. If you let students choose their own topics, you may learn from a single stack of papers what it takes to be a good cheerleader, how to spike your dirtbike tires to race on ice, and how it feels to be gay in a fundamentalist household. If you respond to that first stack with "Who gives a shit?," you're probably in the wrong business. When most of your dinner conversations start with "I had this student paper on . . . ," you're hooked.

Continuously improving. You can always get better as a writer or teacher. We never completely figure out either activity. That can be a frustrating fact for people determined to *master* their art, but it's also a major attraction of what we do. No two classes, courses, or activities are identical. It's always new, and we can always improve.

I'm not big on setting goals; instead, I like to work in particular directions. Students can advance during a semester in so many different ways—in their ability to articulate complex concepts or use lists or write with sophisticated syntax or learn where commas go. I'm happy to help students advance on any number of fronts, just as I'm trying to learn in a dozen directions at any one time myself.

In business, the old concepts of benchmarks and goals have largely been replaced by continuous improvement—constant monitoring of and tinkering with the system to improve it. Don't imagine that all your students will reach a particular level. Just be happy if they all advance.

Helping. Many in our current political and social climate view altruism as a weakness of suckers and bleeding hearts, and some new teachers seem genuinely embarrassed to say, "I want to help people." But that desire motivates every teacher to some degree. Teaching comp provides opportunities to get a kick out of helping people on every level, from being the first friendly, personal face that new college students see, to making a student's day by responding sympathetically to a computer disaster story, to helping a student get over a lifetime hang-up about semicolons. Our job offers plenty of thanks, if we listen for them and learn how to hear them.

Teaching something useful. Our expertise is practical and universally applicable, and it will never become obsolete. With slight twists in our life stories, some of us could have ended up teaching Greek architecture or calculus, and no doubt we would have derived much teacher satisfaction from those other subjects. But because our subject is one of those "basics" that people think everyone else should return to, we don't need to worry about whether composition will go out of fashion or whether the need for our services will suddenly disappear or whether we're teaching something so arcane our students will never use it unless they end up as teachers themselves. There's plenty to ponder when embarking on a career in composition, but you don't need to worry about the importance of the subject.

Enjoying power. I'm particularly drawn to people in our profession because so many of them are peace-loving, anti-authoritarian sensitive feminists who would never think of using power as some of our predecessors did—to get sex or favors from their students. But that doesn't mean we have to hate power. In fact, the attractiveness of power may be one of the biggest surprises for new comp teachers. Some people hate the dictatorial, illegitimate uses of power so much that they may not have considered the benevolent, *fun* ways they can use power. When you set firm guidelines and deadlines for the first paper, you may be amazed that students don't rise up and revolt. Unless your rules are outrageous or you draw a particularly unfortunate group of students, few will complain. They will accept your power and your use of it, and in the long run they will be glad that you used your authority to motivate their self-discipline. And when a student emails to tell you that the resumé or "statement of purpose" essay "worked," got the job or the acceptance, or your insights on how to play the system were accurate, you'll be glad for the power you have.

Having an effect. Power can get students to do the work, but only power used wisely and well can produce the kinds of effects we want to have. Few things are more gratifying than a student's saying with astonishment, "I didn't know I could do that." When you see students' attitudes and writing and even colon use changing, you will get a sense of efficacy that is one of the main antidotes to burnout . . . and it will in turn make you an even more effective teacher (McLeod 117). And, yes, it's fun.

Enjoying the variety. Teaching writing is seldom dull. Well, sure, if you spend more than five minutes lecturing about punctuation, your students will nod off and so will you. And if you assign paper topics, you will get bored with those subjects. But in general, the work of the composition teacher defies generalizations. Whenever the pundits make sweeping claims about "young people today," we know the limits of the claim, and exceptions spring to mind. Whatever succeeded last semester or last period may well flop today. The work we do on any particular day is as varied as the individuals in our classes and unique as the writing those individuals produce.

Of course, you need to keep your eyes and ears open to capture all the interesting moments that keep us awake and amused—the snatch of conversation between the classmates starting to flirt, the priceless malapropism, the shift in a paper that signals a major revision of perspective, the student story that will come to define your thinking about anorexia or the Piltdown man. As long as you maintain your own curiosity, composition will retain its fascination.

Bonding with peers. Camaraderie may be the most alluring and addicting aspect of the comp teacher's job. An unusual and powerful bond develops when you wander, punchy and bleary, into your neighbor's office after you've both survived a day of three classes or twenty-seven conferences. Or when you suggest just the right activity when your office mate rushes in, frantic for ideas, ten minutes before class. Or when you spend two hours and $10 of beer money grousing about the student who won't shut up or the class that won't talk.

I was intensely grateful for this community of the trenches during my twenty-plus years as an adjunct, and I miss it now that I'm a faculty member, a "real person" with a private, semi-permanent office on the first floor. I don't romanticize the comp slave's life enough to return, at age fifty-two, to the fourth floor and a four/four load. But I do know what I've lost, and the casual professional respect of my current peers does not make up for it. Some of the relationships developed in the comp ghetto survive; most evaporated as we went our separate ways. But for a semester or a decade, they were intense, meaningful, and real, and I would not willingly lose the memories of climbing the stairs into the composition attic, feeling the way many people do when entering their favorite bar or club.

If you're lucky in your first year or two, you may develop a close relationship with someone who doesn't live in the trenches—a "real" professor, perhaps one of the writing program administrators. Such relationships can be tricky, because you may have to shift roles almost instantly, from talking like equals at lunch, to becoming a staff member again when your boss runs the staff meeting, to regressing to "student" in a class you're taking from your professor friend. But if you're careful about observing the boundaries of each different pair of roles, a personal relationship with someone further up the hierarchy can be rewarding for both of you—and can be a major asset in your career advancement. (See "Mentors" in Chapter 3.)

Creating a writing community. We create our own microworld in our classes, and it can be profoundly gratifying if that world is more friendly, cooperative, and creative than the "real" one. Many people invest considerable time in building such a community (see Chapter 4), and I've seen some new graduate instructors ready to burst with pride when relating how their collection of twenty-two first-year students became a supportive, productive, caring group, able to mix work and fun, respectful of each other, their teacher, and writing in general. Students who learn the joys of writing and of talking about writing in such communities will seek out similar experiences in the future . . . and form other writing groups.

Reveling in favorite things. Many teachers feel guilty if they let their life creep into their classroom. But whatever your passions—Romantic poetry, mystery novels, The Simpsons, black-and-white photography—you can productively bring them into the comp classroom. Don't create an intellectual wall between your classroom and the rest of your life. (See Chapter 11.) You won't necessarily share the love poems you're writing to your latest crush or your thesis on Anthony Trollope. But don't rule it out. Look for connections, relevancies. Students love enthusiastic teachers, so if you can increase your classroom enthusiasm by including Trollope, maybe you can wake students up, and maybe you can find a way to use his prose to talk about style. I wrote a whole book—*From Dylan to Donne*—about my habit of bringing music into my classes; maybe the pedagogical uses of your passions deserves a book too.

Ironically, the trickiest enthusiasms to bring into your composition classroom may be ones most closely related to the class topic—journalism and "creative writing" for instance. Both of these siblings of composition have much to teach us. If fiction, for instance, is your passion, you may well find that you can use both the analytical and the creative tools of fiction writing to great advantage in a composition course. The problem is remembering that few of your students will ever write a short story. So, fun and enlightening as they may be, the techniques of fiction writing deserve a place in a comp class only if they advance the goals of composition. It is easy to get lost in the enticements of the activity and forget that it needs to be fun *and* meaningful.

Thinking. In discussions about career choices, inevitably the question comes up, What's the smartest way to think about a career? Many of us move in a particular direction because of someone else's sense of our aptitudes or interests—Barto does well in math, so people tell him to be an engineer; Sonja pursues a business degree because people told her it would make her rich. I'm wary of anyone making important decisions based on others' biases and judgments—even my own, say, in this book. But what's a better way?

I pondered that question one evening after class. It wasn't that I *had* to answer it; no one had asked it directly, and a perfectly legitimate answer would have been, "You've got to figure that out for yourself." But the question interested me, and I wanted an answer for myself. After all, when applying to college I had put "chemistry" in the "intended major" box; my math aptitude was higher than my verbal. And here I was, forty years old, making half my age despite my Ph.D. and years of experience. In those days, career questions were never far from my mind. Finally, I had a moment of epiphany. The right career is one that gives you material that you enjoy pondering, not because you *have to,* but because it's interesting, meaningful, maybe even fun.

Although that was a particularly productive pondering session, it didn't differ radically from what I do almost every night during the school year—rethink what went on during the day's classes. Sometimes I imagine what I could have done differently, but mostly I sketch out what I should do during the following classes to build on, modify, or transform the previous class or reading. The thinking that my job requires engages me on many levels. I miss it during my summers off, and often I find myself planning fall courses long before I need to.

My realization about careers may not be "right" or even particularly useful, but the scene demonstrates the mental delights of teaching comp. Look at the kinds of thinking embodied in this anecdote:

- Connecting the immediate and the long-range. I'm not sure this rates as "fun" for everyone, but if you do it fairly consistently, it protects you against the feeling that you're lost in the trees and can't see the forest.

- Seeing the parallels between my life and my students' lives. I steer students away from teachers who give the impression of handing down wisdom from their throne of knowledge, infinitely elevated above the classroom rabble. I can imagine that that kind of power trip might be attractive, for a while, but it would almost certainly become boring. If you know all the answers, why not write them down, hand them out, and go home? Teaching fascinates when we're tackling a problem that engages our own imagination as well as our students'.

- Creativity. (See above.) Many writing teachers—who should know better!—conceive of creative work in stereotypical ways, linked solely with "creative" arts. But the thinking involved in planning tomorrow's comp class is as creative as it comes. It requires not just talent and training but a willingness to experiment and to move beyond or around traditional, received ideas and attitudes. Every day, we respond in novel ways to novel situations, whether the problem is finding a way to explain "coherence" or figuring out what's "fair" to require of a student hurt in a car crash. At first, such thinking on your feet, without any reliable guide or precedent, scares most new teachers, and you may yearn for the straightforward simplicity of scanning a barcode and counting out change. If you're like me, you may never completely get beyond rethinking your spontaneous decisions and finding better solutions for the illusory "next time." But I hope you'll also find exhilaration in such quick thinking, you'll keep a mental notebook

of your own and others' clever solutions to difficult student problems, and you'll begin to feel that a day of teaching is akin to a
day of surfing or skiing, staying on top as you hurtle along, accepting the falls as all part of the sport.

• Organization. Many people who go into composition teaching
  identify themselves as the artsy, disorganized type, the type that
  can't keep appointments straight and who lose three grade books
  each year. But if you're going to survive as a teacher, or in just
  about any other independent job, you'll have to find ways to get
  organized and keep track of things. And I'm betting that you'll
  actually enjoy it.

  Most aspects of teaching composition could be described as
  barely controlled chaos: the classroom itself, often a five- or six-
  ring circus (though the ringmaster doesn't have a whip); your
  gradebook, where you may try to keep track of everything from
  who talked on what day to what subjects everyone's working on;
  and of course the papers, perhaps multiple drafts of the same
  paper, some coming in, some headed back to students, some just
  waiting to be marked in the book. You may borrow organizational
  ideas from this or other books or from peers or mentors, but
  within a year you'll have a system different from anyone else's,
  and you'll be modifying it for the rest of your career. This prospect may strike you as anything but fun, but remember: it's the
  chaos, and the prospect of dealing with chaos, that is so daunting.
  Taming that chaos, making it orderly, is fun. And the process may
  show you strengths you never knew you had, strengths that can
  carry over to other areas of your life.

*I urge those who are wondering about it to become writing teachers. Few things in our
society are less alienating, less immobilized by competition and greed, more likely to bring
us in contact with those from all parts of society, more likely to make it possible to par-
ticipate in both individual and social growth, more involved in exchanging important
thoughts and feelings with others, more relaxed and intense at once, and more joyful and
less sad even in frustration and failure. (David Bleich, 62)*

WHAT STANDS IN YOUR WAY?

The rest of this book attempts to identify and slay (or at least sneak by)
the demons that make it difficult for some people to enjoy teaching

comp. Most new writing teachers share very similar worries, yet often they feel alone with their worries and silly for having them. So I want to list a few right off the bat. I'll provide some quick antidotes now; look for others as you read on.

1. Fear and lack of confidence

Everyone starts here. I'll never forget the secretary laughing at me as I hyperventilated in the courtyard before my first class. And the reassurances—"You'll do fine!"—made me feel as bad as the laugh. So this book will take your fears seriously, present some worst-case scenarios to keep you from being surprised, and try to separate legitimate fears from worries that will likely prove groundless. One piece of advice for now (and this will be my prescription for many problems mentioned in this book): find a sympathetic veteran and share your fears. Get them out of the closet, name them, laugh at them. The worst thing you can do is live alone with your fear.

Susan McLeod offers a valuable metaphor:

> The choir directors of my youth used to say we should be keyed up rather than nervous, so as to perform at peak. Channel that energy, they would say—make your butterflies fly in formation. (1)

New teachers must transform the nervous energy we all feel into the classroom energy that many students love and most students count on. Get those butterflies into formation and you may turn that incipient nausea into enthusiasm.

2. Time

Yes, if I had a way of stretching time, I wouldn't be sweating in front of a screen writing books about composition. Much of my *Composition Instructor's Survival Guide* focuses on saving time, and I will give as much advice as I can in this book. But no one ever conquers the issue of time.

I can almost guarantee that you will be astonished by the amount you can get done in a semester. I still look back on some semesters and ask, "How did I make it through?" The first step in feeling less oppressed about time should be identifying what's crucial for the upcoming semester and where you can cut some corners. Desperate, many new teachers assume that "work" is crucial and "life" can be sacrificed, but for grad students, even that flip answer doesn't suffice. Your graduate advisor will remind you that you are, first, a student; your writing director may argue that your own students come first. Thinking ahead about how you're going to reconcile those incompatible claims on your time may save you some agony later.

3. Volume

We're overwhelmed. The problem isn't just time and organization; it's the sheer volume of stuff—stuff that your writing director wants you to learn (like the difference between reader-based prose and writer-based prose, or how to teach the insights of social construction); stuff that everyone assumes you know but you don't (like the difference between a gerund and a participle); stuff you feel you ought to know to be a good teacher (like every student's name).

Face it: composition's an overwhelming business. This book will help you sort the crucial from the trivial and give you some handle on the crucial, but the feeling of trying to surf a landslide won't ever completely leave you. Two interrelated "secrets" about this feeling:

- learning to write better is a huge, lifelong task; students could productively take a writing course every semester throughout college without much repetition and without feeling "done." So give up right now any thought you have of covering "everything" or solving all of a writer's habitual problems. No one can, and trying may make you skim everything.

- take it a day at a time. The best anyone can do is to make sure that every minute (well, almost every minute) of the day is productive and students are learning something, whether classmates' names or how to organize a long paper.

4. Imposter Syndrome

We all feel like impostors at some point, and anyone who claims, "I can teach you to write," *is* a fraud, since the best we can do is help people learn, help them improve. But when we feel fraudulent, it's not that generalized, philosophical kind of fraud we're talking about. It's the "I don't know what the hell I'm doing" kind.

I'm not sure I'd trust someone who has never wrestled with the imposter feeling, and no one can seriously claim to know *everything* about teaching writing. I felt most fraudulent myself when I taught my first business writing class, since I had no background in business or business writing and in fact considered capitalism a destructive, immoral force. But the students liked me because I was a voice of warm-n-fuzzy humanism in the MBA world of productivity benchmarks. We figured out together how to apply my knowledge of writing to the writing challenges they faced in the business world.

It's probably obvious to you how much you *don't* know about your job, but think about how much you *do* know, starting with the insights and generalizations that come from attention to your own writing, and including any books and articles you've read, classes you've taken, conferences you've attended. It's worth reminding yourself every day of the simple but fundamental point that Edward Corbett makes: "students can learn whatever the teacher knows that they do not know" (2). And the most important thing students can learn may be the most basic: "a thirst and a respect for knowledge and a sterling set of intellectual and moral values" (4). A sixty-minute writing class might require four or five clever, practical activities. If you can come up with those for each class, you're producing the same kind of course that a veteran creates. Unless you call attention to your unworthiness—a big mistake!—your students will probably never imagine that this might be your first course.

Teachers establish their authority and legitimacy in a variety of ways, and the vast majority of students automatically respect anyone with the teacher label; authority is yours to keep or lose. We'll talk about many ways to maintain that authority, but the key one is simply to act like a professional. There may be questions you can't answer, and you can't necessarily prepare for them. But you *can* always be to class on time, prepared, with everything functioning. You can learn names in the first couple of weeks, return papers quickly, do what you said you were going to do, when you promised it. Your syllabus alone can assure students you're someone to take seriously, as it establishes high, specific standards and assumes sincere, adult work from students.

Professional sloppiness and self-deprecation eat away at students' respect more quickly than an occasional "I don't know." So don't start the semester saying "I'm a greenhorn bottom-of-the-heap graduate instructor" or "I'm only an adjunct." If you project an air of authority, students probably won't question it, and you'll gradually grow into the self that you're projecting. As my colleague Bruce Ballenger says, you need to get students to focus on *their* performance, not yours.

Elizabeth Rankin suggests that the fraud feeling for beginning teachers arises because these teachers "don't yet *feel* the authority they've been given, so they try to act it out in ways that feel false even to them. In the process, what they lose is the chance to relate easily with students, the chance to use their youth and shared culture to advantage in their teaching" (5). Take advantage of your youth (or your wisdom), your cultural knowledge, the things you know that impress students.

When you're feeling guilty one day after faking it once again, consider the glorious consequences of "fudging it." According to Ruth Freeman Swain, "Fudge . . . was probably discovered when a batch of caramels was 'fudged,' or ruined" (1). May all fakes have such consequences.

5. Grammar

The fear of being revealed as a grammar fraud terrifies many beginning writing teachers. We're supposed to be experts on grammar, right? So what do you do when a student asks a grammar question about which you don't have a clue?

First, it probably won't happen. I don't think I've ever had a student ask me, "What part of speech is that?" or "How would you diagram that sentence?" They're as afraid of exposing their ignorance as you are, and they have no motivation to get into the subject in the first place. If a student ever does ask me such a question, I tend to answer with something like "Why does it matter?" Many students have the same warped impression that the general public has about writing—that the most important stuff is what's easiest to test. So a picky grammar question can occasion a quick discussion about the kinds of decontextualized language identification and testing students have been subjected to.

And when you just don't know, it's *much* better to say "I'll get back to you on that" than to give a wrong answer. Responding honestly can teach students an important lesson about writers' priorities: "I haven't done that stuff since junior high; I'll have to look it up. Like most writers, I make that kind of decision by ear or instinct or I check a handbook during proofreading." Even when I have a good answer myself, I may respond to a student's question with "Anybody?" Often a few students at least *think* they know grammar, and they may disagree long enough to give you a chance to come up with either an answer or a way to punt. Make it a research project. "Can you look that word up for us and bring us a definition next class?"

Finally, we should be ready to quote the famous conclusion reached by the authors of *Research in Written Composition* over forty years ago and confirmed by scores of researchers since: "the teaching of formal grammar has a negligible or, because it usually displaces some instruction and practice in actual composition, even a harmful effect on the improvement of writing" (Braddock, Lloyd-Jones, Schoer 37-38). So don't feel guilty if you're not doing daily grammar drills. You're in the best of company.

Figure 1
The Road Signs of Writing

Try making punctuation decisions by thinking of punctuation marks as road signs that give readers quick and accurate information of what is to come. Your options are few and straightforward, and they can be arranged in a rough hierarchy, from periods (which the British call "full stops"), down to parentheses, which some readers barely notice.

.	Full stop. Prepare to shift gears, though you may be able to roll right through.
,	Take a breath, now, and prepare for a curve.
:	Restatement coming: example, definition, or quotation.
;	Reaching the end of one independent clause; prepare for another.
—	Prepare for a sharp curve—watch the cliff on the right!—or a change in road surface.
(	You can ignore this (if you want to).

Examples of the final four:

- We need five things for the picnic: eggs, salt, spoons, cake, and ants.

- He's a no-good man: he dropped her with a thud. *Note that you could also use a semicolon here, but the colon gives the reader more precise information.*

- John Kennedy was right: "Ask not what your country can do for you."

- You can end an independent clause with many marks of punctuation; a semicolon, however, is the only one that assures a reader another independent clause is coming before the period.

- He named his son Walter—his enemy's name!—and his daughter Mourning Glory.

- She moved here from Philadelphia (a beastly place, in my opinion), and she hasn't been back East since.

Because the teaching of grammar frustrates teachers and angers politicians, many smart minds have tackled the issue, and you can find plenty of help if you want to do grammar "right." Constance Weaver's *Teaching Grammar in Context* is a fine all-around source, while Rei Noguchi's *Grammar and the Teaching of Writing* has a more limited focus but includes a wonderfully creative way to teach sentence boundaries. Muriel Harris and Katherine E. Rowan's "Explaining Grammatical Concepts" describes how to set up grammar questions efficiently and orchestrate practice to teach particular concepts.

New teachers are often terrified of grammar because they're well aware of their own grammatical weaknesses, but with some courage, those weaknesses can become strengths, as you explore with the class the difference between hyphens and dashes or the reason we use possessives before gerunds. If you can remember your own frustration when you felt that you wrote well but did badly on grammar tests, and if you can get beyond the punitive feeling—"I had to suffer diagramming sentences, so my students should too"—your empathy will serve you and your students well. And you'll soon see improvements in your own writing and in your ability to explain subtle points to your students.

6. Age

The first class I ever taught was at a community college in rural Virginia. I was twenty-four. The average student was twenty-eight. It turned out to be one of the friendliest courses I've ever taught, and the students gave me some of the best evaluations of my career. Some were young enough to think I was cool, others old enough to pity this scared young grad student. I'm not suggesting this is a typical experience. I just think age—that is, youth—is as likely to work for you as against you. Near the end of his remarkable career, Edward Corbett encouraged composition teachers to "really or vicariously [project] ourselves back into the status of students"(8). If you've recently made the switch from student yourself, that crucial projection should be easy.

You may have a student who doesn't respect you because of your age, old or young. But you also may have a student who can't respect you because of your argyle socks or the cut of your backpack. Youth confers on you advantages that you won't fully appreciate until they're gone. The advantages of experience are more obvious—as your expertise and your resumé grow, you'll be more relaxed and confident in class. But as you get wiser, you're getting older too, and each year your students treat you more like a parent, less like a friend.

7. Fearing the Job Can't Be Done

You're probably well aware of the shortcomings of your own writing, but you may not yet believe what old fogies like me will tell you—that all writers are learners and we never reach a point where we can say, "Now I know all about it and can teach it." It's true you can't teach someone to write, in the same sense that you can't make a horse drink. But if students have even a modicum of motivation, you can help them learn.

Virtually any writing resource can help you help your students; almost every writing text now includes pages of ideas on how to come up with topics, focus, organize, format. You may feel least capable of helping students with their style, but many excellent books are available: Richard Lanham has written a number of books based on his "Paramedic Method," a quick step-by-step approach to making writing more direct and active, and Joseph Williams's *Style* will satisfy any student's curiosity about the subtleties of English.

And you'll probably discover that the "help" students need most is not some kind of linguistic expertise but a willingness to listen, to read carefully and ask good questions, to engage with the ideas. Ironically, people skills may be more important for most writing teachers than writing knowledge. And improving students' attitudes about writing almost certainly benefits them more in the long run than helping them learn the vocabulary of grammar.

8. Lack of Concrete Benefits

This book enumerates scores of benefits of teaching composition, but none are as palpable, as obvious, as universally recognized, as unambiguous as a decent paycheck or a "Professor" before your name. When you're degraded in all the categories that society values most, it's difficult to see the benefits of the job, and even when someone points them out to you, it's hard not to think "what bullshit rationalization!" As David Foster put it twenty years ago, "Teaching writing is [or at least can be] a uniquely thankless job" (2). Or as I put it once, myself:

ADJUNCT

With a Bartleby of Arts
and a doctorate in Denial,
I've survived four chairs,
three deans and

six or eight directors.
Student butts beyond count
have squirmed in my one chair.
My floor is white with dead letters.
My recycling box is always full.
Take the stairs to the top—
no penthouse here—
hang lefts until you see the end.
Where the hallway dies, that's me—
King of the Dead End,
Master of Intermission,
Sultan of Sour Grapes.
The ceiling is low,
the walls very high,
there's a window into a shaft.
The perfboard's covered
with crayoned monsters,
tales of freak beheadings,
the shelves are filled with
books thrown out by those who rose.
Read the screed
outside my door,
genuflect before you knock—
in a year if you're lucky
you'll be on the tenure ladder
at the College of Great Benefits
while I'm teaching your replacement
how to climb.

A large percentage of people who end up teaching composition profess not to buy into American materialist culture. I don't know whether that means that neo-hippies flock to composition or whether everyone who survives in composition does so by becoming cynical about the benefits they're not getting. In any case, you'll be happier at this job if you can persuade yourself that money and status really don't matter. The search for intrinsic benefits will pay off, but the search for professional pay for professional composition teaching probably won't. I'm not saying, "sell yourself short" or "stop agitating for better working conditions." I just don't want you holding your breath until you get what you deserve.

9. The Groucho Marx Syndrome

Groucho famously said that he didn't want to belong to any club that would accept him as a member, and new composition teachers, already feeling like frauds and suckers, getting paid badly for work they're not sure they or anyone can do well, may question the value of the whole enterprise. The secret to combatting this syndrome will become clear to you slowly—while the composition club may not have the cachet of the Shakespeare Society or the theory cabal, comp teachers know that the goal of improving students' writing is practical, reachable, and almost universally supported. Few other disciplines can make similar claims.

10. Your Expectations

The belief that the job is a stopover, a transition on the way to greater things can destroy any hope you have of enjoying it or sticking with it. It's true that few people spend their careers teaching comp, but drifting across disciplinary boundaries occurs in most academic areas, especially as teachers become administrators or researchers. When I was starting out, very few people went to school to teach writing—composition teachers were literary scholars sidetracked by the fascination of their comp classes or the realization that that's where the jobs were. Some people do teach comp for just a semester or two and go on to other things. But don't assume that this will be your route. Put yourself into it, give it a decent shot. And then you can decide where you want to end up.

If you're like me and many other composition teachers, the greatest barrier to your having fun may be your own critical makeup. We remember the one negative evaluation, not the twenty-three positive ones. We berate ourselves for the one typo in the eight-page syllabus. If you tend to be that way, the best favor you can do for yourself is to notice the good moments—the *thank you*'s, the relieved faces when students discover you're human, the sudden small improvements in a student's writing. Celebrate finishing a class right on time having accomplished exactly what you'd planned. Savor those moments, *feel* them. If you can't come to view such moments as *the* reward, you won't last long in composition.

YOU KNOW YOU'RE IN THE WRONG JOB WHEN . . .

Teaching composition isn't for everybody. Even those of us who devote an entire career to composition wonder on occasion if we really should have pursued that interest in glass blowing. So how do you tell if your frustration with your teaching now will last for years? If you're really not cut out to read seventy-three ten-page essays over a weekend?

I gave one answer, the most serious one, at the end of the first section of this chapter: if the job engages your imagination, if you're thinking about it at night, on weekends, during the summer, then you've found a profession. But if many of the following seem familiar to you, it might be time to reconsider plan B.

Avoiding the Stack of Papers in the Study Has Led You to Clean the House So Maniacally That You Break a Knuckle on Your Scrubbing Hand Trying to Get the Grout Behind the Toilet.

All teachers get tired of grading papers, no matter what clever alternatives to traditional grading they use. I get antsy about reaching the bottom of the stack, but I seldom have to fake interest in the next paper. If you really don't give a shit, five hundred more papers over the next few years will not change your mind.

All Your Students Irritate You, and You Find Yourself Wanting to Respond to Their Incessant Self-Centered Griping with "Whatever."

Perhaps some quantitative comp person could devise a way to measure a teacher's level of unhappiness by determining what percentage of the class currently drives the teacher crazy:

95% look for other work

50% you've got a few more years in you if you can concentrate on the good students

0% you must be onto some good drugs.

All of Your Students in One Course or One Semester or of One Sex Blend Together into One Undifferentiated JanelleJanineJayneyJudyJill.

The vast majority of students who move through our classes are pleasant and reasonably well motivated. They don't cause problems. They don't demand much from us, and they may even thank us on the course evaluations. That can be great, but what keeps most of us teaching, I think, are the individuals, the two or three each semester that connect with us in important ways, the ones we know we've affected. Worry if you can't remember a single outstanding student from a recent class.

Your Inner Sadist Has Begun to Love Teaching. "Squirm!" Has Become Your Favorite Silent Command.

I sometimes feel that students treat me like a dartboard, and that makes me want to yank the darts from my own head and send them back. I need to catch myself when I find myself gleefully marking down another "late" in my book, knowing that the infraction will push the offender to another level of punishment.

Words Bore You.

It's not a crime to be uninterested in language. I'm not interested in opera, and I'll still show my face on a big-city street, at least during the day. But if you don't like playing Scrabble or Boggle, if figuring out how to put it just right always frustrates and never rewards, if you tire quickly of your friend's clever punning, if you just don't care about the different uses of "which" and "that," then you might be smart to get out of such a word-oriented business.

You Survive by Hoping for Tomorrow, but Tomorrow Never Comes.

This delicate issue requires some soul-searching. It may even be a religious issue, since it comes down to a question of living for the present or living for some imagined future.

I taught composition as an adjunct for nineteen years. The pay improved slowly, we finally got benefits, I expanded my repertoire of classes . . . but my job was never going to change in a significant way. And I wasn't holding my breath. I thought the work intrinsically interesting enough, and valuable enough, to be worth doing as I was doing it . . . and I was lucky enough to have a spouse who made "real" money (for academia). I had lots of other jobs on the side, and figured I was just as likely to write the Great American Novel with teaching as my day job as I was to do it making ten times as much selling insurance.

What I'm saying is: that decision—to try to be happy with my head pressed against a glass ceiling—required a particular temperament and a particular set of circumstances, and I'm not by any means advocating it for everyone.

You need to become aware of what you're feeling as you work—a time when you're usually too busy to monitor your happiness level. For me, the clearest indication that I don't like the work is that I become hyperconscious of time. The clock refuses to move and the bell refuses to ring, as happened as we waited for lunch hour in high school. Five o'clock starts looking so good, I can't believe it will ever really come.

Teaching composition—and especially holding conferences—makes me punchy, hyped, exhausted, euphoric, depressed . . . sometimes all at the same time, but it doesn't leave me craving five o'clock.

●　　●　　●

There's nothing wrong with seeing this job as a phase. But if it's a phase from hell, you need to transition quickly.

2
PREPARING

Some people postpone worry and stress by simply not thinking about upcoming tasks until they absolutely have to, then running around frantically trying to get everything done, hoping that nothing breaks or goes awry and that they've accurately predicted how much time they will need. This chapter, and indeed much of this book, is not for such people. It's for worriers like me, people who are quite certain that something will go wrong and who can best reduce their stress by imagining what will break and readying the materials they will need to fix it or head off catastrophe.

One word of warning: it *is* possible to overprepare. You may be overdoing it if

- you've rehearsed what you're going to say so often that when it comes time to say it, your voice does the job without towing your brain along. Your lecture comes out of a zombie's mouth

- you've got every minute and detail so well planned that one deviation, one adjustment, sends you into a tizzy

- you know the answers to your questions so well that you save students the effort of thinking and just give the answers yourself.

Get the picture? The problem isn't really overpreparing, it's that you've shut your mind off, so you're not actively engaged in teaching. Luckily, in your first year you'll have so much to do to get ready for your courses that you won't have time to overprepare.

Assuming you're not a last-minute person and you do want to spend some time to reduce the chaos and trauma of the first week, what should you do?

TAKE THOSE SILLY WORRIES SERIOUSLY

That's what Chapter 8 is about. I try to imagine the worries that you might have (I'm a professional worrier, so it didn't take much imagination) and suggest how to combat them. But even a professional worrier can't predict everything that will make you lose sleep. Spend some time with a sympathetic piece of paper that won't laugh at your worries. If confronting them on paper doesn't help, find someone who can face them down with you, perhaps in the pages of Wendy Bishop and Deborah C. Teague's *Feeling Our Way: A Writing Teacher's Sourcebook.* In it, fifteen new teachers describe some of the things that bothered them in their first year of teaching, from worrying about their nipples showing to debating whether to try to hide their accent.

For me, confronting worries on the day before helps me avoid too much trauma on the day itself. For instance, I determine ahead of time what to wear. My advice for the first few days? Whatever makes you most at ease. That doesn't necessarily mean the clothes that are most "you," the ones you wear to putter at home. I know some normally casual men who wear a sport coat and tie the first day of class, just for that little boost of authority. You don't want to be asking yourself, in the first fifteen minutes of the semester, "Does this shirt really go with these pants?"

Another issue that you don't want to confront on your first day: What will students call you? Again, your comfort should be your guide; there's no right and wrong, no rules to follow. I feel uncomfortable being called anything but "Brock"—especially because everyone butchers my last name. However, colleagues I respect and admire insist on being called "Doctor" or "Ms."

All such decisions involve adjusting distance, and there's no way to determine the ideal distance from your students until you've taught for a while. Some teachers close to students in age and outlook prefer to have students use a title, while some whose demographics now make them alien to their students try to close that gap by insisting on first names.

Take some time to go through the first day in your mind, note anything that worries you, and figure out how to relieve that worry. Afraid you'll forget something crucial? Start a list right now of the things you want to bring to class and add to it whenever you obsess about something new. Uptight about repeating yourself (Wilkerson 10)? Don't be. Supervisors encourage it and students expect it.

Worried about equipment? Find the room you'll be in and check everything from the placement of electrical outlets to the presence (or absence) of chalk or markers. (I always keep extra markers in my pack; you never know when the previous teacher will walk away with them.) Try out your voice in the empty classroom, find the closest bathrooms, determine whether there will be distractions from a noisy hall or people outside the windows.

"Memorize your first sentence; everything will follow after that," advises a consultant with the University of Virginia's Teaching Resource Center, which recommends that new teachers "use many acting techniques such as relaxing, energizing and warm-up exercises; breathing techniques; and vocal practice" (Wilkerson 11).

Few of us ever become the smooth-tongued orators that we'd like to be, and for a few semesters I'd try not even to think about your imperfections as a lecturer. If you're in a program that videotapes new instructors, you'll have to confront soon enough your failings as a stand-up intellectual. (When I first heard myself on videotape—and only Pennsylvanians who remember Mayors Frank Rizzo or H. J. Tate can appreciate the depths of despair here—my reaction was, "He sounds like he comes from Philadelphia!") You know the obvious do's and don't's of public speaking: face your audience, make eye contact, don't mumble or go too fast, don't fill empty moments with self-deprecation (Wilkerson 11). Practice that first sentence, and when you get to the end, with your list of the day's activities in front of you, imagine what it will feel like to soar into the role that you will almost certainly love.

Once again, your imagination is your friend.

WORK FOR COHERENCE, SHORT- AND LONG-TERM

No, I'm not adding yet another worry to your list; I'm encouraging you to plan, so that you can avoid lots of little worries throughout the semester, especially worries of the "Why am I doing this?," "What should I do next?," and "What's the point?" variety.

Long Term

Nothing more debilitates or demoralizes us as teachers than feeling, in the mid-semester doldrums, that we're just making busywork, finding things to fill time, randomly appropriating exercises. It's a struggle to do much about that feeling when you're in the middle of it, lost in the trees and unable to see the forest. But if you spend an hour or so planning in the summer, you'll be confident throughout the semester that you can answer those questions—in fact, you did, back in August.

What Kind of Coherence Am I Talking About?

First, the whole semester needs some kind of shape or form; assignments, activities, emphases need to be sequenced in a way that makes sense to you and your students and that builds toward major assignments and projects. You could certainly create a course out of thirty or forty-five discrete days and activities, unrelated to each other or to any larger whole. Assuming you chose the individual activities well, students might learn a lot from such a course, but I don't think it would feel intellectually satisfying for most of us. And while students might recall individual activities, a class of fragments wouldn't build students' overall base of knowledge as well as would a class in which everything ties together. To remember something, we have to link it to something we already know. If a student gets introduced to the concept of "writing process" on day one and engages in some kind of writing process activity almost every day for the rest of the semester, she may retain some knowledge of the general concept, some sense that she can approach any writing task in a variety of ways, even if she forgets all the individual activities.

What Shapes Could a Composition Semester Take?

When I was just starting out, a colleague, Dan Regan, suggested a sequencing strategy on which I still base most of my writing courses: make the semester itself mirror the writing process for an individual paper. Start with ways of coming up with ideas, move to approaches for sorting those ideas and choosing a good one, on to focusing, developing, researching, peer reviewing, revising, proofreading, publication. Of course, in practice, this process is somewhat recursive (as are most writing processes)—half way into the course you might be helping students come up with ideas for a new paper on the same day as they proofread a paper they began in week one.

As a general scheme, this one has great advantages. It's simple and commonsensical, so teachers and students have no problem remembering it; it's flexible; it provides teachers with ready answers to the question, "What should I do next?"; it helps align students' priorities by focusing on content and ideas for weeks before turning to grammar and punctuation; it can easily expand or contract and mesh with other schemes.

You can take a class through an entire process in an hour, writing for two- or three-minute blocks on note cards, or show students how someone writing a book might expand the process to well over a semester. If the course mixes literature and writing, you can go through one process starting with the students' own ideas, then another one that starts with responses to literature. The simple principle, which could be phrased "start at the beginning and move to the end," provides a logical basis for endless variations.

Many teachers develop long-term coherence, too, by creating a logical progression of paper assignments. Almost any progression would be defensible; you just need to have a logic for yourself and for your students. My logic depends on my goals and what kinds of writing my students have experienced. I most often start with a personal paper—something students can write pretty much out of their own heads—and then move to progressively less personal assignments, ending with a research paper or researched essay that combines traditional "objective" research with the personal. Personal papers aren't necessarily easier for students to write than research papers; in fact, some students in the sciences, used to writing research papers, find it very difficult to express opinions or write about themselves. But I start with the personal because it forces students to see right away that their own ideas and experiences do have a place in college papers and can provide the basis for much academic writing. It would be just as logical to start with an external focus and move to the internal.

Another approach is to organize by workload. Students haven't read enough or discussed enough to write big papers at the beginning of the semester, especially research or response-to-literature papers. On the other hand, students often complain about having too much work due at once at the end. So in a reading-oriented class, I plan the bulk of the reading for the first half of the semester, with only short reading responses, and then space the major papers out over the second half. In a student-friendly variation, students write the bulk of the papers before the last month, then revisions or smaller papers in the final weeks. In courses with less reading, I space big papers evenly throughout the semester and plan smaller assignments in the off weeks. It's always good to space papers relatively evenly, so students have time to get feedback and perhaps do revisions on one paper before they focus on the next.

You will, of course, never please all your students; some will have two exams and a paper due for another class in week eleven, which you had figured would be a slack time when you could require extra work.

Or you can organize by student roles. I've used this principle most often in upper-level courses with students who are planning to be teachers, but it could be a way to think about any course, especially if the course includes a public-speaking or presentation component. At the beginning of the semester, students naturally slip into the traditional "student" role, relatively quiet, passive, and obedient. As the course progresses, students can take on more responsibility, more autonomy, more control of what gets said and done in class, moving from closely supervised small groups into more independent small groups, and climaxing in groups or individuals leading whole segments of the class.

Many teachers' default mode of achieving coherence is to follow the text. If you rely heavily on a text, it makes sense to use it as your course backbone, rather than have two different skeletons underlying everything you do. Authors put together some texts so intelligently that their organizational scheme becomes an important focus of class discussion. Moffett and McElheny's *Points of View,* for instance, is a reader that follows Moffett's taxonomy of narrative perspectives, from interior monologue to "anonymous narration—no character point of view." Bruce Ballenger's *The Curious Researcher* takes students through a non-traditional research-writing process, first asking them to question all their assumptions about research papers, then helping them build a researched essay based on their own interests and predilections.

However, instead of bending everything else to fit a book's organization, I feel more comfortable coming up with my own coherence for the semester and fitting textbook chapters into it. So I would follow the text, but with these caveats:

- Determine the book's main goals, and see if they resemble your class goals. Maybe the book emphasizes writing with style (with lots of pointers about creating tight, graceful, elegant sentences), while you concentrate on writing to learn, and you want activities that will help students brainstorm, focus, organize. Or maybe you want to make literature a larger or smaller part of the course than the text does. I'm not suggesting you should throw out the textbook and wing it; I'm just saying that if you know where you and the text are headed, you can work out the best convergence.

- Be sure the text itself has an organizing principle that you understand and accept. Some older writing texts began with an emphasis on the word and then built to sentence, paragraph, and finally whole papers. That quite logical organization would be disastrous in most teachers' hands.

  It's too easy to assign a chapter each week without asking "Why is the book ordered this way?," "Is it the best order for my class?" and "Does each focus deserve the same emphasis?" If you discover the organization of the book only when your students do, you're not going to be able to make the best use of it.

- Question each chapter. Individual chapters wind up in a textbook for all sorts of reasons, many of them having nothing to do with pedagogy—maybe documentation issues are fashionable among publishers, or an editor is fascinated by logical fallacies or writing about films. Unless you're only using one book and/or it's short, you probably won't have students read every word. So pick and choose.

A word about teaching with a text (or even a syllabus) given you by your department or program: unless the writing directors are obsessive micromanagers, you'll still have plenty of freedom, and you may come to appreciate having some decisions made for you. Find out from veterans and administrators what's required and what's just suggested, what your boundaries really are. If you're told what kinds of papers to assign, you can probably still choose whether to emphasize voice or persuasiveness or style or organization. Even if you're given a grading rubric, you can still exercise creativity and choice in *how* you teach students to achieve the prescribed organization or style.

The same holds true for the readings. If you're told to teach an essay you're not crazy about, you can have students critique it, find its strengths and weaknesses, knock the professional author off the pedestal. It's always good for students to see that even published essays fall short and could benefit from revision. You can use the reading as a model, good or bad; have students expand on it or argue against it; study its lead, end, or general persuasiveness; analyze how the author creates its voice. The possibilities are endless.

In any case, don't let yourself be bullied by a text or a syllabus; if you see yourself as mechanically carrying out the instructions of an author or writing director, you won't enjoy your job and you probably won't do it well. I'm not suggesting that you fight city hall, at least in your first semester; respect the limitations you work under, but see them as a challenge, perhaps even a spark, to your imagination. All writers are used to working under various kinds of restraints—of form, material, length, time, audience. We just accept those restraints as a given and strive to make, for instance, profound beauty out of the seventeen syllables that haiku "allows." The same holds true for teaching. If the restraints make you feel straitjacketed, ask veterans where they find wiggle-room.

Far from being mutually exclusive, these organizational principles work well together. In fact, this last one would almost certainly need to be combined with one of the others. And I'm not advocating rigid adherence to anything. But you'll feel better about your whole course if you always know how a particular activity fits into a larger scheme. If none of the above appeals to you, look around; almost any recent writing text includes suggestions about the movement of a semester and the sequencing of assignments. James D. Williams, for instance, develops a rationale for sequencing assignments very different from mine (282-288).

Short Term

So you've got the whole semester moving logically and you feel good about the course goals. Why worry about day-to-day coherence?

Again, the answer is less stress for you, more learning for students. To make a class or a week of classes coherent, simply pay attention to connections. Of course, planning can help—choose the perfect reading to dovetail with a particular writing assignment, or read the speaker's work just before he or she gives a talk. But good planning doesn't necessarily eliminate the gaps between the day's classroom activities. I observe a lot of seasoned teachers who no doubt planned the day's activities based on a sense of continuity and thematic ties, but they don't emphasize those ties during class, so the class session sometimes feels like a series of discrete segments. Such a class may leave the teacher dissatisfied, and since students often don't see the big picture no matter how well it's presented to them, they're almost certainly going to miss it if we don't point it out . . . which most likely means they'll forget the day's activities within hours. As E. M. Forster said, "Only connect." You can link almost any pieces of a class, and forcing yourself to summarize and show connections may yield some surprising insights. Just ask yourself what the links are, then let students know about them in overviews and reviews and in transitions from one segment to the next. Sounds rather like writing a coherent paper, doesn't it? If we taught the way that we advocate students should write, we'd all be stars.

HANDOUTS AND OVERHEADS

In the weeks before your first class, scope out how the department gets text to students. I'm a fan of the copy machine (and the recycling bin), but budgets and departmental histories and biases probably determine copying policy more than convenience. Does the department expect you to do everything on overheads? If so, does every classroom have a functioning machine? Are you encouraged to make a course packet and have students buy it from the bookstore? Does everyone post material on a class website or use the library's electronic reserves?

As online courses have proved, it's possible to run an excellent writing course without using paper at all. Finding that terrific article you want students to read is often as easy as Googling the title and then posting the URL for students or copying the whole text to your website. If you have access to a scanner and can make pdf files, you can transfer anything on paper to a website. The most important resource I offer the new teachers I supervise is to enter them as "students" into the staff website I've created, which includes everything from syllabi to favorite readings to student papers from the past. But before you invest the time into creating such a website for yourself, consider its limitations. Do you want students to bring copies of some of the materials to class? If so, does the website just shift the copying burden from your department to your students? Plead as you might, you will never get all your students to come to class armed with the crucial handout if each student has to print it out. So sometimes relying on online materials has the appearance of saving paper and money but the effect of leaving less diligent students in the dust.

Under any copying policy, go into the first month armed with handouts. (For the rest of this section, I'm going to use "handouts" meaning "or overheads, electronic reserves, etc.") A meaty handout can anchor extended discussions and therefore act as your spare tire when something else goes flat or blows out unexpectedly. Students like to have something in hand or on screen when they're trying to follow what you have to say. Besides, the thought that goes into composing a handout helps expand and clarify our own ideas and plans.

While you'll never have a full semester's handouts ready to go before the first class, it's worth spending some time gathering and creating them before you start teaching. It will help you feel more secure, and it will improve your thinking about subjects that at the moment may be just notations on a schedule.

Should you "gather" or "create" your handouts? All teachers use handouts, and most veterans have a huge collection. Though I can't speak for the comp teacher down the hall, the composition world in general has a long history of sharing, so most colleagues will gladly let you use their handouts. You can probably collect most of what you need for the semester in a few minutes of asking around.

On the other hand, it's difficult to teach someone else's lesson. We have to make it our own, and sometimes that takes using it three or four times. Besides improving your understanding of the subject, creating your own handout will give the handout your own stamp, as it is written in your voice, for your purposes. So while I would encourage you to gather as many handouts as possible during your first year, I would wager that in the long run, you will end up remaking many of them.

A special word about coursepacks, a popular option for schools that can't afford big photocopying bills and for teachers who like to supplement a reader or replace it entirely. It's terrific to have a set of readings and activities in students' backpacks from day one, especially since the readings can be your favorites, things that you feel confident about. But schools and copy centers differ radically in how they deal with the issue of copyrights. Some may still assume (wink, wink) that you have clearance for the material in your packet, and they'll run off your copies in a couple of days. Others take copyright law very seriously and will not copy your material until they've gotten written clearance from publishers or authors, a clearance that may come months late and with a hefty price tag. So if you intend to use such a packet, find out how the copy center handles it, and be ready to submit it many weeks ahead of time if you include copyrighted material.

SYLLABI

You've dealt with plenty of syllabi as a student, but if you've never created a syllabus, you may find the task daunting. Keep in mind three fundamental truths about syllabi that you probably didn't think about as a student:

1. Making up a syllabus is the best—for some teachers the only—way to plan your class. So yes, it's a pain, but each syllabus is easier than the last (partly because you can create boilerplate parts to move from one to the next), and if you do it well, you'll have much less to worry about for the rest of the semester.

2. The syllabus, a quasi-legal document, lays out a sort of contract between you and your students. So when students complain that they didn't know about certain rules or dates, you can respond, "Look what it says in the syllabus." But it works both ways—students can hold you to your syllabus—so you need to be sure that you mean what you say.

3. Many students will only glance at the syllabus. That is, in general, their problem, but it means you can't put something in the syllabus and forget about it, assuming everyone got it.

Crucial Details

Because of the first two points above, every syllabus should include a number of crucial details. You need to make up your mind about them and you need to alert students to them in an official way. To get a sense of local syllabus traditions, ask some veterans to show you theirs. If the program offers a core syllabus, *use it*. Look it over very closely and make modifications if that's acceptable. You'll have plenty of other chances day-by-day to be creative. Almost certainly, your syllabus will need the following.

Your information. Name, office number, phone number, email address, office hours. (Some teachers give out their home phone number, something I discourage. And I would definitely not list my home address.)

Class information. Course number, section number, meeting place and time.

List of books and other materials required for the course and where students can or should get them.

Course objectives. I used to make these short and simple. Having recently dealt with outside accreditation and assessment, I now realize that the easiest way for an administrator to "prove" that a particular course includes a particular element is to find that element in the course syllabus under "objectives" or "goals." I'd be surprised if one student in one hundred paid any attention to the objectives, but listing them may help you clarify in your own mind what you're trying to do, and it may also keep your boss happy.

Course grading procedures and standards. I usually provide descriptions of A, B, C, D papers. I'm not sure they really help students, but pointing to them provides one quick answer to the "What do you want?" question. Including in your syllabus specific rubrics for particular assignments can save you headaches later. (See Figure 7 and Anson and Dannels, "Developing Rubrics for Instruction and Evaluation.") You also need some system of weighting each graded assignment, whether you give a percentage or a number of points to each paper. Make sure you include everything that you want to affect students' grades. Students will question this section of the syllabus more than any other, so it's worth thinking through a number of times and perhaps running by some peers.

Consider including your stance on issues such as: Do you consider improvement or effort? Do you use the same grading scale throughout the semester? Can the same grade mean very different things in terms of the strengths and weaknesses of the paper? (See Chapter 5 for more on grading.) What does "late" mean? (Wilhoit 39-40) (Say "due at the beginning of class" so you don't have students skipping class to show up with a paper at the end of the hour.)

List of crucial due dates. I usually start my planning by figuring out what papers, exams, and major readings I want students to do. I try to spread them out more or less evenly over the semester. Don't rush this step; think through it from all angles—How much time has elapsed since the last big assignment? Will students have done all the prerequisite work? How will you deal with students who neglect the day's reading or don't even show up for class on a due date? What else is going on in your life on the due date? Will the spacing provide time for students to rewrite and for you to respond?

There are advantages and disadvantages to detailing in the syllabus what's going to happen every class day of the semester. Scheduling each day can make you feel boxed in, and if you don't leave flex days, one unavoidable change—a snow day, a sick day for you, a holiday no one told you about—can render the whole schedule useless. On the other hand, it's a great relief to go into the first day of class knowing that you have at least a skeleton for the whole semester, and all you have to do day to day is put flesh on it. I sometimes try to have it both ways by jotting down for myself what I plan to do each day but putting only the major due dates in the syllabus that I give students.

Descriptions of assignments and requirements. To sharpen your thinking and improve your communication with students, make your assignment descriptions as detailed and complete as possible. You need to see, and be able to communicate to students, the connections between assignments, the progress or development from one assignment to others, the skills that students will practice in one assignment and need for the next. You won't see many of these kinds of connections until you've gone through your assignment sequence at least once, but thinking about them before you teach will help you see coherence in the whole semester and alert you to the issues that link one assignment to the next.

It's up to you whether you put the detailed descriptions in the syllabus or just summarize the assignments in the syllabus and hand out a full description later, when you start talking about the assignment. If you put the whole thing in the syllabus, count on calling attention to the assignment description weeks before the particular project is due; otherwise students won't read it.

In the assignment description, you should articulate your stance on any of the following that you haven't covered clearly and completely in class. Often only the best students read and follow the assignment

directions, but you still want to have them written down so you don't have
to repeat them to each student who asks.

- Paper length: max and min? Because padding to reach a page
  minimum encourages terrible writing, I avoid setting minimum
  page numbers for any one paper, requiring instead that each
  student turn in a set number of polished pages over the course
  of the semester. And unless the assignment is a summary or some
  other task that tests students' ability to compress material, I usually don't give a page maximum.

- Due date and time. (If your syllabus doesn't already state your late
  paper policy loudly and clearly, state it here.)

- Goals, objectives, context, audience for the paper. How does this
  paper relate to what you've covered in the course? What are its
  purposes (always plural, to my mind)? What skills do you want
  students to practice as they write it? (Ideally, all papers should be
  learning opportunities, not just substitutes for tests.) Should the
  paper stand alone and make sense to anyone who happens to pick
  it up, or can the author assume that the reader knows a certain
  body of information? Do you have a particular audience in mind?
  Can students choose to write for a specific audience (high school-
  ers thinking about going to college, for instance), or do you want
  them to write for a general audience or perhaps an audience with
  a certain knowledge background?

- Grading criteria. You may want to create a grading rubric or
  matrix for each assignment. (See Figure 7.) In any case, give students as clear an idea as possible of what you'll be looking for.
  Imagine the shortcuts that a clever or lazy student might take and
  head them off. For example, in my Teaching Writing courses, I
  ask students to research a thorny issue in the discipline so they'll
  understand the various sides and see the issue's complexities. But
  the first time I gave the assignment, a number of students found
  an easy answer to their issue—like "Let's just abandon grades!"—
  without considering the other side, the consequences of their
  stance. So now I include two or three sentences about engaging,
  not evading, that thorniness.

- Your preferences on
  - format

- use of title page
- name, date, section in particular places
- summary, abstract, or overview necessary or preferred
- documentation (prefer a particular style?; in-text or footnotes?)
- use of "I"
- use of personal anecdotes or opinions
- single-spaced vs. double-spaced
- particular kinds of analysis or organization
- use of headings, subheadings, lists, bullets
- particular terms or concepts necessary (ie. should students use the terms they've been studying?)
- specific number and types of sources (eg., can they all be from the Internet?)
- getting help from classmates or other students
- using work from another class
- folders, staples, paper clips, plastic covers

You can't assume that students "know" about any of these issues or that their previous teachers agree with you. If you don't care, say so. But do some soul-searching before you announce your preferences to students. Perhaps you think it's too fussy to insist on a title page, but if a nice clean title page gives a paper a positive boost in your eyes, you need to tell your students. And give some thought to what you're calling this assignment, what type of paper you want to get: an essay? a personal essay? a researched essay? an argument? a response? an analysis? Students tend to fall back on the labels and approaches they're familiar with; I never use the phrase "term paper" in my classes, yet students often do, and they bring with that label assumptions inappropriate to my class.

Your definition of a successful paper. Again, you can't assume that students or their previous teachers share your ideas about what makes a good paper. Consider whether you feel strongly about any of the following and/or borrow some from this list and articulate your own priorities. Some teachers feel that a good paper should

- demonstrate an understanding of class concepts and successfully use class terms
- answer completely the question(s) asked in the assignment or posed in the paper's first paragraph

- be well written, with no unnecessary words and no mechanical mistakes
- be original and creative in form and/or content
- reveal complex thinking by the writer
- leave the reader thinking
- be clear and easy to read and grasp
- demonstrate a solid grounding in relevant literature
- have a strong writing voice, perhaps using humor and figures of speech
- challenge the writer and reader
- effectively blend in other voices from sources or interviews

My colleague Keith Grant-Davie suggests that teachers should engage in some serious self-scrutiny to determine what they really grade in students' papers and then pass that information on to students. He also asks a series of questions to help teachers perfect their own assignment descriptions:

Could I suggest ways for my students to choose and focus their topics?

Could I prime their thinking by suggesting questions for them to consider?

Could I define the parameters of the assignment more clearly by suggesting or requiring that students follow specific methods of research and analysis, consult certain sources, or include particular material in their papers?

Is there any other information I could give students about the assignment that would help them learn from it?

Small but important issues. What's your attendance policy? (I suggest something like "Your grade will fall after 3 absences, and anyone who misses more than six classes may fail the course.") Your tardiness policy? Do you accept late papers? (I do, but I lower the grade one-third of a letter for each late day. I seldom articulate this fact to the whole class, but when you grade portfolios at the end of the semester, as I usually do, so students have a chance to revise their papers and improve their grades, lateness penalties become almost moot.) Do you grade participation? If so, how? And can you explain why? Do you grade every paper that students turn in? Do they get a chance to revise? Do you insist that students with planned, excused absences turn in the work they will miss *before* they leave? (See Chapter 5 for a thorough discussion of such issues.)

In general, it's a good idea to be tough about such things in the syllabus; then you can bend in individual cases. I feel *very* strongly that

---

Figure 2
Sexual Harassment (Modify for your school.)

Sexual harassment is defined by the Affirmative Action/Equal Opportunity Commission as any "unwelcome sexual advances, requests for sexual favors, and other verbal or physical contact of a sexual nature." If you feel you are a victim of sexual harassment, you may talk to or file a complaint with the Affirmative Action/Equal Opportunity Office.

Figure 3
Students With Disabilities (Modify for your school.)

Reasonable accommodation will be provided for all persons with disabilities in order to ensure equal participation within the program. If a student has a disability that will likely require some accommodation by the instructor, the student must contact the instructor and document the disability through the Disability Resource Center, preferably during the first week of the course. Any request for special consideration relating to attendance, pedagogy, taking of examinations, etc., must be discussed with and approved by the instructor. In cooperation with the Disability Resource Center, course materials can be provided in alternative format, large print, audio, diskette, or Braille.

---

you should spell out a tough attendance policy. I'm less clear about late papers. When I was a student, I hated it when I worked hard to get a paper in on time only to hear the professor tell a lazier student, "Sure, turn it in tomorrow." On the other hand, some lateness excuses can melt your heart, and you'll sleep badly if you have to say "sorry, can't bend that policy" too often. Perhaps the most inane "education" policy of recent years has been "zero tolerance," which equates a nail file with an assault rifle and ibuprofen with cocaine. The stupidity of "zero tolerance" highlights the need to make decisions based on all the circumstances in a particular situation, not hide behind unbendable rules.

Accommodation and discrimination information. This is another quasi-legal aspect of the syllabus; your state or school may require—or at least recommend—that all syllabi contain sections about sexual harassment, discrimination, and accommodations for persons with disabilities. (See figures 2 and 3.) Even if it's not required, get it in your syllabus somewhere. It may be relevant only once a year, but you don't want to feel that a deaf student or a rape victim suffered through your class because they didn't feel welcome to come talk to you.

Plagiarism definition. Students can't be told too often, or too strongly, about plagiarism. Check out what the school catalogue says about it and use the school's language or make up your own. My school doesn't prohibit self-plagiarism, but I consider turning the same work in to two different classes unethical. So my definition is broader than the school's. (See Chapter 9.)

GENERAL ISSUES

Short Versus Long

I've seen one-page syllabi that read like introductory letters between friends-to-be and twenty-five-page syllabi that present a good chunk of the course through everything from quotations to comics. My own syllabi tend to be in the middle of that range—eight pages or so, with all the crucial information I've listed above, plus more on how I grade and a page of my philosophy. Many teachers set down some of their assumptions and guiding principles in their syllabus to encourage students to open up ("I believe that all opinions are valuable") and to head off potential problems ("I will not tolerate language that is demeaning to a particular sex, race, nationality, or religion.")

Although I feel guilty asking students to read eight dull pages for the first night's homework, and I love the feeling that a short, endearing letter gives, I would feel naked creating only a one-page syllabus. I would want to follow it almost immediately with something like "rules, assignments, and requirements," and that would defeat the purpose of keeping it to one page. I see the advantage of creating a mammoth syllabus—it saves time later, ensures that students have the crucial materials that they need, and "saves me from writing on the board," as my wife puts it. But I don't usually want to scare students away by presenting them with a massive tome on the first day, and I don't know with certainty everything I plan to do in a semester.

So there's a lot of latitude with syllabus length. I would encourage you to be meticulous about including the crucial stuff and then just add anything that you want everyone to know from the outset.

Voice

You probably think of a syllabus as having as much voice as the tax code, but consider that the syllabus introduces you to students, and the sense they get of you from the syllabus may be lasting. I think of my syllabi as fairly dry and businesslike, but students have told me that they decided to take my class because of bits of humor or humane policies in the syllabus.

So shaping the voice of the syllabus is a tricky business. You don't want to sound like a comedian; sometimes teachers try too hard to be funny or chummy and end up sounding frivolous. Others are so intent on putting the tough foot forward that they sound like ogres, an impression that may be slow to dissipate. Make your policies tough, if you wish, but there's no reason to give the syllabus a drill-sergeant voice. Be yourself—a tightly written, well-edited self.

Don't leave your syllabus to the last minute. That will mess up your planning and make you stressed in ways you may never recover from.

Do proofread your syllabus over and over, and get some help. If your first offering to students sags with errors, how can you hold students to high standards of editing and proofreading? Anyone can help you with proofreading, but another teacher can also look at your syllabus for problems, omissions, contradictions.

Do make copies well before the first day of class. You can bet there will be a line at the copying machine on the first day . . . if the machine hasn't chosen that day to give up the ghost entirely.

Emphasis

Your dream may be to teach Romantic poetry, Marxist theory, or self-actualization, but you have to remember that yours is a *writing* course. There's room to use some of your favorite literature as models or to spark ideas, but you need to monitor constantly the time students spend in class and on their own, making sure that the vast majority is *writing* time. In the simplest terms, we learn to write by writing; even rhetorical analysis has limited value in the composition classroom if it doesn't contribute directly to students' writing improvement. I fret when a new teacher's syllabus seems to be creating a literature course under the guise of First-Year Writing. Don't worry your supervisors; and even if you think this is the only writing course you'll ever teach, give yourself a chance to see how interesting it can be to put writing in the spotlight.

THE PLEASURES OF PREPARING

You'll hear veterans complain about having three or four "preps" in a semester (meaning that they teach that many different courses, rather than multiple sections of the same course). And when you contemplate everything I've mentioned in this chapter, you may find the prospect of preparing to be overwhelming.

There *is* a lot to do, but preparing can be calming and reassuring rather than onerous. As with any large task, you need to divide it into small pieces and start as soon as possible. I think you'll find as you check each small task off your list, you can erase corresponding anxieties in your mind. We fear the unknown, the uncertain, the uncontrolled. Once you've learned, for instance, the department's approach to handouts, actually producing the handouts—whether by making overheads or by trundling your work to a copy center—becomes just a chore, much lower on the anxiety scale than "What am I going to do about . . . ?"

Just as important, preparing allows you to daydream about the possibilities, what you *could* do, and what a blast it would be if everything went according to schedule, you found the perfect word and the perfect example each time, and every face mirrored your enthusiasm. It *may* happen that way, but even if it doesn't, it's healthy to dream a bit as you prepare and to revel in the feeling that you can do it, you will be prepared, and it will even be fun.

3
RESOURCES

I am a self-sufficient loner. I hike alone, I ski alone, I play music by myself. I change my own flat tires, I read maps rather than ask for directions, I'd rather drive by myself for days than play elbow hockey with boorish cell phoners in germ-drenched airplanes.

But I don't teach alone. Yes, I'm usually the only "professor" in the room. I don't team-teach or borrow lesson plans anymore. But I feel very lucky that at the formative time of my career, I got to work with the world's most generous mentor, Don Murray, and a writing community that I still see as ideal. Because most comp teachers work at the bottom of the academic ladder, we tend to bond with each other, help each other, and share. And even if you're more of an anti-social individualist than I am, you're not going to survive in this business unless you can learn to find and use help.

PEOPLE

I hope you're lucky enough to be working in a school that respects and values composition. Freshman English at my grad school was seen as the academic equivalent of taking out the garbage. The only idea exchange I saw was of the macho "I'm teaching in five minutes, what should I do?" variety. Almost no one, faculty or grad students, saw improving our writing pedagogy as an issue worthy of serious thought and research.

But that was thirty years ago, and now most universities at least pay lip service to the importance of composition and devote some resources to it, if only because the writing program, with its writing lab fees and summer courses, may be the only money-making arm of the English department. In any case, your institution almost certainly has the most important resource for your growth and development as a comp teacher—people willing to help.

Secretaries

This may seem an odd category to start with, since most secretaries never teach, but if you're going to make one friend during your first few days on campus, it should be the executive secretary of the department, the person who probably assigns offices, hands out keys, and knows everybody's business. Unlike the front-desk person, who is paid to be pleasant and patient, the head secretary may well have a personality with an edge to it—an attitude—and may enjoy wielding her (they've always been women, in my experience) considerable power. Such people sometimes scare new instructors. But you need to remember that however much bluster and bravado she greets you with, she's almost certainly poorly paid, underappreciated, overworked, and perhaps badly treated by some of the faculty. So you may be able to make a permanent friend by treating her with respect, showing an awareness that she's overworked and probably doesn't have time for your trivial problem, perhaps thanking her for mailing you something during the summer or making the moving-in process easy. Sympathetic humor melts a lot of walls.

Making friends with the secretaries will make your life substantially easier. They call the room coordinator when another class shows up for your room and time. They know how to get the overhead projector fixed, where the A/V cart is supposed to be, which professors will be sympathetic to your need for another thesis committee member, how to get a good parking sticker. And they're often wonderful people. My wife and I named our daughter after the first executive secretary we worked with in New Hampshire, Larkin Warren, who taught me to do an undervalued job with dignity and class.

Administrators

One of the important favors a secretary can do for you is help you assess the department's administrators and decide which to approach with your particular need. (Personal caveat: the first secretary I talked to at UNH told me to avoid that mean Don Murray—advice which, if I had followed it, would have blighted my career.) Know something about the background of administrators before you begin bringing problems and requests to them; you can easily find such information from published records, likely to be on the department's website, and from your peers in the program.

Key questions:

Who handles what issues? In my current department, the Head assigns offices, the associate head assigns classes, and the executive secretary assigns phone and copy machine codes. The logic to such divisions of responsibilities escapes me, and you're not likely to understand them in your school either. But to save yourself time and embarrassment, know who does what before you start asking administrators questions.

Do the administrators have degrees, teaching experience, and research interests in composition, or are their backgrounds strictly literary? Someone with a composition background should take your questions seriously and have some useful answers, but that person may also have strong opinions about the ways things should be done in a composition classroom. You may need to be careful how much you reveal about yourself, your approach, and your weaknesses. Literary scholars may know little about what you do and may not want to learn; sometimes such people are forced to run writing programs and feel bitter about it, trapped in a composition backwater when they want to teach seminars on *Finnegan's Wake* to five enthralled grad students. (Be wary of such generalizations, though; my current department head specializes in obscure eighteenth century Scottish texts, but he's very supportive of the writing program.) Do your homework so you'll know what kind of language you need to speak.

How "busy" are they? I put "busy" in quotation marks because I see it as a state of mind rather than an objective measure of activity. You'll probably never run into an English professor who'll say "I'm not busy" (except possibly one on sabbatical, and then you're not likely to "run into" them at all). But some administrators will use "busy" as a cudgel to make you feel guilty and beat you out the door, while others will always make time for a question or a quick friendly chat.

Do they have a political axe to grind? Some administrators with roots in composition may believe that allowing narratives into academic papers has led to the decline of western civilization. Others may feel that you should take your kind of question to your peer mentor and not bother them with it. Or they may immediately try to recruit you to be on the "right" side of an ongoing political rift. In some departments, a meeting of a hiring or promotion committee may turn into a debate between long-standing foes.

Is there bad blood in the department? You probably won't get a good answer to this kind of question until you search out the department's best gossips and earn their trust. Affairs and professional insults most commonly set faculty at each other's throats, and finding out about them can help you avoid sticky situations.

Do you need to be a squeaky wheel to get a tolerable office or a functioning computer? As an administrator, I know how difficult it is *not* to give unfair attention to the squeaky wheel, the person who comes to you with a problem to fix and a sad, urgent story. Most administrators try to avoid the squeaky wheel influence by having a system for distributing all the department perks—a ladder for the next office opening, a merit pay rating rubric, a "next computer upgrade" list. But the person in charge of such things in your department may think only of the needs of the person in the doorway at the moment. If so, you may have to darken that door.

But don't worry that your request will seem outlandish or unreasonable. Any seasoned administrator knows that new people fret about keys, phones, paychecks, respect. Whether that understanding and potential guilt makes the administrator generous or rudely defensive, only the administrator's therapist knows for sure.

Do some administrators have odd hours and other quirky habits? One nationally famous scholar where I went to grad school told his classes that they couldn't get in touch with him in the morning because he didn't have an office, and they shouldn't get in touch with him after noon because he'd be drunk. That's an extreme example, but it's fairly common for some people to get to work at seven a.m. and others to be hitting their stride at seven p.m. The best administrator for you to work with may not be the person whose work most closely resembles yours but the one whose schedule most nearly matches yours.

Mentors

You probably don't have to be told that mentors are the best thing since in-text citations. You need to find one. Or, more commonly, have one find you. Mentors may be the single most important factor for keeping a teacher's spirits up, especially in the first few years. You can't calculate the value of having someone at least slightly more powerful and successful believe in you and help you succeed. Most of us aren't brash enough to walk up to a strange and relatively famous professor and ask, "Will you mentor me?" A mentoring relationship usually develops naturally while the mentor and the mentee work together. So accept any offer to work with a more experienced person and nurture all your relationships with potential mentors.

If that sounds like a creepy dating game, remember this: most successful people have mentors, at least during one important part of their lives. Not long ago, today's mentors couldn't get the time of day from anyone . . . except their mentors. Most people will pass on the favor. My wife, Melody Graulich, is a superb mentor, in part, I think, because her mentor, David Levin, was so generous, himself. Most academics have a soft spot for the older person who gave them a boost, and if you're careful, you can tap into that good feeling.

Beyond the obvious ones related to sexual harassment, no rules govern mentoring, and the relationship can develop from a wide variety of activities. Melody and I used to do minimum-wage odd jobs for David Levin and his wife Pat. I never worked a lick for my mentor, Don Murray, but we've eaten a lot of lunches together, something I seldom do with the people I mentor. Go figure.

William Broz reminds us that not all of our mentors need to have lunch with us or even meet us. If you read a good deal of a writer's work and think about how it applies to you, you may find that what Broz calls a "distant mentor" can affect your thinking, perhaps give you a form or approach that you can imitate, maybe even make you feel validated. We're lucky to be working in a field whose best practitioners tend to be terrific writers and can mentor us through words on the page.

Colleagues

Colleagues are your most important resource and a primary source of the fun you should be having. In this category, I include everyone who teaches "with" you. I don't differentiate by rank, because I think the only two defining factors are experience—veteran or novice—and attitude. You may find someone who's famous and on the verge of retirement easier to talk with than your same-year office mates.

Peers

You can find great relief in sharing the sense of bewilderment, of being overwhelmed and run ragged, with someone who knows exactly what you're talking about. Peers are your support group. Use them. Help them move into new offices, go to their bratwurst parties, read their bad poetry. When you come back, ashen-faced, from your first confrontation with an angry student, only a peer can say "that asshole!" with the proper outrage.

You probably don't need encouragement to rely on peers because you don't have much choice—they will usually be the closest people when you start sinking and grab for a hand. I'm going to spend much more time talking about veterans, because your links with them will not be as automatic but may be even more important, at least for your professional development.

Veterans

To a novice, someone with three or four years of experience may appear infinitely wise, and the naive novice may imagine that the veteran commands a robust salary and cross-campus respect. Because you don't see them suffer and doubt, as you probably do your peers, you may think that veterans don't share your worries and frustrations and therefore have no interest in talking to you. Some veterans may feel they've conquered your demons, but consider: who but a novice like you can really appreciate a veteran's brilliant solution to a first-year composition teaching dilemma? Many veterans delight in having an appreciative audience, talking to *somebody* who thinks what they do is interesting.

This is not a minor issue, so I'm going to take some time to try to convince you that you should overcome your shyness, your sense of being an ignorant pain in the butt, your feeling that a huge, unbridgeable gap separates you from people with only a few more years of experience. (Maybe you don't feel that way. Maybe you think you've got it all figured out and don't need any help; in which case, get real and listen up!) So why should those busy, overworked, underappreciated compositions veterans want to work with a greenhorn?

You make them feel successful and important. Because most students can't judge knowledge and expertise and wouldn't articulate their judgments if they could, they seldom keep healthy the egos of even the best teachers. And while you may be awed by *their* knowledge and abilities, administrators and tenure-line faculty don't pay much attention to composition instructors of any rank.

So the veteran's most likely source of the admiration and appreciation we all treasure is a novice colleague—a person who has enough experience to know what a difficult, complex job teaching comp is, and who is eager to snatch up any pearls of wisdom that veterans drop. I well remember when I started to make the transition from greenhorn to old hand: the writing director began asking me to lead staff meetings and other instructors started inviting me to their classes to be "guest writer" or "blues expert." I was tremendously flattered and felt that I had in some sense arrived. At UNH, we had a voluntary mentoring program (a great idea, if you can get your program interested in it), and though it involved giving up a few hours at a time of the semester when no one had any to spare, we never had any trouble finding experienced teachers willing to work with new ones. Don't underestimate the desire to be appreciated.

Veterans remember and have sympathy. For twenty-five years, I've struggled with having too much to do in my classes, rather than too little, but I still recall the awful feeling of needing to fill time and being hesitant to turn to others for fear I would be exposed as an unimaginative slacker. I still get a big kick out of running into new teachers after their first few days in class and hearing the surprise in their voices when they say, "They listen to me! They don't think I'm a fraud!"

They like to help. The previous point is just a particular case of the general: we teach because we enjoy helping. You may find some exceptions—particularly among graduate students who see teaching comp as just a way to stay fed while they earn their degree and become Famous Professors. But as you already well know, the job comes with few extrinsic rewards; nobody does it for long unless they can survive on gratitude and hope.

They like to share. You may not believe it at first, but comp teachers share. Novelists love to satirize English departments because of their nasty battles over nothing, not because of their spirit of cooperation. Yet it is the norm in the composition programs I know to be unselfish with your brilliance.

Why? Part of it is trench camaraderie. Some may be a result of the models set by composition leaders like the late Wendy Bishop, who edited enough books to employ and inform thousands of comp teachers. Some of it may be the nature of our work. There aren't many scoops in composition, no patents or literary breakthroughs, like finding a lost Mary Austin novel in the Huntington Library. We may come up with brilliant classroom strategies, but they gain us recognition only if we share them. Only peers really appreciate them, and who has the time to turn them into those articles we're always saying we're going to write?

Sharing may also result from our recognition that each of us has a limited imagination, and teaching comp requires as many great ideas as we can amass. Some people come up with stimulating writing prompts, others with clever ways to help students know each other, others with ways of engaging students in discussions about literature. We become a kind of collective imagination and memory bank, learning from each other and passing the benefits on to our students.

This atmosphere means that novices can often contribute as well as veterans. You may not know much about comp teaching yet, but if you've just served a stint at a summer camp, you're probably up on the best ice-breakers and team-makers. Or your undergraduate thesis on Calvin and Hobbes—as well as your xeroxable collection of scenes suitable for office doors and overheads—may make you popular. And who wouldn't be impressed by your clever use of your languages background to show that we all *do* know something about Latin? There's room for a million different expertises in composition. You almost certainly have some; you just need to make them visible to others.

You may not be aware of the sharing already going on in your building. Is there a lesson plan repository somewhere? A website? An informal library of journals and texts? Collections of past syllabi? A bibliophile on the staff who owns everything and loves to lend?

Are there reading, writing, teaching, or debriefing groups that would welcome new members? Start one of your own if you need to. Since people are the most important resource in this business, you need to figure out how you can regularly interact with at least a few people who can listen to your ideas, read your work, and check on your sanity. The best writing groups include members from outside the writing program and the English department. People from art or education or history or even phys ed may take their own writing seriously and work to improve their students' writing, even if such work doesn't appear in their job descriptions or their syllabi. Such people can give you valuable new perspectives on writing and can help you avoid the serious mistake of assuming that the writing program has a monopoly on teaching writing expertise.

Your Students

Yes, students are a terrific resource. "If we keep our antennae tuned to their frequency, we can learn much from them that could convert us from being merely competent teachers to being great teachers" (Corbett 9). Collectively, they provide an institutional memory that no one person can equal. Someone in class will know all the computer clusters on campus, the library hours, who uses the classroom before you do.

More importantly, students can help you monitor and improve your class. Don't wait until the semester-end evaluations to find out what they think. A quick mid-semester survey can allow you to change aspects of your class while you can still make a difference. I sometimes ask students to write me a weekly or bi-weekly letter, noting what's going well and not-so-well, what they're confused and worried about. Reading them and responding in any fashion takes considerable time, but students will tell you things in such notes that they won't say in class or face to face, enabling you, magically it seems, to tailor the class to students' needs.

Students can also provide a tremendous amount of help for their peers. I'm wary of having students correct each other's grammar, but in small groups or as a whole class, they can bounce ideas off each other, read and respond to drafts, help each other understand the day's reading, direct each other to useful library resources.

Using students as a resource is *not* a cop-out, and I doubt very much if any of your students will see it as such. Helping a classmate organize a paper teaches the helper invaluable lessons applicable to the helper's own papers. It's a sophisticated teaching technique that makes students feel important and empowered and, coincidentally, gets you off the hook a good bit of the time. (See Rebecca Moore Howard, "Collaborative Pedagogy.")

OFFICES

You may never need to talk to people at the Affirmative Action office or the Disability Resource Center or Veterans' Affairs, but you need to know that such places exist and that contacting them may make your life easier.

A student asks for more time on all assignments because, he says, he's ADHD, and they always get more time. Do you take him at his word and give him the break? Do you make your own evaluation of him? Do you send him off for testing somewhere? No. On my campus and many others, students with special needs get special accommodations from faculty only if they register with the Disability Resource Center, whose people are trained to deal with special needs.

Similarly, the counseling center exists to handle the personal problems that appear in student papers and make us say, "I can't cope with this." Most schools have special rape hotlines or sexual assault counselors. And the Affirmative Action/Equal Opportunity Office takes on issues of discrimination too tricky for us to feel confident about.

If you have athletes in your classes, you may want to contact advisors from the athletic program—or they may contact you, since their job is to make sure that athletes pass courses like yours. Athletes often have access to tutors, so you may be able to get help for an athlete who writes poorly without having to invest all the time yourself.

The power, scope, politics, and funding of such offices varies widely across the country, but don't assume that they're too busy and don't want to be bothered by one more new teacher with a student she's trying to help. The funding of such offices often depends to some degree on the number of students they help, so they may be eager to add your student to the day's tally. One phone call or email to one of these offices can save you a lot of time and stress.

THE WRITING CENTER

This is an office that deserves special attention. You may be asked or required to work in the writing center; if so, you'll soon know what resources it offers besides a staff dedicated to helping student writers. Does the writing center office, or some other back room in the building, house a collection of *College Composition and Communication* and other journals?

Does it have model papers, grammar handouts, a library of writing texts, an administrator who's glad to come talk to your class about the center?

Writing center people can probably point you to plagiarism web sites, help you with arcane questions of grammar, suggest approaches to working with particular students. (Our writing center saved my sanity a few years ago simply by letting me know that their tutors were having as much trouble with a particular student as I was.) Though this may be changing as the number and size of writing centers grow, in the past, writing centers have often struggled for a sense of legitimacy, and their personnel have been glad to be treated with respect by other professional writing teachers (that means you).

Best of all, writing centers can help you reduce the amount of time you spend working with students on their writing, without lowering the quality of students' papers or their learning. Writing center tutors can be your stand-in for almost any one-on-one work you'd like to do with students except grade discussions: tutors can listen as students brainstorm ideas for a paper, help students build the paper a spine, read the rough draft and suggest ways to improve it. If you ask them nicely, most tutors will even help cure students of semicolon phobias or annoying addictions to passive verbs.

Students generally won't go to writing centers on their own, even if they're convinced a visit to the center is a good idea. That's why many writing teachers require a visit or two to the center, giving points just for showing up and working with a tutor. Experience will have to teach you whether the combination of writing center reputation, student motivation, and your own persuasive skills will lead students to the center more than once without further arm-twisting. If students see their work at the center as the direct outgrowth of their work with you—if, for instance, you help the student untangle some key sentences and send the student to the center for further untangling—they may be less likely to resent your suggestion that they pay the center a visit.

If you have doubts about the effects of writing centers, read something like Muriel Harris's "Talking in the Middle: Why Writers Need Writing Tutors."

WEBSITES ABOUT STUDENT DEMOGRAPHICS

In terms of your interactions with a particular class, national trends don't really matter: you need to deal with the students you face when you walk into your classroom, whether they're part of a demographic tide or furiously swimming against it. On the other hand, especially as you get older and gaps develop between you and your students, you may want to remind yourself how different today's students are from you and your peers. Our unexamined assumptions can derail our teaching, and we base many such assumptions on the tacit belief that today's students resemble us at college age, only geekier. Knowing how wrong that assumption is can help us start to see who our students really are.

If you're interested in what current nineteen-year-olds think and believe, start with your own school's website. It may list recent survey results under "assessment" or "demographics" or "students."

Next, try the Higher Education Research Institute: www.gseis.ucla. edu/heri/findings.html. HERI conducts assessment surveys for many schools across the country.

The National Center for Educational Statistics at www.nces.ed.gov/ publishes a "Digest of Educational Statistics" that includes general trends in college enrollment over the past thirty to forty years and more specific recent information. At the same site, check out the Integrated Postsecondary Education Data System.

The Chronicle of Higher Education, a widely read and well-respected journal, offers advice to adjuncts as well as national data on college enrollment trends, faculty salaries, test scores, degrees awarded, tuition and fees, spending on research and development, and student aid. www. chronicle.com.

BOOKS AND ARTICLES

Rather than outline an ideal composition library for you here, I have indicated throughout the book where you can turn for further reading on particular subjects. If you're going to read anything but student papers during the school year, you're going to have to be efficient about it. That may mean reading the article instead of the book; the summary of the great theorist rather than hundreds of pages of the theorist's impenetrable prose; the conclusions but not the discussion. And it will almost certainly mean getting over the English major's hangup about reading everything the "right" way—cover to cover. Use indexes, in this book and others. You need context in order to understand the passage that the index directs you to, but you don't need to read the whole book. Always know why you're reading, what you're looking for, and when you find it, stop. Remember, I'm not talking about reading novels, or even the composition reading you might do on vacations; I'm talking about the reading you do during your harried semester to make your courses run more smoothly.

A word about *handbooks.* You need one, an up-to-date one with lots of information about analyzing and citing websites and preferably with detailed examples of two or three citation formats. Whether or not you require your students to get a handbook, they will be asking you things like "How do I cite an email interview?" and for your own peace of mind, you need a place to find an answer. If you're buying a new handbook, look for features that may help you on special areas that you're not comfortable with. Is there a chapter on graphics and images? Are there good discussions or activities helping students understand concepts like plagiarism and website credibility? Are there CD ROMS or websites associated with the handbook? These ancillaries don't necessarily increase the value of the handbook, but if they're good, they can save you time on some of the more mundane and less interesting aspects of composition.

Besides the journals and books published by the NCTE (discussed in Chapter 10) and other composition journals like *Composition Studies* that your library probably carries, you might want to pay attention to publications that target your status. *The Adjunct Advocate* lives up to its name. Visit www.adjunctnation.com. Gappa and Leslie's *The Invisible Faculty* is the best scholarly look at adjunct status, while new graduate instructors can consult books like Good & Warshauer's *In Our Own Voice: Graduate Students Teach Writing.*

Composition is no longer a fledgling discipline whose important works could barely fill a single bookshelf. What you want to know is out there, somewhere, in print.

•   •   •

The wealth of resources now available for new composition teachers and the general awareness that new teachers need mentors won't necessarily make life easy for you right away. All those books and ideas can be overwhelming and lead to the feeling that you *must* read everything right now and incorporate all of those wonderful ideas into your next class.

Forget it. The field is so large now that it's virtually impossible for anyone to stay on top of it. Sure, you need to keep learning, but do it incrementally and start locally, with the people in your department. Find out what books and articles the people around you are reading and using, and if a number of people mention the same text, read it when you have a chance. Determine who the resident writing gurus are and introduce yourself. Go to the resources listed in this chapter when you need answers or suggestions, not because you *ought* to be reading more or changing your approach. Trust your instincts.

4

THE FIRST DAY

First days are the worst days. A good mantra if you have a bad first class. Amid the inevitable confusion and chaos, we have little chance to make real contact or get the grateful feedback that sustains us. Foul-ups with the roll, the room, or the equipment eat up time, and even veterans often feel frazzled.

I fear only experience can bring the alternative view of first days—to look out on the sea of new faces and guess and wonder. Who will be the smart ones? The good writers? The friendly, appreciative ones I'll always be glad to see in my office? The skeptics that will have to be won over? I often wish I could videotape the faces that first day and record my guesses about how each of them will turn out. It's a fun game, a bit like a first date. It's just too bad we don't have the chance to sit back and appreciate it.

Chapters three and eight attempt to prepare you for the first day by suggesting—and by asking you to brainstorm—what might go wrong and what you can do to prepare for it. This chapter will focus on a variety of different ways to get off on a good foot. Forget the traditional first day activity—going over the syllabus section by section. It bores students and gives them a bad impression of the class, and no one remembers anything from the syllabus anyway. Instead, do something interesting and fun with writing the first day, and assign a close reading of the syllabus for the second class period, asking students to write down questions as they read. You will probably have to call roll, give your name and office number, and do a few other business and housekeeping duties. Write your name and the course number on the board, which will cause a student or two in the wrong room, on the wrong day, or on the wrong planet, to slip out. Write up the homework for the next few days; few things establish authority faster than reminding students "I'm in charge of the work you're going to do."

But that should still leave you with at least half an hour to set the right tone for the course. Here are some ways to use that time.

CREATE COMMUNITY

The success or failure of a writing class often depends on the interpersonal dynamics among classmates—the "chemistry" of the class. We can't control all the elements of that chemistry, but we can create the best chances for positive interactions by establishing early on that

- civil, supportive, and sometimes constructively critical relationships are crucial to the functioning of the class and the learning of individuals

- getting to know each other's names and styles is not just friendly, but it's also important for students' growth as writers

- every voice and every idea deserves a respectful hearing, but no idea and no person is above challenge

- as I believe Yvor Winters said, a victory for one writer is a victory for all. In the ideal writing community, everyone eagerly helps everyone else and cheers every well-written sentence, including the teacher's. If you portray yourself as a struggling writer, your students may well invest themselves in your struggle. But on a day when the whole class seems to have conspired to make trouble, you may find it difficult not to see your students as the enemy. Resist that urge. Few students will expend the energy necessary to conspire against you unless they feel that you've already cast them in the "disruptive student" role. And once you think "me against them," your semester may never recover.

Such ideas presented directly to the class won't have any effect, but if integrated into a day or two of community building, they may start to take on meaning for students.

How do you build community? Our culture overflows with ideas, from doing ropes courses together to playing silly games. Ironically, I find that a group develops best when we focus on individuals. So I usually spend a day (not necessarily the first, if lots of people are adding and dropping) just having each person introduce him- or herself with some basic information—major, hometown, campus residence—and something quirky, memorable, unique ("I once toured the world with Up With People"; "I can bend my thumb back to touch my wrist"; "I went to six high schools.") I encourage "pointless" conversation in response to these introductions: "Do you know So-and-So? She would have been a year ahead of you" or "I

went to seven high schools and this is my third college." The quirky, tenu-
ous bond developed by such a connection may provide the foundation
for a good peer group.

Variations on this kind of introduction abound. Students can interview
each other, then introduce their interviewee to the class and perhaps
write a profile for their first assignment. The class can play a name-learn-
ing game, in which each person tries to recite the names of everyone
who has gone before. You can gather information from each student and
then quickly create a treasure hunt: "Find the person whose parents were
both in the military"; "Who in the class speaks fluent Portuguese?" Or
you can set up a kind of cocktail party scenario (perhaps even with bagels
and orange juice cocktails) in which everyone tries to meet and find out
information from as many people as possible.

Use your imagination and your experience in scouting or church
groups or elementary school. Silly is good. Maximum laughter is good.
And be sure to include yourself and try to be as open as possible. I often
mention as one of my "unique" characteristics that I have an adopted
Korean daughter, and that creates an instant bond with anyone who is an
adoptee or has one in their family.

QUICK PROCESS OVERVIEW

The problem with doing a community-building exercise the first day is
that your community is not stable yet, and the students, flustered about
their schedules and antsy about the first day back at school, will not
remember names and details as well as they will once things calm down.
So while I recommend devoting a day to community building, I prefer
to do it some time in the second week, and to use the first day to give
students a quick sense of the kind of work (fun work!) we'll be doing
throughout the semester. In a writing class, that means a speedy introduction to writing process.

Students should know from the outset that writing process activities are
not *exercises*, like playing scales, but practical steps that actually accomplish
writing work, more analogous to learning the first few bars of a musical
piece. Therefore, even on the first day, if I ask students to do some think-
ing-on-paper, I try to make it contribute to the first assignment, so they'll
finish the day feeling they accomplished something useful.

For example, if the first paper is a personal essay, the first activity will
be a listing of subjects that might turn into such an essay: conflicts or
questions or traumas or favorite people, places, or things. Right from the

start, I want students to view their lives, opinions, and ideas as valuable ore from which they can refine writing that others will want to read. And I do my own list on the board.

I allow three or four minutes for that first list, then I follow it with three minutes devoted to each item in a series of activities like the following:

- choose one subject from your list
- freewrite on your subject
- read over the freewrite and mark anything interesting, especially surprises
- jot down 6-8 key ideas about your subject
- write as many titles for an essay about your subject as you can in 5 minutes; choose one
- write a short paragraph about your subject
- reread and revise your paragraph
- read the paragraph aloud to the class or a small group.

You can explore endless substitutions, variations, and condensations of this sequence. I don't aim to give students *the* process to follow in the future, but rather to expose them to the idea that writing can proceed in small, relatively painless steps, and that they can produce a finished product in a very short amount of time. Subsequent classes can build on the end product or on any of the steps.

As they explore the surprises that inevitably pop up in such a process, students may start believing that writing is thinking. "I'd never thought about that!" many say as they leave class, and if they grasp that writing made them "think of that," they'll begin to see how important writing can be to their academic and post-academic lives. Most students reach college thinking that writers simply encode already-completed thought, and students who aren't in the humanities may consider writing a necessary evil that they'll be done with as soon as they complete their "gen ed" requirements. It probably doesn't do much good to *lecture* students on the importance of writing, but revealing it to them can become a major focus of the first few weeks of class.

DIG RIGHT IN

I like the process overview to be practical, oriented toward future assignments, but it *is* an overview, covering an unrealistic amount of material quickly. If you want students to take a significant step into the work they'll be doing for the course rather than understand the whole writing process, you can have them do any number of activities even though they may not yet have purchased books or looked at a syllabus for the class.

First, find paper topics. Different schools of thought point novice writers in different directions to explore for subjects. Some say "Write about what you know." Most of us write most comfortably from knowledge, but we also find it easy to get up on a soapbox and preach already-formed conclusions, and such a rant usually does not make an interesting paper.

Another approach: write about what you don't know; explore and question rather than preach. Great research papers can come from trying to answer questions that intrigue us. A useful compromise: have students write about a subject they're familiar with but choose an aspect of that subject that they don't know well. Figuring out something that bothers you, pursuing a real question or conflict, produces the best papers.

In any case, I want students to find enthusiasm and energy, so I try to help them locate a subject that they *want* to write about. An authority list is a great first step: students write down everything they know more about than does anyone else in the class. Terrific subjects might arise from it, but more importantly, students need to realize that they *are* authorities on subjects worth writing about; they don't need to live ten more years or travel the world before they find a subject. Often they're inspired by what I put on my list—when they see that a professional writer thinks he could write an essay on growing giant pumpkins or the joys of Scrabble or the difficulties of raising one adopted and one biological child, they begin to see more possibilities in their own lives.

You can spend the whole first day listing: an authority list, a want-to-know list ("I wish I understood the theory of relativity"), a conflicts and questions list ("Why do I have such trouble getting along with my mother-in-law?"), a traumas list (accidents, family deaths, muggings), a things-I-feel-strongly-about list . . . . I usually give six to eight minutes for each list and assign students to "finish" the list—come up with at least 25 items—for the next class meeting.

My current favorite listing-for-topics approach borrows from Don Murray's concept of writing territories (1999 18-19). Murray points out that most of us write about a finite number—maybe five or ten—of general "territories." (Mine include writing, music, teaching, family, hiking and skiing, psychology, politics.) To come up with a list of their territories, experienced writers can look back over what they've written and put the specific texts into general categories. Novice writers have a slightly more difficult job, thinking about the things they *would* write about if they had the time and motivation.

The list itself can be useful, but I always ask students to go one step farther and connect the territories, sometimes simply by closing their eyes and randomly drawing a line between two or more items. Our uniqueness resides not so much in any individual interest we have but in the confluence, the overlap of those interests. The overlap contains the subjects we can write about that will most likely be unique *and* very much us. For instance, millions of Americans share my interest in music, millions more teach, almost everyone cares about families, and many are fascinated by writing. How do I find something new to say in any of those very popular areas? I search the area where all four overlap, a smaller area not nearly so well populated. And out of that area have come two articles, several presentations, and a book.

I make that point with my classes but also do what I ask them to do—randomly connect territories. Hmmm, skiing and politics. Not subjects you see put together often. No obvious overlap . . . except if you think back to the 2002 Olympics, which took place just down the road from where I live, and the fact that a formerly sleepy, mom-and-pop ski area, Snow Basin, became glitzy and expensive, with amazing new lifts and a controversial new federally-funded road, just in time for the Olympics, and if you know that the owner of the resort was also on the Olympics governing body. . . . Many of my students have come up with productive paper ideas by making similar connections.

QUIRKY ACTIVITIES

Consider doing things on the first day that surprise students, shake them up (maybe with Diesenhaus and Leary's "electroshock therapy"), make them rethink their assumptions about English classes and possibly about college in general. Besides tearing students loose from their preconceptions, unusual opening-day activities can open students' minds to ideas that they might use throughout the semester. Writers and English classes always hunger for subjects, and subjects can be anywhere; therefore we can justify analyzing and hunting for subjects in almost any area of human endeavor.

With Music

My favorite quirky area is music. I begin almost every class period with music, and I find that simple act sometimes wins over students for the semester. As Edward Corbett says, teachers "are more likely to succeed if they resort to the medium of sound than to the medium of print" (5). My book *From Dylan to Donne* suggests many course-starting musical activities. I'll just sketch two here.

Before I play any music myself, I ask students to jot down the name of a song or two that's in their heads at the moment or that they'd like to hear on the radio driving home . . . not necessarily "my favorite song of all time," but something they're currently attached to. Then I play a song from my past and explain how analyzing my attraction to it helped me understand some part of myself. Sometimes I use Dickey Lee's "Patches," a maudlin tragedy about the girlfriend from the wrong side of the tracks who kills herself because the upper-class narrator's family prevents him from visiting her . . . so the narrator pledges to "join" her, presumably by drowning himself too. It seems a silly, embarrassing song now, easily dismissed. But it was my favorite at age ten, on the first album my brother and I bought with our own money, and when I realized recently that for almost thirty years I've been playing the same model guitar that Dickey displays on the cover, I decided to mine the connection. I fear that the "Patches" view of romance—as frustrating, hopeless, ultimately tragic—has had a huge influence on who I am and on my expectations about relationships.

After I've told my story and explained what I learned from analyzing the song, I ask students to figure out the meaning of their song choice. Besides shaking up students' ideas about what subjects merit inquiry and analysis, this activity has two fundamental goals: it often leads to interesting essays (in my case, I could pursue an essay about why suicide is considered romantic, or perhaps do a Marxist analysis of elements of our culture that warn us that crossing the boundaries of class leads to death); and it demonstrates to students that analyzing their own interests, tastes, and passions has value and might teach them something.

Another musical starter: I play a song that no one knows and ask students to jot down not an analysis but an initial gut reaction, an "ugh" or "wow" or "I don't get it." During a second playing of the song, I ask students to find a particular detail of the music that provokes the reaction. We then go through steps very similar to those I use for beginning any literary analysis: students freewrite about the connection between the detail and their initial reaction, then they distill their thinking into a single assertion remarkably similar to a thesis statement. Without planning to, they come up with something: a thesis plus a detail, feelings, and intellectual thought to back it up.

Figure 4
Writing Process Self-Analysis

Answer the following questions about a paper you've written recently. (Choose the one that you remember best.) After you've answered the questions, go back over them and determine whether you think your answer to each question is typical of the way you work or unusual for you. Finally, note answers that you wish were different and why you would like to change them.

1. Why did I write this paper?

2. How did I come up with the subject?

3. Whom did I talk to about my subject?

4. How did I refine the subject?

5. What did I do to plan the paper before the first draft?

6. What tools (eg. red pen, yellow pad, computer) did I use?

7. How did I make the first draft into a final draft?

8. How did I come up with my opening paragraph?

9. Who read the drafts?

10. What reaction did I get from my teacher or other reader?

11. What parts of the process were difficult or painful?

12. What parts were easy or enjoyable?

13. What is usually the hardest step in the writing process for me? Be ready to discuss in conference ways to experiment with that step to find alternatives.

14. What is my personal writing goal for the semester?

While particularly appropriate for a literature class, this process benefits any class that involves analysis because it underscores a crucial point that many students won't at first believe—that most analysis, even literary criticism, begins not with the head—knowledge and critical scrutiny—but in the gut, with some kind of felt response. As neuroscientist Antonio Damasio argues, "if we didn't have those gut responses, we'd get caught in an endless cycle of analysis, drawing infinite pros-and-cons lists in our heads" (qtd. in Johnson 46). Most students get to college distrusting their gut responses—too many times in school, the teacher's "correct" inter-pretation contradicted their reaction to the text, and they concluded that their own thoughts were useless. Many are shocked and delighted to find that they can start with something they really feel, pin their impressions on particular details, create an assertion or thesis statement about their ideas, and then flesh out the assertion. If they can learn to believe in—or at least take seriously—their gut reactions, they will be significantly closer to becoming better, happier, readers and writers.

With Other Media

Before I began to concentrate on music as my quirky opener, I started every class with what I called "Tales From the Outside World." I would read or paraphrase a news story to bring up an issue that would lead to a discussion or that I thought students might write about. Bill Strong, in *Coaching Writing*, suggests some wonderfully useful and amusing activities with strange newspaper stories, having students rewrite the story from an unusual perspective, for instance. And most students enjoy reverting to grade school and making collages with scissors and a stack of magazines. As long as we remember that in most cases we're not training journalists, we can do an almost infinite number of things with print media.

The same holds true for film, art, TV, photography: if you're sufficiently interested in it, you can think of ways to use it in class, and your enthusiasm for it might make it a fine way to start off your course. In his book, *Tune In: Television and the Teaching of Writing*, Bronwyn Williams makes an extended and convincing argument for the value of analyzing television programs in composition class. You could open your class with a scene from "The Simpsons." We accomplish a lot if on the first day we can stretch students' ideas of "English class" and broaden their definition of "text."

With "The Arrowmaker"

Probably the most clever and literary class-opener I know, and the one with the longest-lasting effects on students, was developed by Charles Woodard using an excerpt from N. Scott Momaday's *The Way to Rainy Mountain*. The activity demonstrates to students, in vivid symbolic form, the importance of speaking up, in class and in life. It requires students to dust off their critical reading skills, and it can lead to a rousing class debate. Dr. Woodard has kindly given me permission to reprint his whole original article in Appendix B, and I strongly urge you to read it and try it out . . . if not on the first day, then sometime in the first two weeks of class.

With Other Key Readings

Troll your memory for short readings that have meant a lot to you and might be a perfect starting point for your class, either because they immediately raise a theme you want to build on or because they attack a belief you want to challenge. Billy Collins's poem "Introduction to Poetry," for instance, quickly and humorously raises the question of how we should respond to poetry or any other creative writing and warns readers against beating the meaning out of a text. Marvin Swift's article, "Clear Writing Means Clear Thinking Means . . . ," argues persuasively that writing and revision create and change meaning, not just style, and reading the article can be an effective first salvo in the battle to convince students that writing isn't just transcription of already-formed thoughts. Bruce Ballenger's "The Importance of Writing Badly" can relieve students of some of their anxiety about being less-than-perfect writers. Reading a Dave Barry column can allow you to assert that good writing can be fun and funny. Follow your enthusiasm. Start with something you enjoy.

•   •   •

I don't like slow "introductions," either in essays or courses; I like to get right to the important stuff, even if that means spending the first day building community and good feelings. Often on the first day, I'll ask students to sign up for a conference sometime later in the week, giving me a chance to meet everyone by the second or third class meeting. I also always hand out a questionnaire (see Appendix C) for students to fill in before their first conference, to give me a head start on finding out who they are and what they might write about. In addition, I give writing students a questionnaire about their writing backgrounds, asking them to think about a recent paper they've written and the process that led to that paper. (See Figure 4.) Asking themselves, "How did I write that?" is a good first step for students, most of whom need to become more aware of their writing processes, especially ones that have worked for them.

Don't fall into the trap of thinking that first days are automatically lost time, treading water until students get the books. Accomplishing something, however small, on the first day will make you feel much better than just dismissing the class early; it will leave both you and your students expecting each class to be purposeful and worthwhile.

5

GRADING, ATTENDANCE, AND OTHER PAINS-IN-THE-BUTT

Teaching in the age of litigation sometimes becomes a defensive game. We have to establish rules and policies not for the one hundred students each year who act like reasonable, civil human beings but for the one per year (or decade) who acts like a bad lawyer on steroids, tries to get away with dereliction in your class, and then searches your syllabus with a magnifier to find the loophole that permits loutish behavior.

So in grading and other crucial issues, we need to prepare for the worst. While that may be a depressing task, it helps us not to worry about the worst for the rest of the semester. We can lean on a good syllabus. Constructed with care and a certain degree of paranoia, syllabi help us through difficult times.

In our syllabi and elsewhere, we need to be proactive and open about our grading and other policies, rather than downplay our role and pretend we're not the gate-keepers, the grade-givers. It helps no one to be dishonest with ourselves or our students about the place of grades in our classes. As Elbow says, "The more I try to soft-pedal assessment, the more mysterious it will seem to students and the more likely they will be preoccupied and superstitious about it" ("Embracing" 153). We may want to eliminate grades from our courses, but we have to be realistic about how we compute them and how they affect our students. "You can tell students anything you want about 'taking responsibility' and 'thinking for yourself,'" Jerry Farber says, but "the grading system you employ—a middle finger extended before them—is always more eloquent still" (274).

RANDOM GRADING TIPS

Grading is a hugely complex subject. If you want to dig deeply into that complexity, try Tobin's chapter "What We Really Think About When We Think About Grades" (57-74). If you give yourself a hard time because you find yourself so conflicted when grading, read Tobin's "Thirteen things that I think about when I give grades that teachers are not supposed to think about when we give grades" (65-66). I wouldn't trust anyone who said grading was easy.

Figure 5

An Attempt to Explain My Paper Grading Approach

Grading papers is a complex and somewhat mysterious process, even to people who do it often. As I read a final draft, my grade estimate gets swayed subtly by a large number of factors, some of which I've listed here. The qualities above the line pull a paper up toward an A, while the qualities below (and, usually, the opposite of the "good" qualities, e.g. "lack of clear focus") pull the grade down toward D.

---

a well-developed and well-supported thesis or point • insight • interesting information • unique or unusual ideas or perspectives • humor • successful metaphors • telling details • effective organization • lively language • clear focus • good use of quotations • originality • challenge • distinctive personal voice • thought—writer's and reader's

---

spelling and proof reading problems • wordiness • grammatical errors • confusion • logic problems • oversimplification • fog • punctuation quirks, especially run-ons and fragments

---

To avoid having this section take over the whole book, I will assume that you don't have control over the entire grading system and the question "To grade or not to grade?" is moot. These "tips" cover aspects of grading I feel fairly confident about. The next section, "Grading Dialogues," digs into thornier issues about which reasonable people disagree.

Listen to What Others Have to Say

I've never met a writing teacher who enjoyed grading or who had discovered the perfect way to do it. So many of us keep trying new approaches. For your first semester, you'll probably want to use the grading methods most popular at your school, but when you get a breather, you may want to ask around and/or do some reading about alternatives. When you're gnashing your teeth about grading, it's comforting to know that old timers do that too—I go through what my wife calls "the week of sighs" at the end of the semester when I have to come up with final grades. Read Elbow on "Ranking, Evaluating, and Liking" or James D. Williams on peer-based holistic grading (317-328) or Stephen Tchudi's book on alternative grading methods. You may find a method that appeals to your personality and fits your situation.

Figure 6
Brock's Grade Book

Names: Wait until the third or fourth class meeting to write students' names in your grade book. Otherwise, you'll have cross-outs and names out of order. Take the time to write the names clearly and include nicknames. In a couple of years, when a former student asks you for a recommendation, you'll need all the precise, memory-jogging help you can get. Use the whole gradebook page; if you can give each student two or three lines, all the better.

Attendance: If you quietly record attendance at the beginning of every class, you won't need to remind students that it matters to you. Note lateness, too, in this column.

Participation: As soon as possible after class, note everyone who contributed for that day, so you have a relatively objective basis for participation grades.

Grades: Obviously every time you give a grade for a paper or presentation, it needs to go in your book. If you grade two versions of the same paper, will you cross out one and squeeze the other in, or record them in separate columns?

Paper Content: Even if you keep a separate log of each paper and its strengths and weaknesses, record each paper's contents in shorthand in your gradebook.

Participation Estimate: At the end of the semester, before I add up the times a student has participated, I jot down my general sense of how that student has contributed. I don't like basing the participation grade solely on my memory of who talked on what days. I may forget to note participation on days when a particular student speaks up, or the student may carry a discussion one day and then be silent for a week, and I want to leave room to reward participation quality, not just quantity.

Participation Number: Make sure all crucial grade calculations appear in your gradebook, in case you need to go back months later and reconstruct a grade.

Name	Attendance	Participation	Grades	Paper Content	Participation Estimate	Participation Number	Participation Grade	Total Pts	Brownie Pts	Final Grade
Adams, Eve	✓✓✓✓✓	✓✓✓✓	A-	guns	A	12	A	93	+	A
Bard, Will (Billy)	✓✓✓✓✓	✓✓✓	D+	shoelaces	C+	3	C	78	–	C+
Cox, Alice	– – ✓✓	✓✓✓	C-	divorce	B	8	B+	86		B
⋮										

Here, add up the student's participation checkmarks (and perhaps subtract participation minuses if the student was disruptive).

Participation Grade: I reconcile the last two columns and come up with an overall participation grade (my version of checks and balances). At the top of this column, and every other column that has a direct bearing on the final grade, put the percentage that this number contributes to the final grade.

Total Points: If you give points for each assignment, you'll need a column in which to total the points before you convert them to a letter grade. Even when I've given everything a letter grade, I usually convert all the grades to numbers so I can easily compare students' overall performance.

Brownie Points: As objective as we might want to be, every teacher is affected by factors that are difficult to put into numbers—attitude, effort, and improvement, for instance. I sum up such factors, as well as attendance, in this column.

Final Grade: Make sure you label this column clearly. It's embarrassing to return to last year's grades and not be able to tell instantly which is the crucial one.

Use Pencil

It erases. Read over and correct your comments before you turn the papers back. You don't want to sound as foolish as the professor who wrote on a student paper, "proffreading is important." Also, we don't want to add to the generations of student writers who have been turned off by teachers' "bleeding" on their papers in red ink.

Keep Tabs

Keep as much information on students as you can. Either in a grade-book, on a computer, or on a sheet you construct for the purpose, list all the students in the class and keep track of things like

- the subject, length, and grade of each paper
- attendance
- participation
- lateness (to class or with papers)
- a few strengths and major weaknesses of the papers
- number, type, and effectiveness of all revisions
- grades, even those estimates you may be forced to give orally

After you teach for a few semesters, you'll know which bits of information you actually make use of, and you can stop gathering the worthless stuff. Having data to support our grading and classroom management decisions can make us feel confident and reduce worries about grade gripes.

Don't Estimate

Students will want you to take a quick look—or even a long look—at a paper and give them an estimated grade; after a discussion of a draft's strengths and weaknesses, they'll ask, as they stand up, "So what grade would you give this?" Don't fall for it. I always regret giving out estimates. Say "At least a D" or "It'll pass" if you want. I wouldn't be surprised to find that "reading to respond" and "grading" use two different parts of the brain; they're two different functions, two different approaches to a paper. When I'm reading a draft to respond to, I'm trying to find what works, what can be built on, and I often ignore the obvious problems. But when grading, I can't ignore those problems.

Don't Make Spot Decisions about Grades

Students sometimes challenge grades on papers or for the whole course and want you to reconsider the grade on the spot. In the pressure of the moment, it's easy to say "Ok, I'll raise it," or to give a blanket "No." I've made mistakes in both directions. Saying that you'll reread the paper(s) and reconsider the grade almost always mollifies the student. I find that when I'm uncomfortable with a grade, I spend so much time rethinking it that I *want* to reread the paper to become sure enough of the grade that I'll stop losing sleep over it.

Beware of Responding Defensively

I know this one intimately because I'm still very susceptible to it myself. If you worry too much about students' challenging the grades they get on their papers, you will concentrate your reading and probably your response on the reasons the grade isn't higher—the paper's shortcomings. But it's bad pedagogy to mention more than two or three weaknesses in your response, and you always want to mix the criticism with praise. If you have reason to believe that the student may challenge the grade, keep a record for yourself (i.e., not on the paper) of the 101 other reasons it didn't earn an A, and bring it out only if you have to.

Grade Both Relatively and Absolutely

Don't imagine you'll find the one perfect, "objective" grade, but work toward a grade you feel comfortable with. "Don't be objective; be fair,"

Murray counsels. Your own standards and priorities will evolve, and, to encourage that process while you're grading your first sets of papers, you might want to start sketching out your own particular way of grading.

I like to have a sense of absolute standards—the paper I'm giving a B-minus would be mediocre no matter where I encountered it, no matter who judged it. But after I've developed preliminary grades based on my sense of the paper's absolute worth, I often put all the papers in piles from A's to D's and then skim through, asking if these three A-minuses have equivalent strengths and weaknesses and whether the errorless bullshitting argument truly deserves more credit than the heartfelt but barely literate personal essay.

You'll also eventually need to calibrate your grades against others' and make sure your average isn't radically different from everyone else's. Your writing program may hold such calibration sessions during staff meetings or orientations, when everyone will grade and discuss a few papers. But for the time being, be content to work on internal consistency.

Be Flexible in Responding to Grammar

I used to refuse to give above a C-plus to any final draft that contained a sentence fragment or a comma splice. At the time, I felt a bit righteous about having "high standards," but I now think I punished some good writers unfairly. Is "unimaginative research, no idea, and excellent polish" necessarily better than "good research, interesting idea, and poor grammar"? Such uncertainty has led me to favor holistic grading—a grade applied to the whole interacting mishmash of factors—rather than attempt to break the process down into individually graded parts. You can't ignore grammar errors—at least not many, not at the college level—and yet you have to avoid turning into a grammar cop. In the large grey area between those extremes, most of us feel our way toward a grading intuition. We need to keep monitoring our reaction to mechanics and make sure we're not just reenacting what our own teachers did to us.

Grade a Paper's Risk or Degree of Difficulty

Sometime in your first semester, you're likely to encounter a paper that seems flawless—tight, polished, errorless writing that fulfills the assignment—but says nothing, goes nowhere. There's nothing "wrong" with it, so you have trouble not giving it an A, but how can you give it a top mark when others in the class have done so much more with their papers?

To head off such problems, I always include a "degree of difficulty" or "risk" factor in my assignment descriptions or grading rubric. Students have no problem with the concept (most have watched Olympic diving or gymnastics), but they may never have encountered it in a writing class. I usually mention a couple of examples to get the idea across—should a flawlessly written paper describing how to bake a cake from a mix get the same grade as a flawed but provocative essay that sets forth an original peace plan for the Middle East? Make sure you talk about this issue before students choose their topics, so they don't automatically fixate on the simplest and most manageable topic.

Don't Get Caught in the Time Trap

Teachers tend to be sensitive, sympathetic souls, and we don't want to treat our students the way some professionals treat us, with a minimum of time and attention. With that mind set we end up agonizing and guilt-tripping ourselves whenever we ponder not rereading the fifth draft quite as carefully or not writing another two-page note to a student who didn't learn from the last one.

It's very easy to overwhelm students' capacity to accept and use even positive, constructive criticism. Two good sentences about a paper's key strength and key weakness may be more helpful than two pages, and the student will almost certainly greet them with more enthusiasm. Similarly, very few people have the strength to look at every marginal comment and correction on a well-marked-up paper. And students value a quick response at least as much as they value an accurate grade or a sensitive comment.

So what does this mean in terms of hours and minutes? How long should it take you to grade a batch of five-page papers? I've never seen a study that asked that question, so I can only guess. If you're just grading, no comments, I think you could handle six to twelve papers per hour. Grading *and* writing comments takes me twenty minutes per paper minimum—and often much longer. But remember, no one else has any way of gauging the time you spend on a paper. So there's nothing wrong with skimming a paper that you've already read and coming up with a quick grade.

Separate the Personal from the Academic

If you give students control over the subjects they choose to write about (something I strongly advocate), you'll inevitably face a heart-wrenching paper about death, desire, or divorce and you may find yourself saying, "I know this incident forever changed your life, but—as a paper—it's a D." If

I have a chance to communicate with a student about such a paper before I have to grade it, I ask, "Do you want just to *talk* about this subject, or do you want to deal with this as a paper?" Often the student volunteers that it isn't much of a paper but he or she just needed to write about it. If the student asks to deal with it as a paper, you can talk about coherence and transitions without feeling callous.

If I don't have a chance to give feedback, I may refuse to grade the paper, giving the student credit for it but saying, "It would demean this subject to criticize this paper." In almost every case, the student wants, first, to have the importance of the subject recognized. Once you do that successfully, you can discuss grading issues with less trauma.

Accept Grading's Subjectivity

The subjectivity of responses to writing and the lack of universally accepted and assessable goals and standards worry both students and teachers. Students complain, "She just didn't like my style," and teachers worry, "How can I justify giving this one a B-minus and that one a C-plus?"

Some schools seek to avoid the subjectivity of grading by using exit exams or having teachers grade other teachers' students. I'm not going to discuss those options because there's little chance that you will have any choice about whom you grade. I mistrust such systems because they treat our subjectivity, the humanness of the bond between comp teacher and student, as a problem rather than an opportunity, a weakness to be avoided rather than a strength to be exploited.

To my mind, the relationship between student writer and writing teacher resembles all the other important writing relationships a writer must deal with—student/professor, writer/editor, employee/boss. We write almost nothing for a general, objective, faceless audience. Instead, we write for multiple audiences—usually ourselves and maybe some idealized "general audience"—but most particularly for the one person who will pass judgment or take action on the piece of writing.

So rather than being an ivory-tower anomaly, the writing teacher/student relationship resembles all writing relationships, with one important difference—the writing student can *learn* about writing relationships in a way that an employee is unlikely to learn from a boss, or a writer from an editor. The writing student can plumb the teacher's priorities and standards, negotiate form and content, and learn from all the interactions between writer and audience, interactions which, outside of the writing class, tend to be hidden from view. The student may find it irritating to have to conform to the teacher's eccentricities, but doing so will prepare the student for the eccentricities of other important audiences in other "discourse communities" less likely than the writing teacher to have reasons for their biases and to be willing and able to articulate them.

Therefore, my advice to those worried about their subjectivity is to engage students in a discussion of the subjectivity of audiences—they will almost certainly have stories about Teacher X demanding one thing and Teacher Y something quite different. Help students see that the two teachers did not want opposite or contradictory elements in a paper; they probably both worked from a similar list of "elements of good writing." That one might put "creativity" at the top of the list and the other "polished surface" should neither surprise nor disturb us. Discuss the complexities of writing for multiple audiences and be as clear and open as possible about what you as a teacher look for in papers. If you're a stickler about spelling, format, or comma splices, say so. I believe that just about any grading emphasis can be justified *if* the teacher explains the emphasis to students. As former NCTE president Victor Villanueva (2002) says,

> Grading is based on a Platonic sense that we know good texts when we see them. This is every bit as subjective as students accuse it of being. A teacher must establish his or her criteria and subjective quirks from the outset and remain consistent. (100)

Don't be embarrassed about your subjective reactions to students. Recognize that the personal, subjective bond you develop with students allows you to personalize your pedagogy, to be more human and less like a Scantron, and to help students study and understand the kind of writing relationship that will probably never be as transparent for them again. (See "In Defense of Subjective Grading" in Appendix D.)

GRADING DIALOGUES

I'm setting up the next section of this chapter as a dialogue between two voices because these issues are complex, and I don't want to pretend that there's a right way to handle them. Every teacher reaches a slightly different point of stability within these dialogues. But I will mention my own default way of handling these situations, in case you don't have time at the moment to bother with the complexities and want something approximating an answer right now.

Should we grade improvement and effort?
    Yes.

- If we don't grade improvement and effort, only English majors may get top grades.

- Students who improve but still don't receive good grades get discouraged.

- We should encourage advancements in process, skills, and attitudes, not just ability to complete assignments well.

No.

- It's almost impossible to judge how one student's effort compares to another's, and gauging improvement is almost as difficult.

- It's a shame to discourage untalented writers, but it's even worse to punish writers just because they wrote well before the semester began.

- We can and should analyze and work to improve writers' processes, but ultimately the best measure of the process is the product, and it would be crazy to punish a good writer for having created a product in an unconventional way, even if "unconventional" here means "seemingly without effort or improvement."

Default: Grade the product, but make students aware that effort and improvement affect the "fudge factor."

Should we maintain the same writing standards throughout the semester instead of raising the bar higher as writers improve?
Yes. Standards should be consistent throughout.

- Students need to deal with a realistic assessment of their abilities. Realism may discourage some, but it may light motivational fires under others. An early A may give some students the false impression that they can just cruise through the semester.

- While it may be psychologically difficult for both student and teacher to face a low grade in September, it's more important to feel in December the satisfaction of improvement.

- I wouldn't want to explain to a student that a paper that earned an A in September gets only a B-minus in December.

- You can avoid discouraging students by not grading early papers, or by grading them and emphasizing the chances for revising the grade upward.

No. Grade easy at first.

- High early grades make students enjoy writing more and increase the likelihood that they will put time and energy into it.

- The worst thing we can do to struggling writers (about 98% of the population) is give them a grade early in the semester that says "you can't do this."

- Grading easy at first doesn't mean you're a pushover for the course. There's plenty of time in a grading period to raise the bar.

- We can start off lenient in specific ways—like not counting off for mechanical errors—and then get tougher as time goes on.

Default: Work for consistency.

Should we grade class participation?

Yes. And we should let students know what we're grading and why participation is so crucial to their learning:

- Students can often learn as much from other students as from the teacher; a silent student receives but doesn't give.

- When students ask questions and get answers, or make statements and get feedback, they tend to remember the whole discussion much better than if they just listen.

- A relatively small composition class may provide the best chance that normally shy students will ever have to change their image; if they leave college still timid about speaking in public, they may find themselves too often sitting silently in corners.

- People who assert themselves in class get practice which should help them assert themselves in their writing and education.

No. We shouldn't grade participation because

- We're all liable to see and count some kinds of participation and miss others, like small-group work.

- We should encourage multiple forms of participation, possibly including shared journals, that could substitute for traditional discussion participation.

- Some terminally shy students would be so stressed by a participation requirement that they might drop the class.

- We're not teaching public speaking. You get those classes in the Communication department.

Default: I grade participation, but it can also fit easily in the "fudge factor" category.

Should we take and grade attendance?
Yes.

- In an ideal world, students would come because they're fascinated, but the lure of the Game Cube is always going to beat us out.

- Absences change the class dynamic; if the group gets too small, the teacher and the remaining students have to work hard to keep the energy level up.

- Every English class is at least partially about process and methods, not about facts that can be memorized and tested. Not counting attendance makes as little sense as not counting an exam.

- In any course, students learn how to be "good students," a step toward being "good employees." We don't do students any favors by making college a "no fault" zone where you show up when you feel like it.

No.

- Grading attendance is high school stuff, an insult to both teachers and students.

- Some students argue that if they do the required paperwork for the class, there's no justification for their having to sit there as well.

- Grading attendance gets us into the sticky moral and practical territory of judging whether a grandparent's funeral is a better excuse than a faulty alarm clock or strep throat.

- We should make each day interesting enough, and important enough to the overall course, so students don't have to be coerced to come.

Default: Make attendance part of your "fudge factor" and/or outline a vague but potentially severe missed-classes penalty in your syllabus, like my "missing more than 3 classes will lower your final grade." And I would add to that "or being frequently late." Tardy students are more disruptive than absent ones because they make you wonder whether you should start the class again or fill them in. Other students notice if you tolerate lateness, and the problem can become an epidemic.

Should we grade everything?
Yes.

- Because many students pay attention only to graded assignments, any serious assignment has to carry a grade.
- The more information we can give students about our grading priorities and standards, the better. And the more grades they get, the more they know about how they're doing, the less surprised they'll be at the end.
- It usually takes less time to come up with a grade than to write comments, and a grade may communicate more.

No.

- Why spend the time, when students hate being battered by grades anyway? And responding without a grade is much easier on the teacher psychologically.
- Students need to accept that writing has intrinsic value even without a grade attached.
- Usually we can make the ungraded material into necessary steps leading to the graded material.

Default: For homework or journals, just record who did it. Grade everything else that's not officially designated "rough draft," but don't feel you have to come up with letters or numbers. "Check," "plus," and "minus" are useful as well, and for papers that can be revised, let students know that the grades can be revised as well.

Should we grade drafts as well as the final paper?
Yes.

- If you don't grade early drafts, students won't take them seriously.
- A grade is the one unambiguous part of your response. Good teachers always find something to praise in a draft, but students may misconstrue that praise to mean "an A for sure."

- Students get antsy if they don't get grades until the end of the semester.

No.

- We shouldn't let grades interfere with learning until absolutely necessary.
- We can give students the option of having their drafts graded; most won't take it.
- Grading is much more stressful than responding; why start that stress early?

Default: Grade an early draft, but do it quickly, grade low, and make it count only 1/4 of the paper's total grade.

Do we grade the person? Consider life history, effort, enthusiasm, and improvement, unavoidable drains on the student's energy, the effect the grade might have on the student's motivation and future?
Yes.

- To be fair, we must look at background and previous experience to judge a student's work in the class.
- We shouldn't be slaves to numbers, denying a student the crucial A because the numbers don't quite justify it. Often, ignoring the arithmetic is the most fair, humane, and pedagogically sound thing to do.
- Grades don't measure anything perfectly and always have political elements and political effects. So we don't *make* a grade political by, for instance, giving a break to a good student who needs a certain GPA to get a scholarship. We just change the political equation slightly.

No.

- We can't possibly grade "the person" fairly. We know the life stories of some students and nothing about others. How can we determine which lives deserve breaks?
- Giving extra points for particularly helpful or enthusiastic students brings elements into the grading mix not listed in the syllabus. And it encourages students to be suck-ups.

- In the long run, doing students favors with grades does not help them. You might be tempted to give a break to particularly good writers, but they need to learn the lesson of deadlines the same as anyone else. For her own good, the brilliant procrastinator may need to get the B she really earned instead of the A that many teachers would give her by bending the rules.

Default: Be able to justify any grade with calculations, but if your gut gives you a strong message about a student's grade, fudge the numbers a little so the calculations agree with your instinct.

Should we worry about grade inflation?
   Yes.

- Grade inflation punishes the outstanding students. If mediocrity gets an A, brilliance goes unrewarded. We need to remind both ourselves and our students that most universities define C as average or competent work—no real problems but no outstanding features either.

- The administration—*"they"*—might care. I've had wonderful colleagues who routinely gave everyone A's and went on to live productive lives. But I never knew how seriously to take their students' enthusiastic evaluations.

- It can be embarrassing when the press gets hold of the stuff that passes, or gets an "A," in our classes. A "B" should mean something.

No.

- We want to encourage revision by grading final drafts, and revision inevitably leads to higher grades.

- Any college student should be capable of turning C-plus writing into B work over the course of a semester, and we don't want to punish everyone in a class just because many of them did the necessary work.

- A writing teacher can encourage with a high grade and save the constructive criticism for comments.

Default: Don't worry about grade inflation now. Try to make sure you give a range of grades on the first paper, and at some point you'll need to do some cross-grading with others to make sure your grades aren't too far from your school's norm.

COVER YOUR ASS

We write mostly, I fear, to cover our butts, to provide documentation or support in case of future challenges, whether lawsuits from customers or dunning notes from the boss. You may be getting a Master's in English because you want to write novels or critical theory, but you will actually devote much of your keyboard time to more mundane writing tasks performed primarily to prove that you did it. And, sorry, I'm not going to encourage you to fight city hall and ignore all that "busywork." On the contrary, since I aim to help you worry less about your teaching, I encourage you to CYA in as many ways as possible at the beginning, then perhaps reduce the paper volume as you become more experienced and more adept at solving problems spontaneously. So how do you CYA?

What to Get in Writing

Syllabus

I detailed in Chapter 2 and earlier in this chapter the things I put in every syllabus. As you make up yours, do some soul-searching and figure out what rules really matter to you. Anything you don't get into the syllabus will be hard to enforce later. Do you feel strongly about attendance, tardiness, deadlines, offensive language, plagiarism, participation, group work? Put your feelings and requirements in writing. You can always back off and bend later if you want.

Assignments

Whether or not you make assignment descriptions part of the syllabus, for your sake you need to put these things in writing: dates (of first drafts and revisions), page limits, format requirements, content requirements. Assume nothing. Yes, you'd think that anyone writing a "response to literature" paper would know that they're supposed to talk about some literature, but. . . . Unless your students are much better than mine, you will never create an assignment description clear enough and thorough enough to make sense to everyone. But if you put the crucial parts of the assignment in writing, you'll at least be able to point to them when a student says, "But you never told me . . ."

Plagiarism Statements

When I began teaching, discussions about student plagiarism involved mostly shame and pleas for mercy. Now, perhaps because plagiarism has become so commonplace at the highest levels, students may respond to a plagiarism charge with "So?" or "You didn't tell me that was wrong" or "Talk to my lawyer."

This kind of attitude means every writing teacher must have a clear and detailed definition of plagiarism in the syllabus. But for many teachers, that isn't enough. When, in the process of prosecuting a plagiarism case, the questions arise, "Did the student know what the word 'plagiarism' means?" and "Did the student promise not to plagiarize?," teachers may need written proof that they can answer "yes" to both. Some of my colleagues include fill-in-the-blank plagiarism statements in their course packets and require that students sign and turn in a statement with every paper. Others have students read a definition of plagiarism, or go through plagiarism exercises (many publishers now provide them on book-related websites), or sign a blanket statement indicating their understanding and promising not to plagiarize throughout the semester.

Doing such things will seem to be a time-wasting pain early in the semester. But if your students do cheat, you'll be very glad you put in the effort. Your institution probably has established ways of dealing with plagiarism. Find out. (See Chapter 9 for more on plagiarism.)

Changes

Very few students will complain if you push back a paper due date, but you probably need to document and perhaps even get students' signatures on other substantial changes in requirements, assignments, grading, and deadlines.

Special Exceptions and Excuses

I generally believe what students tell me; I don't want to investigate whether their grandmother really did die or make a traumatic situation more difficult by asking for a doctor's note confirming the "procedure." But you should make clear in your syllabus that anyone who expects to be excused for absences—primarily for athletic events and other school-sanctioned activities—should present you with a written schedule of when they will be gone. And you might want to make a form for them to sign each time they're going to be absent, indicating why they will be gone, taking responsibility for making up the work, and stating when they will turn in any assignments that will come due while they're away. (Many teachers will accept such "missed" assignments only if they're turned in *before* the student leaves for the activity.) You might teach for years without ever seeing much value in such forms, but then you may run into an athlete who uses the "I've got practice" excuse to miss class after class.

When you make exceptions, try to do so in writing—perhaps by emailing the student and sending a copy to yourself. You won't remember by the end of the semester whether you excused the student for one day (as you think you did) or indefinitely, as the student claims.

What to Document

Besides creating your own paperwork to try to prevent—or give yourself the best defense against—student complaints, you should get in the habit of keeping copies of all relevant documents whenever a problem seems to be brewing. That means, when dealing with possible plagiarism, keeping a copy of the original paper, any sources you turn up, any plagiarism statements the student has read or signed, emails or notes you or the student writes.

Plagiarism probably creates the greatest need, but other issues should be documented as well. Keep notes on all inappropriate comments, especially sexual ones, and save any letters or notes that students send you. Sexual harassment is not dead on campus, and it can be very frustrating to know you've been harassed but not to have all the evidence because at first the harassing comments seemed trivial. Many campus disability or equal opportunity offices now insist that students be given special accommodations only if they present the teacher with signed paperwork from those offices. No one wants individual teachers trying to judge whether a learning disability or medical problem justifies exemptions or accommodations.

Require students to put any official business in writing as well. "Asking a student to write a one-page explanation of why a paper deserves a higher grade is a technique that both discourages shallow challenges and encourages introspection and analysis" (Wilkerson 11), and the same holds true for most complaints. You can defuse some tense moments with students by insisting that the discussion shift to paper.

What Not to Sign

Especially during the first few weeks, students will crowd your desk after class wanting you to sign things, principally add and drop forms.

While I can't see any harm in letting someone drop—it's not our job to argue with students about priorities or remind them they can't complete their major without our course—be very wary of signing anyone into your class. At some schools, the teacher has complete control of the roll; at others, like my own, the computer has control, and if I—or students—try to bypass the computer's control with a signature, the computer will ignore me and double-book the opening in my class. So this is another good time for "let me get back to you." Ask someone how the system works.

What to Tell the Boss

As a writing administrator, I would like to think that my colleagues trust me and see me as a problem-solver, not a problem-creator. But I know that the teachers on my staff don't want to bother me with trivia and hesitate to mention to me problems that might put them in a bad light. Administrators certainly appreciate teachers who can handle their own problems, but at the same time, they don't like learning about a student's unhappiness when a parent or the university's lawyer calls. So part of CYA is FYI—sending copies of memos and emails to your immediate boss when you think there's any chance that the boss might eventually become involved in the situation. That means making copies for your boss of any correspondence involving grade disputes, plagiarism, or other cheating; responses to students' claims of discrimination or unfairness; documentation of students' disruptive or unruly behavior; and other special cases.

•　　•　　•

Any time you talk to a veteran writing teacher, think about expanding this chapter, adding the tips that you glean from the conversation. But don't accept uncritically the advice offered. Teaching is a system of interrelated issues, and the DNA of that system is you. The system is and should be a reflection of you. So you may not know if a piece of advice will work for you until you try it out or think through how it fits with the rest of your practice and philosophy.

6

WHAT YOU NEED TO KNOW
ABOUT THEORY (FOR NOW)

I suppose as an undergrad I heard the word "theory" and perhaps fret-
ted that I didn't know enough about it. But I wasn't forced to confront
theory's haughty stare until my first semester of graduate school, when
I took a course in theory taught by E. D. Hirsch, Jr., later to achieve
national notoriety for his books about cultural literacy. Hirsch assumed
you knew the ideas of Heidegger, Husserl, and the hermeneutics crowd,
and I quickly found myself drowning. On the first paper I got a "pass"
(which at Virginia was failing), and I knew I had to get a "distinction"
(an A) on the second paper or lose all hope of gaining "permission to
proceed" to the Ph.D. So I wrote on the brilliant validity theories of a
certain E. D. Hirsch, Jr, and how they incorporated and linked the more
limited theories of other thinkers. I got my A and my permission to proceed, but for decades I feared theory as the enemy of common sense and
good teaching.

I know I'm not the only one who started teaching composition with
a fear of theory. Despite or perhaps because of Hirsch's course, I wasn't
sure what the word meant. I knew I was supposed to care about theory,
and I knew that writers like Don Murray who weren't sufficiently theoretical (the word here meaning, I think, "incomprehensible") shouldn't be
taken seriously. But I couldn't imagine what those effete Germans had to
do with my writing courses. As soon as I picked up the chalk in my own
classroom, I became a composition practitioner and forgot about the big-
name theorists in Hirsch's class.

Resistance to theory is common in composition programs. Ironically,
it may result either from lack of theoretical knowledge, or from being
"inundated with theory in graduate courses" (Neeley 21). In either case,
it can be debilitating and self-defeating.

Luckily, I eventually learned that while it may be fine for a composition teacher to ignore particular literary and philosophical theories like
hermeneutics, all good teaching is theory-based . . . which is just another
way of saying that good teachers know what they're doing and why.

Theory helps us make effective minute-by-minute decisions and construct intellectually coherent classes. To teach effectively, we need theory's "generalizations about an area . . . in terms of which descriptions of phenomena in that area can be couched and explanations can be offered" (Gee 12). Gee says, "there is no escape from theory" (5): the question is whether our theories are conscious and explicit or tacit, implicit. If we don't make clear to our students why we're doing or advocating something, they'll construct their own explanations, their own theories. Students learn "rules" like "You can't start a sentence with 'because'" or "You should never use 'I'" when we don't provide—or students don't hear—a full, nuanced explanation. Without any sense of the theory behind what we do, our classes become a series of shot-in-the-dark exercises—busywork, as our students complain.

We always need a thoughtful answer to "Why am I doing this?" If we ignore modern composition ideas, naive and tacit theories (Gee 12-13) will likely guide our thinking: "The way I was taught is the best way." And that's a problem. I don't want to pass Warriner's *Grammar* on to another generation. Theory allows us to see what else we might do; theory tells us, for instance, that direct grammar instruction is largely futile, and that frees us to find or invent other modes of helping students learn grammar and to choose to concentrate class time on other things.

[margin note: role of theory]

Historically, composition has had an uneasy relationship with the word "theory." Composition's practicality and perceived lack of theoretical foundation long justified keeping it in the attic of the ivory tower, the poor relative of literature. This situation began to change in the mid-1960s, and by the late 1970s, "compositionists" began demanding academic respect, Ph.D. programs with "composition" in the title began springing up, and theories of composition began multiplying. In fact, according to James Thomas Zebroski, "the field of composition appropriated theory far faster than literary studies" (31). "[T]he very folk castigated by some High Theorists, those lowly writing teachers of the 1960s and early 1970s, might well have started a 'chain reaction' that made Theory possible" (45). (Reciting the history of composition is popular these days, but beware: all such histories reflect the beliefs and biases of the historians.)

[margin note: History: theory vs practice]

Although composition is a more mature discipline today, it still holds a unique position in the academy because

[margin note: Position of comp program]

1. Its subject is writing, the most concrete mode of human thought, so any body of theory—from psychology to communication to

anthropology to sociology—has relevance for the composition teacher and can be incorporated into composition theories.

2.   There are still relatively few departments of composition. Writing programs tend to be housed in English departments, sometimes dominated by literature faculty who may view writing classes as the fourth floor cash cows that they would prefer not to talk about. (Composition tends to bring money into English departments because universities often require—and *fund*—first- and second-year writing courses.)

3.   Because most colleges require a semester or two of composition, writing courses constitute a huge percentage of the overall English offerings each semester. The fourth floor cash cow may have enough weight to affect first floor policy.

4.   Graduate instructors and adjuncts teach most comp courses, while the tenure-line compositionists who write articles for *College Composition and Communication* teach methods courses and seldom show up in first-year English classes, which means that, as far as I can tell,

5.   Most composition courses still focus on the practical—what works? what will engage my students today and get them writing?

I reveal my own biases and background when I say that such a preference for the practical is not a bad thing. Battles among theorists can be fierce, with advocates of the reigning theory belittling those who came before and leaving teachers confused about what they should teach. As much as I'm cautioning against creating a theory-less writing course, I'm saying too much theory is also a widespread problem; theory-minded teachers have used their classes to experiment with or proselytize about their particular theoretical orientation, sometimes teaching their students nothing but their fixation on a particular idea.

Luckily, there's plenty of middle ground. When it comes to pedagogical practice, many of the approaches advocated by particular theoretical positions are useful for any composition class and composition student. Feminists want more collaboration in the classroom; multiple-intelligences experts want us to use images and get students moving around; the constructivists want us to help students see that they are products of the world around them. Each approach can be valuable for all students. And some teaching strategies are accepted almost universally. Everyone believes in giving student writers personal attention, for instance—if only we could find the time for it.

As I read different writers on composition, I try to find overlap and consistency where the writers themselves may see only difference. Disagreements are often matters of emphasis: e.g., is it more important to encourage student growth and self-knowledge or to help students understand academic discourse? To almost all such questions, I answer "both," and I vehemently reject the idea (see Farris) that we harm students if we are theoretically eclectic, drawing our class activities from different theoretical camps. I applaud teachers who refuse to get caught up in the movement of the moment and steadfastly ask, "What will help my students write better tomorrow?"

We can answer that question best by relying on our own experience and that of our colleagues, but some general principles—whether or not one calls them theories—inform the work we do. I certainly don't advocate making comp courses "theoretical"; rather, I think we need to be constantly asking ourselves "Why am I doing this?" and "Why do I think this will work?" and coming up with answers beyond "It will be fun" or "It will keep them busy for fifty minutes." "Theory" doesn't have to refer to incomprehensible European abstractions. "Students improve their writing when they're working on something meaningful" is a theory too, a very powerful one.

How does a teacher choose from among the many competing theories the best one to guide classroom decisions? We first need to be clear about our own beliefs. Theories connect our values, our goals, and our experiences; as one changes, the others change. I'm determined to improve writers' attitudes toward writing because (I theorize from experience) attitude affects every aspect of a writer's performance. As I summarize some of the theories important to composition in this chapter, you will see that I tend to highlight those aspects of the theories that offer ways to make students more comfortable with writing. A teacher determined to prepare students for academic writing might draw on different elements of the same theories. There is no generally right or best theory, though there may be a best one for a particular situation. So know your goals and priorities before you venture into theory . . . and be ready to amend those goals as different theories offer you new insights. We always need to keep an eye on the larger picture, so we don't just repeat for our students the experiences we had in school or borrow activities from friends with no thought of how they fit our own goals.

This chapter will not guilt-trip you about all the dense academic books you should be reading or even try to give a thorough overview of all the theories that have some bearing on composition. Instead, I'll trace the development of the theories that have affected me as a teacher in the past thirty years. Perhaps reading about my own path will help you choose yours.

PROCESS, MY FIRST CLUE

I well remember the "thin ice" feeling of pretending to teach a composition class without knowing answers to any of the "Why?" questions. I had my Ph.D. in hand, I could spot a passive verb at fifty paces, I was using the top-notch reader and handbook that the writing program recommended. But I had no rationale for what I was doing. I felt like such a fraud that I canceled some Friday classes because I couldn't justify a third pointless hour of class.

Enter the process approach. The most earth-shattering change in composition during my lifetime seems, in retrospect, the most simple and obvious. When I was growing up in the 1960s, writing was a great mystery. We were given an assignment, turned it in, got it back with a grade, some red marks, and a short comment, and then somehow were expected to do better on the next paper. Between "get assignment" and "turn it in" was a large black box that no one talked about, although everyone knew that's where writing occurred (Bizzell 110). A history teacher gave me the one piece of writing advice I remember from secondary school: "Create the frame, then fill in the picture." I remember the advice because it shed a tiny sliver of light on that black box. He was talking about process.

At about the same time, other, older minds were advancing beyond the old questions—"What's right and wrong about this writing product?"—to the central question of the process movement—"What does the writer do to create a good written product?" Peter Elbow began his search as he struggled to overcome the writer's block that was holding up his academic career: "I couldn't study, couldn't figure things out, couldn't write anything" (*Contraries* xii). Donald Murray, a Pulitzer-prize winning journalist turned writing professor, tried to help student writers by examining his own processes in his 1968 book, *A Writer Teaches Writing*. And in 1971, Janet Emig published *The Composing Processes of Twelfth Graders,* bringing a researcher's rigor to the question of what student writers do to get their papers written. In England, James Britton was arguing against traditional writing exercises, which he called "dummy runs," and championing the expressive function of language (Joseph Harris 8-9). No one person can claim to have invented the process movement; at more or less the same time, a lot of observant people realized that the old assign-and-correct system wasn't working, and they all, to use a Murray analogy, started trying to figure out what was going on when the ball went through the hoop for a writer.

The 1970s and 1980s saw an explosion of articles and texts about writing process. What steps should writers take, and in what order? How do the processes of professionals differ from those of novices? When should teachers intervene in a student's writing process? Is there a "best" writing process for each writer or each assignment, or would the ideal process vary with assignment, writer, and situation? (See Lad Tobin, "Process Pedagogy," for a history and bibliography of the movement.)

We still lack firm answers to most such questions, though it seems clear that no one process works best for every writer or every assignment. Because many advocates of "process" also encourage students to write from their own experiences and develop their writing voice, "process" became associated in many minds with "personal writing" and "expressivism." This association seems to me a silly mistake. Every piece of writing, no matter how formal, academic, and impersonal, results from a writing process. Examining and possibly altering that process might benefit the writer and the writing product, whether that product is a personal diary or a business plan. As Anne Ruggles Gere puts it, "Elements of the writing process, whether they are called prewriting, drafting, and revising or incubating, writing, and reworking, can be adapted to any model" of composition pedagogy (22). As an advocate of the process approach for twenty-five years, I'm clearly biased, but no matter what new fads may sweep the composition world, I think we should always be asking the process question, "What's a good next step for this writer to take?"

A process emphasis carries enormous practical implications, and all comp teachers should at some point immerse themselves in process pedagogy. For starters, I will list some of the key ways in which the process approach currently manifests itself in many composition classrooms.

1. We explain, demonstrate, provide time for, and encourage many different writing strategies, from freewriting for ideas, to finding a focus, to ordering the material, to revising. No one activity will appeal to every student in a class, but if students leave the course feeling that two or three approaches "work" for them, that may be the biggest gift we can give them.

2. We help students become aware of their own writing processes and the effects of those processes on their written products. A sloppy, error-filled paper may indicate that a student just can't write, but before you wade into cataloguing the paper's problems, ask about the process that led to the paper. Chances are, the student started writing just hours before the due date and knows the paper is a disaster, so you need to talk not about punctuation but about procrastination. Similarly, when a paper succeeds, we need to help the student writer figure out why and remember the lesson for next time. Some critics accuse process-oriented teachers of ignoring the product, but in fact we can judge the success of a process only by looking at its product . . . and by asking the writer how the process felt.

3. We intervene with particular process suggestions when students flounder. Knowing what to suggest, depending on the student's own diagnosis and progress, takes experience, but a quick look at Chapters 2 and 3 of Murray's *A Writer Teaches Writing* (2nd ed.) can provide more suggestions than any one writer could possibly use. If a process seems to be working—if the writer likes the written products and doesn't fret too much during the writing—I'm inclined not to meddle with it, even if parts of it seem inefficient.

4. We keep reminding ourselves and our students that no one process works for every writer or every writing task. The process varies from writer to writer, task to task, time to time. What works smoothly for me may be useless for you. The lure of presenting *the* way to do it is powerful; some textbooks prescribe process steps as rigidly as others prescribe grammatical correctness.

5. As I mentioned in Chapter 2, the writing process provides a convenient and logical organizing principle for a class period or an entire course, starting with methods of coming up with ideas and ending with editing activities. Once I started using this process logic, my courses made much more sense to me.

The process approach rescued me when I was just starting out, and it still gives me a rationale for the work we ask students to do—if an activity helps students with the writing process, if it teaches them something about prewriting, drafting, or revising, if it results in titles or leads or outlines they might use in their papers, it is worthwhile. That a process orientation will always be valuable seems to me unassailable. Writing teachers could no more ignore the steps that lead to a finished writing product than an automotive engineer could ignore the steps used to build a car. But perhaps because the idea of process has taken such strong hold in writing teachers' minds, someone had to attack it.

"POST-PROCESS"

The term "post-process" has never made sense to me. Everything is a process, even death and decay. You can't get "beyond" or "after" process. To understand the term, you have to know that "post-process" theorists have created a caricature of writing process theory and pedagogy, a travesty that, unfortunately, now gets cited as if it were the real thing.

In the introduction to his widely read book *Post-Process Theory*, Thomas Kent lists what he calls "the central tenets of the writing-process movement": "this process is generalizable, at least to the extent that we know when someone is being 'recursive' or to the extent that we know when to intervene in someone's writing process or to the extent that we know the process that experienced or 'expert' writers employ as they write" (1). I don't know any process theorist or practitioner who would agree with Kent's statements, yet they seem to have become gospel for post-process thinkers, who viciously attack the idea that there is one right writing process— ignoring process advocates' consistent assertion that the most appropriate process depends on all the elements of the rhetorical situation. As Lee-Ann M. Kastman Breuch points out, "post-process scholarship has ignored process as how-centered and has curiously assumed that process is content-based"—thus effectively reversing the common-sense meaning of "process" (106). Since the insights of the post-process movement "have been present in previous scholarship about composition pedagogy, alternative pedagogies, and pragmatic theories dating back to John Dewey" (118), don't spend your precious theory-reading time on "post-process."

EXPRESSIVISM

"Process" gave me a justification and organization for my courses. "Expressivism" motivated me. Despite my adjunct's pay and status, I continued to teach, and stay reasonably sane, for twenty years largely because I was, long before the word was coined, an "expressivist." I encouraged students to write about things that mattered to them, and as a result, their papers, however badly written, were almost always interesting enough to keep them writing and me reading.

Expressivists theorize that writing is fundamentally a generative act and is deeply connected to cognition. They believe that giving students a chance to express themselves is a valuable goal in and of itself; that the best student writing, even the most academic and impersonal, grows out of the student's own interests; that writing courses should encourage writers to develop interesting and unique writing voices; and that growth in a young writer's character, maturity, and vision may be more important (and more interesting for the teacher) than progress in the writer's grasp of sentence fragments. (See Gere 20, and Burnham.)

Critics of expressivism complain that the world doesn't need another paper on anorexia and that we should be teaching sentence structure, not self-analysis. It's true that some paper topics are as hackneyed as moon-June rhymes, but for a particular student, the cliched subject may be new, and writing about her sister's anorexia may be the only thing that gets a student to care about writing. Few writing courses are purely expressivistic; most teachers use expressive assignments to engage students and then move on to drier, more technical matters. Once engaged, students are more likely to care about structure and grammar and therefore more likely to learn.

SOCIAL CONSTRUCTION

At about the same time that process thinking and expressivism were becoming popular in the world of composition, theories that rejected the notion of the individual as unique, *sui generis,* began to take hold in a variety of humanities and social science disciplines. Modernism was a celebration of the individual artist, but postmodernism, particularly social constructivism, challenges the autonomy of the individual, asserting that we are all products of the groups and cultures that have socialized us, and "our" thoughts are fairly predictable results traceable to the ways we've been "constructed." Constructivists assert—accurately, I think—that constructivist insights may elude writers trained in Romantic, expressivistic classrooms. Expressivist writers in their cold lonely garrets may cling to the notion that their thoughts and writing are uniquely theirs, but writers blind to how much their ideas have been influenced by others, particularly by the dominant culture, are not in a good position to question or break free from that culture. Therefore, some constructivist teachers who help their students recognize the influence of the dominant culture see themselves as "liberating" their students, practicing "critical pedagogy," encouraging "critical literacy" in the "social-epistemic" tradition, "inviting students to engage with ambiguity, multiple perspectives, and open-endedness" (Duffelmeyer 70), "to unify and make connections in one's own experience and academic studies . . . to form sociopolitical opinions based on open-minded and autonomous reasoning rather than on prejudice and authoritarianism" (Lazere 56, qtd. in Duffelmeyer 72).

Like many expressivists, I let several waves of social constructivist thought break around me before I paid attention. But finally I couldn't ignore the clamor of voices saying that students need to explore the world around them, not the one inside their heads; that expressivist writing foregrounds the individual and ignores the insights of social construction (and therefore is apolitical); that any college writing course should be preparing students to write successfully in the academic world. Perhaps most important for my own particular bent, social constructivism provided a theoretical justification for talking about a subject that would otherwise be off limits because it would insult my students: how our politics are socially determined.

Social constructivists tend to see expressivists as mushy-headed, touchy-feely romantics. Expressivists see their detractors as prone to the same mistakes that have caused many English courses to make students hate writing. I don't see the two emphases as being incompatible. I try to do as much of both in every class as I can, but of course given the finite amount of class time, some things get more emphasis than others. I usually end up letting students express themselves and their own ideas in at least one paper per semester. I can't tell you the number of students—many of them senior English majors—who have told me they never really cared about what they were writing until they were given free choice to write about something that mattered to them—to *express* themselves.

I now heartily endorse the goal of helping students discover the origins of their own tastes and biases. Even so, my experience suggests that individuals can cling strongly to their sense of agency and uniqueness even when outside observers would see them as culturally determined. And I worry about the teachers, some of them nominally Marxists, who seem intent upon shoving students' social constructedness down their throats in much the same way that other teachers would forcefeed their students patriotism or racism. To my mind, the relationship between teacher and students creates the most important and lasting political effects of a writing class. If we can empower students, making them feel like respected equals in the world of writing, they will recognize and stand up to oppression more readily than students pressured into accepting their professor's view of the world.

FEMINISM

Composition and feminism often share politics and pedagogies: belief in collaboration, emphasis on cooperation rather than competition, delight in the discovery and construction of new meanings. The two disciplines grew up at the same time, and the majority of composition teachers are women, many of whom become politicized by the often-gendered oppression they encounter. As Elizabeth A. Flynn puts it, "composition studies could be described as a feminization of our previous conceptions of how writers write and how writing should be taught" (571). Feminism comes naturally to many compositionists.

Yet even for teachers who consider themselves feminists, a feminist analysis of a class can lead to surprises. As Ritchie and Boardman say, "Questioning assumptions about genre, form, and style, [feminists] have provided an impetus to seek alternative writing practices" (588). Ritchie and Boardman list some of the focuses and concerns shared by feminist thinkers and "emerging pedagogical theories" in composition:

> coming to voice and consciousness, illuminating experience and its relationship to individual identity, playing the believing game rather than the doubting game, collaborating rather than competing, subverting hierarchy in the classroom. (595)

Paying conscious attention to concerns like these improves our teaching—and may help us reach more of the women in our classes. I try regularly to ask myself questions like

- What's the gender balance in my reading list?

- Do I call on female students as often as male? Do I show the same kind of enthusiasm for their class contributions?

- Are women well represented in the music I play and the films I show?

- Do I teach my students about gender-neutral language?

- Do I offer (or draw from students) a feminist analysis of the reading, when appropriate?

- Do I privilege linear argumentation over other ways of organizing writing? Should I?

- Should I tolerate a colleague calling Margaret Fuller "that broad"?

Asking myself such questions leads me to discover good writers, good writing, and effective pedagogy that I might otherwise have ignored. (See my *From Dylan to Donne,* 26.) Misogynists would sneer at the "politically correct" nature of the questions, but as with many ideas currently damned as "p. c.," the goals are sensitivity to *all* students and equality in the classroom—hardly radical ideas. (See Jarratt, "Feminist Pedagogy.")

#6
LEARNING THEORY

I guess you could say I came late to learning theory; I didn't pick up the foundational principle of education until my last course as a graduate student.

Connect new material to what you already know.

This adage seems obvious, commonsensical. We learn "Mama" and "Dada" by connecting those sounds to the two most familiar beings in our life. We begin learning French by relating a French word to an English word we know: "book=livre." And we don't learn quantum mechanics unless we have a pretty good basis of physics to help us make sense of quarks and muons.

Yet no one mentioned this central principle to me in my first twenty years of education, and we routinely ignore it in school, seldom encouraging bridges between disciplines and sometimes even punishing students for bringing into one class material they learned in another.

Keeping this maxim in mind can make the composition teacher's job much easier. When trying to figure out whether something will work pedagogically, we can simply pose the question, Will it allow or encourage students to connect new material to what they already know? For instance, if you want students to understand "classification," simply defining the term and then asking students to classify the poems they've been reading may not work; it may seem like an alien, academic exercise. But if first you engage students in classifying something they already know—types of Magic cards, perhaps, or the best players at each position in the NBA, or current genres of popular music—they'll move more easily to academic classifications. If you want students to learn about comma splices, using textbook examples may work, but finding an example in the student's own paper will probably be more effective.

This adage also reminds us to make overt the connections that may be obvious to us but won't be to our students. You probably choose the five activities for the coming day because they prepare for future assignments or build on things you've done in the past. But unless alerted to such connections, students may see the activities as busy work. We can't assume that students will make the connections; we need to make them ourselves, or at least lead students to them.

This section could be five hundred pages long; in general I think the more you know about learning theory, the better. But for a quick overview, here are some other commonsensical learning maxims that are easy to forget or ignore:

Learning must Be Active

We ignore this intuitively obvious point because it's much easier to lecture, explain, define a topic—say, active verbs—than to engage students in discovering and figuring out the topic for themselves. Often "efficient" is the enemy of "effective."

Attitude/Motivation Is Crucial

As I argued in Chapter 4, sometimes spending time on seemingly pointless activities that build morale or community may result in pedagogical windfalls: good morale affects learning for the rest of the semester. A day or a semester that improves a student's attitude toward writing has not been a waste.

We Often Learn Best from Those Just Slightly Ahead of Us

It's hard for us to accept that there could be substitutes for the words of wisdom with which we bless our students, yet students sometimes learn best from their peers. This does *not* mean that you can leave all grading and responding to classmates, but it does give us options and takes some of the pressure off the paper-reading frenzy.

Our Brains Are Easily Overloaded

Especially when we're being critiqued. This is a hard lesson for new teachers to learn—we think, logically enough, that if a little feedback is good, a lot has to be better. Being English majors and writers, we may have hungered for more critique than we got from our own professors. But students tend to see the volume of feedback as proportional to the number of problems in a paper, and they tune out quickly. So we need to work to find the one or two key, consistent issues in a student's paper and help the student understand them, rather than try to provide complete, thorough coverage of a paper's strengths and weaknesses. (See Chapters 1 and 8.)

Don't be embarrassed to pick up much of your learning theory second hand, after others have translated the theory into specific classroom activities.

Lynn Langer Meeks and Carol Austin have done that kind of translation for teachers in their book, *Literacy in the Secondary English Classroom,* grounding their ideas in the work of Australian Brian Cambourne, whose research led him to describe eight "conditions of learning" that "need to be in place in the classroom and happening in conjunction with one another" if students are going to learn (5). Cambourne's terms provide a convenient checklist for teachers. A good course will *immerse* students in the task, *demonstrate* how to do it well, set high but reachable *expectations* for performance, make students *responsible* for their own learning, give them opportunities for *practice* and *response* to that practice, help students see how the skill can be *applied* outside of the classroom and build enough interest so that students will be *engaged* in it (Meeks and Austin 3).

Cambourne's conditions can be used in planning—making sure that the activities you have in mind follow all or most of the principles. But they can also be used to diagnose what went wrong—what key principle did an unsuccessful activity lack? Meeks and Austin combine Cambourne's conditions of learning with Lauren B. Resnick's eight "principles of learning" to create what they call "a literacy learning environment" (7-10).

Books like *Literacy* can both introduce us to theorists whose ideas we might pursue more fully and make our course activities better anchored in ideas, more fully "theorized."

READING THEORY

I thought my background in literature had introduced me to plenty of reading theory, but I didn't become aware of the theorist whose work most affects my own until I was well into my third decade of teaching. The late Louise Rosenblatt was one of the most important thinkers in the field of English, and for years she was the most neglected. She published the first edition of her seminal work, *Literature as Exploration,* in 1938, but I managed to miss hearing about her until I read Tom Romano's books sixty years later. He gives her the credit that she deserves.

Rosenblatt's genius lies in her ability to describe the reading process in a way that makes sense and that doesn't ignore the reader, the text, or the author. New Criticism advocated a focus on the text alone, declaring irrelevant or distracting the author's biography and the associations that the reader brings to the text. New Critics sought to identify the best interpretation of the text, the one supported by the most textual evidence.

Reader response criticism revolted against New Criticism, bringing the reader back into the picture, transforming the literary work "into an activity on the stage of a reader's mind"; "the meanings of a text are the 'production' or 'creation' of the individual reader" (Abrams 149–150). This emphasis provided relief to teachers who felt pressured to make sure that all readers come to the same conclusions about a text, but in its extreme form, it tends to treat the text as just a springboard for the reader's ruminations and to see all ruminations as equally valid.

Rosenblatt's transactional theory avoids the extremes of both positions; it appeals to me as a teacher because while it avoids calling any interpretation "wrong," it confirms my own sense that some readings are better than others. It accepts the rather obvious point that readers aren't blank slates: every reader brings an entire life history to a text, and therefore the reader's associations with the text and the meaning the reader gets from it differ from those of any other reader. It also acknowledges that reading is a transaction, the reader's associations and sense of meaning changing as the text provides new information. All interpretations have value, Rosenblatt says, because they all say something about the particular reader, but one interpretation is more valid than another if it accounts for more parts of the text and relies on fewer inferences or interpolations. (We don't want an interpretation of *Hamlet* relying on the existence of the prince's previously unknown sister.) Rosenblatt thus avoids labeling anything a "wrong" reading, a label that has shut up young readers for years, while at the same time she skirts the swamp of pure relativism in which all readings are equal.

What does this have to do with the composition class? Many of our students reach college hating English and writing. If you ask them why, most will relate an experience when a poem or short story excited them, but their enthusiasm soured when they were told that their response was wrong. As a result, most assume that their associations with a text—and by implication all their experiences and ideas—are irrelevant and in fact interfere with their ability to arrive at an "accurate" interpretation.

A few minutes spent on Rosenblatt's ideas can banish the judgment, the "right" and "wrong" from the English class and start students on the road to trusting their own intuitions and associations and valuing their own experiences. Students most often resist open or personal essay assignments because they don't think they've done or thought anything worth writing about. Rosenblatt's assertion that their life experiences and "random" associations do have value, and the teacher's aren't necessarily any better, can help students see their own experiences in a new light. It can also help student writers avoid the feeling that they have failed if a reader doesn't get everything they intended to convey.

In other words, though Rosenblatt has little to say about composition per se, how the writer thinks about readers and the reading process affects every decision a writer makes. So sharing Rosenblatt's ideas with the class, and bringing them up during discussions of readings, can free and relax students and leave them feeling that their writing might really matter.

TEXTUAL THEORIES

Theories that explain how a text affects its readers and therefore how writers should construct texts are as ancient as Greek oratory and as new as "discourse communities." Our students need to learn that language is not a neutral stand-in for reality but always has political content and rhetorical force that can be used or manipulated. Some of the concepts of rhetorical theory, like "audience" and "purpose," find a place in every writing course. Discourse theory asserts that the rhetorical moves of a writer take place in the larger context of a discourse community, people who share certain values and modes of communication—an English department (or composition faculty) for instance. And genre theory highlights the rules and assumptions that underlie specific written genres, helping us understand why the writing in a personal essay should be different from that in a resumé.

Some teachers, especially those emphasizing argument, draw from various rhetorical theories to lead students to closely examine language and its effects. Many start with connotation, or the parts of a paragraph we tend to remember (end, beginning, middle), or the rhetorical triangle—audience, writer, and text. Some move on to talk about the three kinds of authority writers use to affect readers—ethos (we believe in the writer as a person), logos (we're convinced by the logic of the piece), and pathos (we're swayed by our emotional involvement). Other popular ways of understanding the effects of language are stasis theory, a series of questions used to determine whether an argument is about fact, definition, evaluation, or policy, and Toulmin theory, which encourages students to study claims, warrants, grounds, and backing (Ramage 79–83). Books like those by D'Angelo or Corbett and Connors can introduce interested teachers to classical rhetoric and its modern applications.

Again, the importance of these theories to any one teacher will depend on the teacher's goals and values. A process enthusiast may argue that a writer experienced in analyzing purpose and audience doesn't need specific training in new genres and discourses, while someone who puts more emphasis on academic writing will want to introduce the concept of discourse communities early in the semester and may provide students with practice in writing in specific genres. (See Covino, "Rhetorical Pedagogy.")

REFLECTIVE PRACTICE

Whatever our interests in theory, we need to engage in the kind of *reflective practice* that Chris Anson advocates: "a realignment of our focus away from abstract theories or the findings of empirical research and toward personally meaningful, contextually grounded teaching experiences (Schön 1987, 1983)" (28). As Nyquist and Sprague put it, "meaningful TA development entails development of reflectiveness" (80); "At the level of personal career fulfillment, the unreflective university instructor will not be intellectually challenged by the unending puzzles that present themselves in our classrooms" (82). Even if you resist being "theoretical," be reflective—being conscious about what we do and self-conscious about learning from our experiences will lead us to discover the kinds of cause-and-effect relationships that theorists want us to see. Borrowing the term "reflective transfer" from Schön, Kathleen Blake Yancey says

> the procedure that enables us to learn from and theorize our practice requires four steps: that we (1) observe and examine our own practice; (2) make hypotheses about successes and failures, as well as the reasons for each; and (3) shape the next iteration of similar experience according to what we have learned; when we (4) begin the cycle again. (235)

Theory is most useful and most meaningful when it helps a teacher understand and account for generalizations the teacher reaches through reflection.

7

CONFIDENT AND HUMBLE
And Other Contradictions We Live By

> *There is a genuine paradox here. The positions are conflicting and they*
> *are true.*
> Peter Elbow, "Embracing Contraries in the Teaching Process"

Composition is a world of contradictions. Perhaps our most popular formula for good writing—"clear and concise"—wars with itself: clear usually means more detail, more length. Teachers who don't recognize the paradoxical nature of our work may get frustrated listening to (or giving) conflicting advice: "Meet with your students as often as possible . . . but you gotta have a life of your own to stay sane." If we recognize the oxymoronic nature of much composition advice—or, to switch metaphors, the delicate balancing act between extremes—we can search for our own balance point rather than be buffeted from one extreme to the other or become so cynical that we see all advice, all generalizations as meaningless. I will try to sketch out the two sides of some of these contradictions, but don't expect me to locate the perfect balance point. There may not be one . . . or the balance may be different for each person in each situation.

CLEAR AND CONCISE

This central tension helps make writing so complex and fascinating: on one side, pressures for more length—"complete," "thorough," "thoughtful," "well-reasoned," "detailed"; on the other, terse words exhorting us to be brief, tight, pithy, succinct. The two sides never call a truce—we're always looking for the document to be a little shorter and a little more informative. But trying to reach both goals at once can lead us to develop sophisticated writing strategies—making a quick, convincing point with a crisp generalization and a striking example, for instance, or using bullets to get all the information across without repetition. Many people value poetry as the most elevated of the written arts because good poetry, short and deep, reverberates through the consciousness.

Of course, as Elbow points out, some student writers don't *want* to be clear or concise; wordiness and lack of clarity may be "part of the 'writing process' considered from a wider angle" (1998, 107.) As Elbow says of his own writing, "My syntax never got clearer until I was finally wholehearted in my desire to *give* myself and my meaning to my readers" (107). I've taught smart, successful students who wrote primarily to demonstrate to others the depth of their vocabulary and the width of their education; they viewed clear communication as beneath them. I couldn't make any headway against that attitude until I understood the contradiction as the student saw it.

GRACEFUL AND POLITICAL

The generic pronoun—"he" used to refer to both sexes—is simple, straightforward writing. No substitute for "Everyone should bring *his* book" does the job with equal grace and brevity. (To my ear, making the whole sentence plural comes closest.) Similarly, "first-year student" is an awkward mouthful compared to "freshman," and "humankind" doesn't roll off the tongue as easily as "mankind." The writer in me says "be direct and brief."

But the feminist in me vetoes any word that contributes to the impression that women are subsidiary, afterthoughts. Though I'm torn, I try to use gender-neutral language exclusively and expect my students to do the same. Fortunately, some terms are both graceful and neutral—"chair" instead of "chairman," "fishers" instead of "fishermen." But sometimes you have to take a stand. Some colleges demand gender-neutral language, as do some state governments. We all need to get used to it.

Debating the politics and style of gendered pronouns should make students wary of other charged words that we use too readily without thinking about their effects. Why do we never call something "terrorism" when a government does it? For whom is "free trade" really free? Is the "reform" really a step backward?

CREATIVE AND COMPREHENSIBLE

The easiest message to understand is the most familiar. For the American motorist, "Stop" or "Pay Toll Ahead" communicate instantly, unambiguously. Such messages also have no originality, no creativity, no sense of authorship. And that's just fine; we wouldn't want our octagonal signs to start saying "Halt" or "Desist."

But while some of the activities we give our students may ask them in effect to create signs that we've all seen a thousand times, most of us, most of the time, ask our students to do original work, perhaps even be creative, push the envelope. Yet to be creative means to experiment, perhaps in nonproductive directions. Some students might want to change the sign to "Put the Kibosh On It" or paint the sign in unreadable psychedelic letters or eliminate the sign altogether just to see what would happen. Occasionally, a particularly creative writer will come up with an original way to be clear, but more often, our students must choose. We need to decide which end of the spectrum we value more and to make clear to students that the choice of ends depends on audience and purpose. If we ask them to be creative one day and comprehensible the next, it's not that we're confused or that we're asking them to do the impossible. We're exercising abilities that they'll use throughout their writing lives.

WRITE FOR YOURSELF/WRITE FOR YOUR AUDIENCE

When we—and our students—sit down to write an essay, who should our imagined audience be? Any rhetorician will tell you to write for your eventual reader, but many who teach for personal growth and discovery argue that writers must, first, please themselves. (See Elbow's "Closing My Eyes as I Speak: An Argument for Ignoring Audience.")

The "first" in that last sentence provides us a little wiggle room in this conundrum. Many writers write first for themselves, with no thought of how they might affect a reader, and only later revise for a specific audience. Though perhaps not the most efficient method, this approach does allow for both the free personal expression of a journal and the audience focus crucial to most communication.

Maybe we should resolve the "Which audience?" dilemma by asking "Which audience *motivates* the writer?" Sometimes student writers need the safety of writing for themselves or a close friend and will be motivated only if they think no one else will ever read their work. Others may get motivated only if they can imagine writing to a specific audience—the coach they admire or the manufacturer of a defective product. In most classes, we use peer responses to give writers a sense of a local writing community that they can write for and get honest feedback from.

Our students need to understand audiences, recognize that almost all the writing they do during their lives will be directed at particular audiences (almost always multiple for any piece of writing), and gain some insight into why and how they write for those audiences. What audience they actually focus on is less important.

DEDUCTIVE AND INDUCTIVE

How do we teach students general truths? The fastest way is just to tell them—e.g., list the most important factors in making a paper persuasive. That takes a lot less time than inductively searching for factors, and the list may be better—more complete, more accurate—than a list compiled by students trying to generalize from their own experience. But will students remember and believe in your list as thoroughly as in a list they generate themselves?

Rather than just present my conclusions, I usually try to make room for students to draw their own, to practice inferring. If students can, from reading editorials, abstract some rules of persuasive writing, they may be able to draw conclusions about, for instance, how writers in their discipline construct and present knowledge. They need to learn to make sense from their own observations rather than run to a book every time a question arises that they haven't specifically encountered before.

But what if they don't reach the obvious, crucial conclusions that we've reached? Worse yet, what if they're wrong? What if they read a couple of essays with surprise endings and conclude that essays should be like detective stories, all false leads and surprises until the end? Their inductive investigation needs to be balanced with direct, deductive instruction, completing, validating, enlarging their ideas. We have no assurance that either method, or any combination of approaches, will work. But teachers need to be aware that these different approaches have different advantages and disadvantages, not all of them readily apparent.

DIRECTIVE AND STUDENT-CENTERED

Teachers who work inductively tend to be "student-centered," a general perspective that appeals to many composition teachers. Student-centered teachers draw answers from students, let them determine the direction of their papers, let them learn the hard way, if necessary. Didn't you learn most of your skills yourself, with the aid perhaps of a well-timed tip? Each student has a head full of schemata different from his or her neighbor's, and therefore learns different things in different ways. Student-centered means encouraging students to find their own paths while we get out of the way.

The extreme in teacher-centered teaching, the lecture, has been largely discredited in composition classrooms, and now we strive for the anti-lecture, where students end up explaining their new understanding to their teachers.

But what happens when the students don't get it? When they're ready to give up on a paper that just needs a little restructuring? When they're never going to write better papers until they can get started before midnight? Do we just hope they learn from this semester's errors and do better next time? Or do we guide them, say "Try this" or "This is where I think you get hung up" or even "I don't think this paper is going to work"?

Don Murray modeled how to work on the horns of this contradiction. Some readers of his books imagine Don to be Mr. Student-Centered, and certainly his work shows an extraordinary respect for students and their writing. He has always preached "let the student speak first about the paper." And yet students always came out of Don's office knowing what he thought. It's a tricky business, balancing the desire to let the student make decisions about the paper with the need to give the student some direction, some help. I find when I'm particularly pressed for time and/ or the semester end draws nigh, I tell the student what I think more often and give more concrete suggestions for improvement. But while students generally thank me for such suggestions and marvel at my ability to see hope and a way out of writing binds, I consider such moments a failure for the writer even if they're a success for the paper.

I strive to make myself unnecessary for the student writer. Ideally, by the end of the semester students have had enough practice in analyzing and improving their own prose that they no longer have to rely on me or my suggestions. Somewhere in that process, they probably need to be shown that there *is* a way out of their dilemma—they can say what they want to say and still write an organized paper. But for this particular paper, do they need a model, a demonstration, or the time and space to experiment and figure out their own solutions?

You can't really go wrong in dealing with this dilemma, even if you go to the extremes. If you solve all of a student's problems, you've helped the student write a better paper and demonstrated that there *are* solutions. And if you refuse to give the student solutions, you've probably helped the student along the path to writing independence.

This apparent contradiction actually has its own logical compromise— instead of being teacher-centered *or* student-centered, we really want our courses to be learning-centered. So we choose whatever combinations of methods will bring about learning.

CHALLENGE STUDENTS AND LOWER ANXIETY

I always include in my opening-week spiel a promise to reduce anxiety in my course as much as possible. Most students have good reasons to be anxious in English class—they fear the blank page, the red pen, the public humiliation of using "bad" grammar or suggesting a "wrong" interpretation, being criticized for habits that may seem to them as unchangeable as the size of their feet. Some writers argue that they need the anxiety of the imminent deadline to get the words to flow, but I'm suspicious of that rationale and certainly don't want to encourage it. In the vast majority of situations for the vast majority of writers, anxiety is the enemy of good writing and learning.

Yet we can't run a college class—at least not after the first few weeks—as though it were first grade, cheering any words that make it onto paper, overlooking invented spellings, rewarding quantity regardless of quality. Some writers *will* improve if they are simply given the time and encouragement to write. But others, particularly better writers, need a push, a challenge, critique peppering the encouragement, a bar raised high enough to require a real leap. And for most people, the challenge of the high bar brings with it anxiety.

To make this balancing act productive rather than paralyzing, we need as much as possible to set ourselves up as coaches, not judges, working with the student to conquer the new height. That means, first, eliminating all the trivial sources of anxiety that set us in opposition to our students—the surprise quizzes, the public humiliation, the red pen. We develop the coaching role through scores of small interactions with each student. For instance, we can frame the student's recurrent writing problems not as weaknesses or immutable character flaws, but as opportunities for rapid growth and improvement, or as dragons that may have been nightmares in the past but that, with our help, the student can certainly slay now. We challenge student writers most successfully not by setting specific targets or exhorting them, but by forming a relationship based on caring about the student and the student's writing.

BE A DEVOTED TEACHER AND HAVE A LIFE

If you have dreams about being a teacher, if it's not just a rung on a career ladder that's headed somewhere else, you probably imagine yourself as one of those life-changing teachers that you may have experienced in your own past and that you have certainly seen in movies, teachers so devoted to their students that they seem available 24/7, so enthusiastic about their subject that they can rouse even the abused and sullen kid in the corner. We want to be the person that kids turn to before they kill themselves or run off to join a gang. Unfortunately, such devotion leaves no room in life for anything else—those super teachers can't have spouses and kids of their own, let alone their own interests that might steal a few hours from their thinking about their students.

Teachers who want to work toward the ideal but also have a life figure out their own compromises, but I think generally the secret lies in choosing how, when, and to whom to be devoted. I will not spend hours—or even minutes—on the phone with a student or meet students for lunch or a beer after class. But I do meet every student one-on-one early in the semester, and I give students as much timely written commentary as they can handle, usually responding to emails within hours, trying to get papers back within a couple of days, and writing lengthy critiques *if* I think the student will make use of them. Each semester, a few students realize how rare and potentially valuable professional feedback can be, and give me draft after draft. I end up spending hours on their work and, from their angle, appearing to be the ultimate devoted teacher. But I don't spend nearly as much time on students who just want to get by and who don't seem to read the comments I give them. It's not exactly that I favor the better students; I'm just willing to match the student's own energy. Sometimes poor writers invest lots of energy and make major improvements.

Other ways of keeping enthusiasm high while not working yourself to death: choose readings that you love, that you don't have to reread carefully, and that are reasonably short, "The Death of Ivan Ilych" rather than *War and Peace*. Don't always prepare for hours; join students in the fun of exploration. Respond to ungraded writing with a single carefully chosen phrase—"you found a perfect example" or "I see the connection between your mother and Mrs. Hopewell."

Keep in mind that what students really react to, what makes us "beloved," is *who we are*. Students aren't grading our on-time performance. Their key judgment is something like, "Do I like and respect this person well enough to take seriously what they're saying?" You'll be the most likable, the most effective teacher if you take some time off, have a life, and bring the energy and rejuvenation of that life into the classroom. The best teachers *live*, inside the classroom and out.

CONFIDENT AND HUMBLE

That phrase may express the ideal attitude for any employee, but it has particular meaning for comp teachers because our attitude affects our students so much, and the combination requires such a tricky balancing act.

We need to be confident so we don't have to endure daily challenges to our authority and ideas, and so we don't give students the impression that they can dismiss our evaluations as just opinions. The nastiest of students feed off teacher insecurity, leveraging it for better grades and special treatment. And apparent confidence begets real confidence—we grow into the roles we project for ourselves. We need to give the impression that we know what we're talking about.

On the other hand, many students harbor lingering resentment against know-it-all English teachers who punish anyone who knows less about grammar than they do. An unfortunate number of English teachers attempt to overcome their general sense of powerlessness by asserting their power in the one sphere in which they have some—"correctness." So an English teacher calls up NPR to tell Dr. Zorba that he should say "healthful" not "healthy," another writes a letter to the editor outraged at the decadence of putting periods outside quotation marks, many give grammar tests to assert their grading power without slogging into the subjectivist swamp inherent in grading essays.

It doesn't help for us to be perceived as grammar police. It's a real triumph for an English teacher to say "I don't know. I'll find out." But if you say it more than once a week, your students may feel that you "don't know" too much, too often. So there's the rub—confidence without arrogance, humility without humiliation.

ENTERTAINING AND SERIOUS

How much energy and effort should we put into making our classes fun, engaging, entertaining? Many people would label that question itself absurd, evidence of what's wrong with education today. English is supposed to be difficult, mysterious, confusing, frustrating—it was in our day, so why should it be different today?

We base our own sense of the right kind of teaching persona almost exclusively, I think, on our teaching models. I had very few entertaining teachers—my best teachers were serious, and they kept things interesting through the power of their ideas, the cleverness of their articulation, the gee-whiz surprise of their connections. Whenever I observe other teachers now, I'm both impressed by and suspicious of the ones who keep students laughing and on the edge of their seats. Sure, if you show Simpsons clips all day, you'll get good evaluations, but is any learning going on here?

Luckily, good pedagogy often entertains. Students generally enjoy and learn more from hands-on activities than from lectures; discovering something ourselves thrills us and makes us remember. Obviously, it would be crazy to leave our senses of humor at the classroom door. But if you find yourself doing something just because you think it will amuse—showing movies or illustrating points solely with cartoons—it might be time to rethink.

AUTHORITY AND PEER

Who are we in relation to our students? In most cases, we're the grade-givers, and therefore the authorities. We need to sit on the highest stool so we don't argue constantly about grades and mechanics, and part of our pedagogy relies on our students' paying special attention to what we say. But few comp teachers feel comfortable being *just* the authority in the classroom; we want to develop a human relationship as well. I know I took my writing most seriously and progressed most when I felt that my writing mattered in the personal/professional relationship with my writing teacher. Students who don't care about the grade or developing the skill may still care about the relationship.

Besides, most of us teach because we like the human contact, and the higher the stool, the less human you can be. Many of my current friends were once my students, so I don't feel the gulf between myself and my students that some teachers feel; because I can easily imagine the role distinctions evaporating, I'm inclined to treat students as friends-to-be. That means accepting their excuses for missed classes, being "reasonable" about deadlines, not asking for signed plagiarism statements with every paper. But most people can remember teachers who were too chummy, and being friendly may make it harder when you need to be tough.

Peter Elbow raises interesting questions about one aspect of this relationship, students' need to resist the dictates of the teacher, discipline, or genre (1998). As teachers, we may find such resistance irritating and perverse, but as Elbow points out, acts of resistance often define us and may be crucial in our intellectual growth. So while it may not feel good to have a student stomp out of our office saying, "I'll do it my way," it may be a productive and beneficial moment in the student's life.

Talk about contradictions: when we feel most hurt, maybe we should applaud.

8
AVOIDING STRESS

I've noticed that the things I worry the most about, and thus waste lots
of time, effort, and sleep on, often turn out to be much less serious than I
originally anticipated.

W. Gary Griswold (qtd. in Haswell and Lu)

Stress is like pain tolerance or writing speed: we'll never know whether
we feel and react exactly the way others do, or whether by the world's
standards we're unique, over- or under-reacting. Is my job more or less
stressful than an air traffic controller's or a wine taster's? I'm clueless. But
I wouldn't trade.

Despite such ignorance, I can compare the stress caused by various
jobs and activities I've engaged in and therefore predict (and sometimes
reduce) the likelihood that I'll feel stressed in a particular week. My list
may be very different from someone else's. I know, for instance, that some
people would rather spend hours on the phone than commit themselves
to paper or email, while I'm just the opposite: I prefer a morning of email
to an hour on the phone. But I hope you can apply my approach to your
own unique stressors.

If you're worried about freaking out, flipping out, burning out, stressing out during your first year of teaching, do some self-analysis. Make
yourself a list of things most likely to bring on the tight neck and the
elevated blood pressure. Be specific. Don't just say "teaching." Is it planning? Grading? Dealing with unruly students? Getting no response to
your questions? Having to admit you don't know the answer to a grammar
question? Forgetting names? Getting blasted on evaluations by students
who smiled throughout the semester?

I've worried about all those things and many more, at various points
in my career. At the moment, it's the last one that sometimes makes me
wonder if I'm in the right business. But that's a veteran's worry, something
that developed over years of evaluations, not something a new teacher
should fret about.

The bits of advice that follow respond to my own worries and those
of people I've worked with. I hope the specific advice proves useful

to you. But more important, I think, is for you to pinpoint your own stressors, to figure out as precisely as you can what's keeping you awake at night. Then ask around until someone comes up with a solution or at least an approach that makes sense to you. As I argue throughout this book, the best therapy may be finding someone who can say, "Been there, done that. It's a pain but you'll survive."

FIND OUT WHAT YOU'RE SUPPOSED TO BE TEACHING

We feel like frauds in part because we sometimes feel that we don't know what we're teaching. What is Freshman English or First-Year Composition? For that matter, what is "composition"?

A huge array of activities takes place under those course titles—everything from old-fashioned critical analysis of literary texts to workshops in which the teacher disappears and students' papers seize the spotlight. The size of that array disturbs some people, because it implies that students who take different sections of the same course within the same university, or who take courses by the same name in different universities, get radically different instruction and therefore practice radically different skills.

Because of that worry, no writing program tolerates *every* possible focus in its composition classes, and you need to find out where your program draws its boundaries. You can learn a lot from whatever material the program provides—texts, generic syllabi, goals, assignment descriptions. But try also to read the syllabi of veteran instructors. How do they break away from the course guidelines? When do they stick to the party line? Do teachers focus on writing as an art, with literary publication the long-term goal? Do they see the course as a game—follow these rules of genre, grammar, and citation and you'll get an A? Or do they see it as a service course, preparing students to negotiate the demands of different kinds of academic discourse? Each is a legitimate focus, and a particular course may try to do all three at once, but usually the writing program will have a fairly consistent emphasis.

You almost certainly won't have to create your own definition of the course, and at this point your main concern should be making sure you don't break any unwritten rules. When you make up your syllabi or assignment descriptions, you'll probably want to run them by a veteran or two, asking them to check for things that the program doesn't condone.

As for "composition," it's a slippery term. As James D. Williams points out, some use "composition" and "writing" interchangeably, while for others, writing "is a broad term that usually refers to fiction and journalism, whereas *composition* refers to academic writing, particularly the sort of writing that students produce in an English or composition class" (2). I'm a literalist about the word: I see "compose" in it and take that to mean that a "composition" class should focus on helping students to learn to compose texts. (A "rhetoric" class by contrast analyzes texts to determine why they're successful.) Find out about the emphases and limitations on the kinds of texts students are supposed to compose—only "academic writing"? only nonfiction? only prose? only responses to literature?

Don't lose sleep if you don't know the answers to such questions before your first class meeting. It's unlikely that the genre police will storm your classroom and arrest you for teaching limericks. But the more you can find out now, the less you're likely to stress from discovering that you're doing it differently from anyone else.

BE YOURSELF

Common as this admonishment is, it sounds pretty stupid. What choice do you have? But because we've all spent so many years watching other teachers, we all have memories or images of good, bad, and perhaps ideal teachers, and new teachers often get bombarded by advice about being anything but themselves: Be tough! Be nurturing! Be cool! Be warm! Be aloof! Be down to earth!

Faking it takes energy and adds stress. Who you really are will come out eventually—and that's a good thing. Ultimately, *we* may be the most important and lasting lesson of our courses. Years from now, our advice about essay leads or paragraphing will have evaporated from our students' brains, but students may still remember, may have internalized, the enthusiasm we bring to writing, our emphasis on discovery, our high standards and generosity. If they like us, they may like our subject, and that is, to a large extent, what it's all about. The "you" that stands in front of a class may not be identical to the you that relaxes with friends over a beer. My teaching persona is more upbeat, tolerant, optimistic, and encouraging than the "at home" me. But that doesn't mean the teaching me is "fake"; it's just a slice of me in which certain traits take the stage and others hide in the wings.

"Being yourself" as a composition teacher is particularly difficult because we play so many roles. As Lad Tobin describes, in a day's work for English 101, we may be asked to be—or feel we ought to be—performers, dinner party hosts, parents, preachers, facilitators, coaches, midwives, drill sergeants, circus trainers, oracles, cheerleaders (82-87). Recognizing the roles you're playing and how they may conflict can help you make more comfortable compromises. If you feel uneasy being the drill sergeant, maybe you should indulge your parental role more often and see how that feels.

Focused on "being ourselves," how do we handle the model teachers in our heads? Think of what elements the great teachers in your past shared. A mental survey of my twenty-one years in school reveals that one characteristic links all the truly outstanding teachers—they all made it clear that they cared about each individual student and what each one wrote. In other words, they were human—generous humans. The other stuff—the intellectual (or perhaps literal) sleights of hand, the clever tying up of the day's discussion as the bell rang, the ability to help us see new things in texts and our own writing and to discover ideas where we thought we had none—all were subservient to, and in some ways an outgrowth of, the simple desire to connect one-on-one. In time, you too will learn to juggle chainsaws in front of an audience; the crucial question now is, Do you care about your students? Perhaps at this second, you're too nervous or too stressed to say, unequivocally, "yes." But if you're still not sure by the end of the year, you may want to reconsider your career direction.

Having the ideal teacher in your head has a positive side: you can ask yourself what your teacher would do in a situation you're confronted with. (Or, as one of my students once detailed in a paper, you can determine how to act by doing the opposite of what your most hated teacher would do.) On the other hand, as Elizabeth Rankin shows in *Seeing Yourself as a Teacher*, comparing yourself to the model teacher can be debilitating and paralyzing. If, during your first semester of teaching, you hold the image of The World's Best Teacher in front of you all the time, the ways in which you don't measure up will be painfully obvious, and you may not last long enough to give yourself a chance to resemble that great teacher. You may admire the brilliant lecturer who could speak for an hour without notes or "ums," but chances are you're not going to become that person. And the star lecturer approach—which might have seemed so ideal in a literature class—would probably flop in composition anyway. I know I'll never be as warm, learned, and patient as my grad school mentor, David Levin. But being Brock seems to work for most of my students, some of whom wouldn't have appreciated David. As Donald C. Stewart says, "Other vocations are about *doing*; we are about *being*. That is why what we do is so important" (30).

Some new teachers fear being themselves in class because they want so much to be liked, and they fear students won't like them unless they sand off the edges of their personalities and put on a smiley face. It may take them years to accept that, as Susan Hynds puts it, "good teachers are never liked by all students. They are often blamed by those who seek mediocrity" (161).

BE HUMAN

That is, when you're faced with a difficult student issue, do the human thing, the humane thing, rather than follow the rules or play the role or keep the boundaries up. As Edward Corbett says, "Mercy is frequently a restorative virtue, . . . intransigence [is] . . . sometimes nothing more than unconscionable rigidity, and . . . a mere pat on the back can often be the impetus that impels one toward the finish line" (8). I'll grieve with the student about the dead cat rather than point out that the paper says nothing and says it badly. Or I'll give a student a break on the final grade so she can get into the nursing program, paying more attention to effort and improvement than output.

There are plenty of good reasons not to take this stance. Answering the desperate midnight student phone call may mean I don't get any sleep that night. Becoming a student's lovelife advisor may commit me to hours of emails. Many teachers legitimately decide they don't have that kind of time and don't want to play those kinds of roles. But I find that refusing to go beyond the official boundaries of my role creates more stress; I worry about the decision and about what I've turned into, and I'm never happy about it. I sleep better if I've been what I consider a good person.

You'll be advised, "Be tough at first, then ease up slowly." We certainly don't want to break our own rules and throw out our deadlines in the first week. And if you can't say "I'll think about it," being tough is probably a better policy than backing down, which could lead to a stampede of requests. Certain students—veteran high school bullies—seek out weaknesses and exploit them. But those same bullies, as well as other students with a strong sense of justice, will rebel against the arbitrary rules, unfairness, and pettiness that sometimes characterize the "tough" teacher. So my advice would be to abandon the tough mask as soon as possible and move instead toward being real and honest. In the long run, students like being taught by people, not rules.

It's not an either/or choice but a balance, as Rankin puts it, of "care and distance" (13) of "struggling always to 'make teaching personal' without 'taking it personally'" (39). "We must make it personal," she concludes, "if we want our work to have meaning" (43).

DON'T IGNORE YOUR COMPLEX FEELINGS

Lad Tobin's *Writing Relationships: What Really Happens in the Composition Class* argues convincingly that the relationships among students and between students and teacher can have a tremendous effect on students' learning and that we need to understand ourselves and our own complex motivations in order to treat our students as fairly and humanely as possible. Tobin recommends that we "pay more careful attention to the research and experience of psychotherapists" to understand ourselves and our interactions with students (29). "By engaging in ongoing self-analysis, by becoming more self-conscious about the source of our misreadings, by recognizing that our unconscious associations are a significant part of a writing course, we can become more creative readers and more effective teachers" (39). I imagine that most of us resemble Tobin: "recognizing and somehow naming the source of" our feelings helps us manage those feelings (35). If you're awake at the wrong hours of the night, stressing about why your students don't respond well to you, analyze your feelings and see if admitting to some will dissipate them.

That's the way I make tough grading calls: I let stress be my guide. If I can't decide on the B-minus or the C-plus, I'll write one of the grades in my book and pretend for a day or so that that's the final grade and see if it keeps returning to my consciousness like the ghost of the improperly buried. Usually, the nagging voice represents an argument that deserves more respect. For instance, Jackie would have had an A-minus for the class if she hadn't gotten a B for participation. But after I wrote the B-plus in the book, the chiding voice kept pointing out that she had been silenced by a dominating group of rude men, and I shouldn't penalize her for my own inability to control the class. So eventually I raised her grade.

DON'T CLING TO "THE WAY MY TEACHERS DID IT"

"We find there is a tendency for graduate students to hold tightly to [what worked for them as learners], distorting information about teaching to fit their personal visions of effective teachers" (Nyquist and Sprague 64).

"One of the central problems of both courses [the preservice course on teaching writing and the teaching assistant seminar]: how to convince new teachers that they cannot rely on their own educational experiences as a guide for teaching all students" (Stygall 40).

Once on their own in a classroom, new teachers tend to forget much of what they've been taught as adults and instead replicate some of the *ways*—and some of the "facts"—they were taught. So they resurrect the five-paragraph essay or hypercorrect their students' papers or spend much too long flogging a favorite story to death—all because one of their teachers did it that way.

Both writing students and writing teachers must learn by *un*learning. What habits or approaches have you unconsciously absorbed as "the way it's done"? Make a list of ideas or emphases that originated in your far past—are they nonsensical prohibitions like those listed in "Yes You May" (Appendix A)? Judgments about the relative value of writing and literature or of various genres? Models of how English teachers behave with students?

Dig especially into clashes between the voices of the present and those of the past. Those clashes create stress. Try to pinpoint why a new idea disturbs you and see if it violates some cherished principle. Then . . . the hard part . . . try to determine if the principle still holds. You'll find that you'll breathe much easier when you accept, despite the outrage of your seventh grade English teacher, that "cutting corners" with headings and bulleted lists makes a lot of sense.

David Smit concludes from work by Hillocks (1999) and Kennedy (1998) that "although English teachers may very well have been taught to teach writing in more flexible and open-ended ways, when push comes to shove, they resort to the same old rigid rules and conventions that have been the bane of the profession since the nineteenth century" (73). Your methods professor probably won't be there to warn you about such backsliding. You need to monitor yourself, becoming more conscious of when and why something pedagogical bothers you.

GO AHEAD, LIKE YOUR STUDENTS . . . AND BELIEVE THEM

We shouldn't need encouragement to like people we're trying to help, but some institutional cultures dictate that teachers distance themselves from students. I don't think you can be an effective teacher for long if you don't like your students, and I see no need to create artificial detachment. You may discover, as I did, that while I wanted to throttle most of my classmates when I was an undergraduate, as a teacher I don't often find my hands straying to a student's throat. Students are much easier to like when you're a teacher.

Peter Elbow did the world a favor in 1973 when he assured us that we don't always have to play the critical, resistant, distanced "doubting" game that we've been raised on, but can instead play the "believing" game; we can believe in and enter into the text we're studying. More recently, inspired by Wendy Bishop, Elbow has written about the importance of liking our students. Read "Ranking, Evaluating, and Liking: Sorting Out Three Forms of Judgment," if you need confirmation that your warm, perhaps unrealistically positive feelings about your students are pedagogically appropriate. Or read McLeod about self-fulfilling positive expectations and especially about the "golem effect" that negative expectations can have on student-teacher relationships (106-113). "The research on teacher empathy suggests that there is a robust positive correlation between high teacher empathy and student achievement" (115). So don't worry if you don't fit into the Gradgrind school of knuckle-rappers.

For me, liking my students extends to believing them. Unless I have a very good reason not to, I believe their stories about dying grandparents and the roommate borrowing the car with the laptop in it. I choose to believe them because I don't want suspicion to warp our relationship and sap my energy. And when students understand that they can win the excuses game without even trying, they often resort to being honest.

USE YOUR IMAGINATION

I've already referred to one rather negative way to use your imagination—to dream up everything that could go wrong, so you won't be unpleasantly surprised and may even be prepared to deal with the nightmares that come your way. Some people find it comforting, in any stressful situation, to imagine the worst that can happen, with the hope that the "worst" won't really look so bad. Knowing that the worst isn't likely to happen should relax us.

Whether or not you can find comfort in self-created nightmares, imagination may be your best teaching friend and stress-avoider. Our business is full of rules and standards, from due dates to grading rubrics to punctuation conventions. Of course, you need to remember the rules you've set up and those that have been created for you by your department or school. But in a stressful situation, thinking outside the box is likely to serve you much better than being able to recall the exact dimensions of the box. You have a "no late papers" policy, but what do you do about the student who works on the school crisis line and gets a suicide call just before class? How do you handle the student who broke her elbow the morning of the final? What happens when the LCD projector breaks and your plan to demonstrate PowerPoint for forty-five minutes goes down the drain?

No amount of worrying can prepare you for all such contingencies, and no one can train you to think imaginatively rather than panic. But I'm betting that you do have the ability, and perhaps the most comforting thing you learn during your first semesters is that you *can* think quickly and creatively in such situations. Things happen so rapidly during a teaching day that you're probably not aware of how many decisions you make and how clever some of them are. Take the time to review each day, not to second-guess yourself but to convince yourself that you *did it* today, you made decisions and survived, so chances are you can do the same thing tomorrow.

KEEP IT SIMPLE

Increasingly, high school and middle school English classrooms look like circuses or rec rooms, with posters, games, "centers" of various sorts, and, in rich schools, computers and audio-visual equipment everywhere. That's wonderful, but I'm grateful that few people expect such extravagance at the college level. While we can make good use of virtually any pedagogical technology, almost everything about writing can be taught—and has been taught!—with nothing more stimulating than pencil and paper. I fear the widespread desire to spend money on computers rather than people has more to do with politicians' warped priorities and coziness with computer makers than it does with any pedagogical logic.

Schools vary widely on how much technology they invest in and how much emphasis they put on students' ability to use it. Obviously, if the course is supposed to familiarize students with certain computer functions, you're going to have to learn those functions yourself. But if you feel no such pressure, you can reduce stress for the first few semesters by not worrying about all the things you *could* do. Get comfortable teaching with the basic tools first. Then gradually experiment with audio-visual-techno aids as the basics become old hat for you—and as both you and your students need new things to explore.

LEARN TO STALL

After extolling the virtues of spontaneous, creative decision-making, I may seem like a hypocrite to advocate asking for more time. But "let me think about it" should be your default answer to student questions that you haven't thought through, requests for breaks and substitutions and special treatment and instant grades. I feel especially strongly on this last point; there's nothing worse than skimming a paper and saying "probably a B-plus" and then later realizing that you'd been trying to see all the strengths of the paper to encourage the student and now when you balance those with the weaknesses, you realize it barely creeps into C territory. If pressed for a grade on the spot, my standard response has become "at least a D"; after that, students are grateful to wait for some reconsideration.

Email has made the stall-for-time answer almost universally applicable. It used to be that the student had to wait until the next class, maybe the next week, for an answer. But now you can say, "I'll email you as soon as I get home," and not feel that you're ruining the student's weekend.

We've got to keep our promises, though. I try to write down some code that will remind me of the student and the request, and not wait for the student to bring up the issue again. I don't want students to start thinking that my "I'll think about it" means "forget about it."

WORRY ABOUT IT LATER

Experience is unquestionably the best teacher, and we don't learn its lessons unless we analyze the day's triumphs and failures. But wait until you get home, take a shower, do your best to induce a state of optimism, so you'll see your failures as opportunities for growth. If at ten a.m. you start thinking about the mistakes you made in your nine o'clock class, you'll have a long day. Serious worriers benefit from setting up a weekly or nightly worry group with like-minded others to laugh away obsessions, perhaps even hold ritual burnings of bad evaluations or obnoxious emails.

CONNECT

That's one of the beat-you-over-the-head themes of this book: connecting with others will keep you sane. Sharing the day's disasters will almost certainly make you feel better about them and worry less about the next day. Of course, you need to find the right people to share with. Do you need the perhaps clueless empathy of other novices? Or the reassurance of a veteran? Sympathy or solution? It's easy to get overwhelmed by others' easy fixes for your insoluble problems. So I'd look for a good listener before anything else.

People who are (or have been recently) in your shoes can help make life easier for you in countless ways, but most novices need, first, someone to confirm the validity, the normalcy, of their feelings. Yes, it's normal to feel that you might throw up before your class. Yes, it's typical to feel crushed between the responsibility and commitment you give your job and the other responsibilities and commitments in your life—to being a grad student, for instance. Yes, it's okay—in fact, it's just fine—to do a little victory dance after a class or conference that felt right.

Seek out the right people to talk to. Of course, you don't have time to be social, but your psyche can't afford to be isolated.

ABANDON "CORRECT" INTERPRETATIONS

There *are* correct answers in English class—to questions like "Who wrote *The Turn of the Screw*?" or "What's the conventional punctuation for indicating that another independent clause is coming?" But I'm talking about literary interpretations. These days, with many of postmodernism's insights now taken for granted, few theorists would argue that there is a single right answer to questions like "Why does Hamlet delay?" or "What's the meaning of 'Once More to the Lake'?" Yet my students report that many of their teachers still spend hours of class time pursuing the *right* (that is: "the teacher's own") reading, so I assume that many people reading this book feel some pressure to come up with a "correct" reading of anything they assign the class.

But take a load off your mind. Abandon the idea of a "right" or even a "best" way to interpret a given text. Forget discerning what the author intended. (See Chapter 6.) Work instead to elicit interesting, provocative, relevant readings, readings that capture your students' imaginations and make them want to read more or write. If you're teaching composition, after all, almost all the reading you assign should lead to writing; I'm suspicious of writing teachers who spend a lot of time on literary interpretation, teaching literature *as* literature. Give up the all-knowing expert role—it scares our students, and trying to live up to it would make anyone uptight. Model instead the curious and inquisitive reader who develops an hypothesis, checks it against the evidence, and delights when the hypothesis leads to new insights.

RESPOND SMART, NOT LONG

For many English teachers, the essence o' stress is the paper Everest growing ever larger on their desk, waiting for response and/or grades. No one can make them magically go away. Even veterans who have been honing their skills for thirty years spend lonnnng hours whittling down that pile. But there *are* ways to make that process less onerous, some of them counter-intuitive.

Separate grading from responding. Ideally, we respond (however briefly) every time a student turns a paper in, but we grade only when it's done

. . . or when a student needs to know how done it is. *Grading* can be a relatively rapid process, especially when you've read the paper before. *Responding* is to help student writers identify consistent strengths and weaknesses and make the final paper better. Thus, everything you say to a student should pass the "Useful for revision" test, and if you find yourself writing a long comment on a paper that won't be revised again, stop. (I admit I don't always follow that advice. I *do* sometimes write long final comments—but they're part of my ongoing dialogue with particularly interested and engaged students, ones I know will read the comments and make use of them.)

Don't mark everything. Occasionally you'll have a student—probably a future English major—who asks you to "mark it up." Some good writers have consistently earned A's yet seldom get the critical push they need to improve further. Marking every misplaced comma is a favor for such rare people.

But the average student gets overwhelmed quickly and probably won't even look at a page with scores of careful editing marks. So the teacher picks one, two, possibly three things to critique and finds three or four examples in the paper. Even some students who say "Mark everything" don't really mean it—they're acting out of a sense of masochism or macho toughness, a feeling that English *should* be painful and discouraging. When you get that kind of request, question it.

Don't get hung up on grammar and mechanics. They're the easiest things to mark, but even if your comment points to other issues, if you mark mostly grammar, students will conclude that's your main concern. I'm not saying ignore grammar. We have scores of clever ways to teach it. But bleeding on the student's paper is not one of them.

Keep your comment short. You may have hungered for teachers' comments when you were a student, but we have to remind ourselves constantly that we are not typical of students or writers. Never skimp on praise, of course—all writers need support (although, as my colleague Denice Turner points out, they need to earn it, the cult of self-esteem notwithstanding). But try to explain the two or three things you have marked, and perhaps hint at something you'll want to cover in the future ("maybe on the next draft we can work on punctuation"), just to make sure the student doesn't get the sense that *"Done"* is just down the road, and move on. Be certain, however, that you're evenhanded with your response, not privileging one type of student or one sex above another—a common English-teacher blindness, as Elizabeth Birmingham points out (2000).

Engage. Students get frustrated when teachers seem to ignore the ideas in a paper and focus only on how successfully they've been conveyed. Students who take their papers seriously have done some important thinking about their subjects, and they want the teacher to acknowledge and engage with that thinking. So be sure to indicate to the writer that you understand and are interested in the ideas—summarize them, ask questions about them, extrapolate logical conclusions, ask for examples, make tentative connections, relate them to your own life and thinking. Without such a base in content, your comments will leave the student thinking that only surface issues and errors matter.

Develop shortcuts. You may feel too busy to do this at first, but take a breather at some point and ask yourself what you've been repeating often in your comments and how you could keep from saying it again. Some teachers create macros on their computers, so they can hit *<alt>P* and call up a paragraph on passive voice. Teachers who require a particular handbook have it at their side as they write comments, and can say simply "read 325-327 on passive voice." Others give students a handout describing common problems and solutions. I do *not* encourage developing your own code where a marginal *P* indicates passive. We're in the business of communication, and students shouldn't need a translator to understand us.

If you develop a rubric for each assignment—a good idea—you may be able to use the rubric as a responding shortcut. Just circle the appropriate description of each of the paper's features. Students who want to know specifically how those general descriptions apply can come talk to you.

You may find the "comment" feature in your word processing program useful, and may discover that you can save time by exchanging papers electronically with some students—especially if you're teaching online. I find that doing anything electronically with students requires either that I take a tough "computer problems are your problems" stance or that I resign myself to spending extra time with the few individuals who can't read my electronic comments or who use some bizarre program whose files I can't open. Use your strengths and abilities, but don't assume that your students have matching strengths.

Use peers. I don't ask peers to grade papers or to look at someone else's grammar, except under very controlled circumstances. But, working in groups either in class or on their own, peers can provide—"free"—much of the feedback that you'd want to give to student writers. You probably can't just turn groups loose on each other's papers; you need to give them some fairly specific instructions. My standard charge to peer

Figure 7

Persuasion Scoring Standard

	A	B	C	F
Evidence	The paper links every assertion to evidence and uses a wide variety of sources and types of evidence.	The paper presents relevant facts and opinions and draws from a number of recent, credible sources.	Evidence is either missing, poorly connected to conclusions, drawn from only a few sources, or drawn from non-scholarly sources.	The paper lacks evidence or assertions or both; convincing only to National Enquirer subscribers.
Argumentation	Convincing web of evidence, tight logic, and gracious acknowledgment of the opposition.	Argument makes sense, without huge leaps or gaps, and shows awareness of opposing views.	Main point is difficult to discern, connections between ideas are shaky, logical gaps and fallacies common.	The paper has no apparent meaning, stated or implied, and makes no attempt to be convincing.
Organization	Lead, end, order, transitions, and structure all support the purposes of the paper.	Structure may be a bit confusing, lead or end may be bland or repetitive, but the reader has little trouble following the flow of ideas.	The reader has to keep turning back to the previous page to try to connect ideas. The paper has little or no skeleton.	Paragraphs could be scrambled with no loss to the paper. Paper reads like a freewrite.
Style/Voice	A recognizable, consistent voice that engages the reader. May approach elegance.	Most sentences read well, and the paper has a very human sound or feel.	Wordiness, sentence problems, cliches, vagueness muffle the voice.	The writer is either trying to be someone he or she isn't, or isn't trying at all.
Technical Details	Grammar, citation form, mechanics flawless and conventional except when irregularities (like fragments) are used for special effects.	Some sloppiness, but generally technique is strong.	Frequent grammar, spelling, punctuation, and/or citation problems clutter the paper's surface.	Surface problems so frequent, they obscure meaning.

reviewers: narrate for the writer the experience of reading the paper—
what raised expectations in the reader's mind, where did the reader get
confused, which questions got answered and which didn't? (See Chapter 7,
"Orchestrating Peer-Response Activities," in Roen for numerous suggestions about using peer groups productively.)

Repeat after me: "Less is more." These suggestions about responding
attempt to pry you away from a belief that's very difficult for many of us
to shake—that we cheat our students if we don't put hours into reading,
responding to, and fixing their papers. I still have that impulse, and when
I'm working with a motivated, serious writer, I sometimes write pages of
feedback, ranging from my own ideas and experiences related to the topic,
to suggestions for further reading, to admonishments about bad habits. But
for the average student, anything more than a paragraph or two of comments and half a dozen marks on the page will be overkill. Any amateur
can trash a First-Year English paper. What takes expertise is finding the key
elements in the paper and creating a short *constructive* response to them.

GET TECHNOLOGY ON YOUR SIDE

I'm at heart a Luddite, suspicious that any new technology benefits only
those who profit from its sale. Unless you're already a techno-wiz, one of
the greatest mistakes you could make would be to try to march your first
classes to the high-tech vanguard. Get the basics of classroom management down before you venture into hypertext.

That said, technology *can* sometimes save time without your having to
invest weeks in learning new programs and training students to use them.
Email is the most obvious example. It allows us to send out instructions
over the weekend with the hope that a fair number of students will actually read them; to confront individual students soon after a class incident,
but without the tension of a face-to-face encounter; to use class time most
productively, turning what might formerly have been a lecture into a
whole-class email. Be careful, though, to set limits; you don't want to be
answering "What did I miss in class yesterday?" emails.

During the semester when we invaded Iraq, I hit upon another use
of email that helped me keep my sanity without coopting class time to
rant about non-class issues. I'm too political and too opinionated to shut
up when my country does something I consider abominable, but simply
bringing up the subject and/or stating my opinion in class doesn't go
over well with my conservative students, many of whom consider it unpa-
triotic to question our political leaders.

Figure 8

Feedback Guidelines and Questions

You can organize and write your response in any way you like, but be specific whenever possible. Enjoy the experience of communicating to someone who cares about something that matters. And somewhere in your response try to do the following.

1. Write a narrative or summary of your impressions of the piece. What happens in this paper? What is it trying to do? What are your general impressions of the voice of the piece and the character of the author? At this point, don't make any judgments or even try to discern a point. You might think of this as the equivalent of an active listener's response: "What I hear you saying is . . ." I often start off my response to a poem with something like "My reading of this is . . ." (Possible beginning of one reader's impressions of "The Inheritance of Tools": "In the first paragraph you connect pain, tools, and your father right away. I thought maybe the paper was going to be about anger at your father. But then in the next couple of paragraphs, you're very respectful to him . . .")

2. Discuss how the piece connects to your life. Does it raise any questions that might be interesting for you to pursue, or offer any answers to your own questions?

3. Provide your own answer to the "So what?" question. What is the paper's point, purpose, reason for being? What takes it beyond being *just* an exercise or *just* an anecdote or *just* a description? Don't give up easily on this question. If at first you see no point, dig, stretch, speculate. Your "wild guess" tells the author a lot about the impression the piece is making.

4. What works? What makes you laugh or surprises you or provides you with useful information? What is concise or insightful, well-phrased or well-thought? What grabs you or moves you or surprises you or makes you stop to think? Don't skimp on this one; it may be the most important. Writers revise and grow by building on their strengths.

5. What might the author add or expand in order to answer questions that the paper has raised? What do you need to hear more about?

6. What sections seem less purposeful than others? Be careful how you phrase this. Just because you don't see the point in a paragraph

doesn't mean that the paragraph is "pointless." Saying honestly "I don't get it" gives a clear but not a harsh message to the author.

7. What confused you? What parts did you have to read twice? Don't be satisfied with saying "Oh, I figured it out." If you stumbled in a certain spot, other readers will too, and the author needs to know that.

8. (Optional and not usually recommended.) Make specific suggestions about changes—offer an alternative title or phrase, or perhaps a source the author might consult. Probably the best way to handle this step is to make notes for yourself about specific things on a draft that you might want to change, then when you get together, ask the author how much detailed critique she or he wants to hear, and what kinds of comments would be most helpful.

So I began sending out emails with the re: line, "War—read only if interested." A student who had never said anything political in class turned out to be an excellent advocate for the administration position, and the two of us carried on a running conversation for most of the semester, with many students reading the exchange, and a few others contributing at times. Being able to rant made me feel somewhat less frustrated about the situation, and the conservative student felt that I was listening and responding to his ideas, which kept him from dismissing me as a knee-jerk liberal.

Be on the lookout for ways you might similarly use technology to save yourself time and hassle. At my school, creating a class website takes one request; customizing it takes about five minutes. But never ignore the time it will take you to learn a new system. Do the cost/benefit analysis, assume it will take you twice as long as anyone estimates, and unless someone insists that your class should have a website, don't bother with it until you can see how it will save you time. I've found the class website particularly helpful when I have to be absent—students can carry on a virtual discussion or respond to posted materials—or when I want students to be sharing things like lesson plans without the expense of making copies for everyone. (See Moran, "Technology and the Teaching of Writing.")

BRING EXTRA

Running out of things to do in class may occasionally please your students, but it isn't very professional, and it's not likely to leave you feeling good about the day. There's no point in worrying about it when the solution is so simple: always be ready with an activity or two that you don't think you're going to need. The best activities for such purposes don't require handouts or preparation and aren't tied to specific issues in the class. No matter what you worked on in the planned part of the class, if you have an extra ten minutes, you can have the class freewrite or brainstorm or do small-group idea exchanges about the preceding work or the upcoming assignment. Once you've taught for a few semesters, you won't need consciously to plan such activities; you'll be doing them enough already so you can add one more without hesitation. But at the beginning, it's probably smart to note on your lesson plan something like, "extra time: list requirements for formal report." Having it there may prevent that jolt of panic when the half-hour activity suddenly ends in fifteen minutes.

LEARN THE PRACTICAL DETAILS

Do your homework on your department.

- What are the photocopying arrangements?
- Is there likely to be a line at the machine when you need to run off a handout before class?
- Where can you go if the machine breaks?
- Where are the bathrooms, the drinking fountains, the nearest coffee?
- Who can help you replace the overhead projector bulb or adjudicate if another class claims your room and time?
- Are sweaters required in certain classrooms, short sleeves in others?
- Who traditionally controls the time between the official end of one class and the official start of the next?
- How do you get a TV and vcr for a classroom that doesn't have them?
- Who chooses and orders books?
- Are students likely to have the class books on the first day?
- How does the add/drop system work? (This can be a major issue; you don't want to add students to your list, thinking you have control, and then find that in fact a central computer rules the class list.)

- When is the paycheck supposed to come, and how can you make
  sure that it does?

Well before the first class, be sure to check out the rooms you've been assigned. If a room is unworkable, you may be able to get your class moved out of it. For me, an acceptable room needs two things: enough moveable chairs and a blackboard or whiteboard placed where everyone can see it. You may not yet have your own list of minimum classroom requirements, but you can imaginatively go through your day's activities.

Where will you sit and stand?

What will you write on?

Are there enough chairs?

Can all the chairs see you and the board?

Can they be moved for group work?

Will you need to bring your own markers, erasers, or chalk?

Are there electrical outlets?

If you like to show slides, are there ways to darken the windows?

Do the location, layout, or features of the room offer any particular advantages? (For instance, some terrible classrooms adjoin comfortable lounges that may be unused during your class time. Or the room may have high-tech features that you'd never dream of "needing," but since they're there, you might find a use for them.)

Again, some pre-semester paranoia can lead to reduced first-day stress. I try to walk through the first day mentally, thinking about precisely what I plan to do when, what materials I will need, and what could go wrong. At least a day or two before the first class, I scope out any new building or classroom to which I'm assigned. Does the door lock? If so, who can open it? Will I have to keep my music turned down low because of an office next door?

Your office (desk, cubicle, cubbyhole, broom closet) deserves some advanced scrutiny too, and again, imagination is your best ally. Is the space big enough and private enough so you'll feel comfortable meeting students, reading papers, writing there? Or should you check out the tables in the student union? If you have a finite number of office mates (that is, you're not in a ghetto of a dozen graduate instructors), contact those mates as soon as possible, find out what their schedules are, when if ever you'll have the office to yourself, what claims they've made on times, desks, bookshelves.

Negotiation with office mates can be a tricky business and is not something to leave to the frantic first day. Since compromise will almost certainly be required, determine before the negotiations what's most important to you—a private desk (could you stand someone else's junk on "your" desk?), bookshelf or file space, control over decorations, the best furniture or the best position? Don't assume that everyone will vie for the same things; people are surprisingly diverse in their office requirements. I'd be willing to give up a lot in order to start off on the right foot with an office mate. If you're flexible and lucky, your office mate will be a key to your sanity, helping you with every other issue in this chapter.

LEARN THE PECKING ORDER

Unless you're in an unusual institution, the composition program is not the most high-status academic unit on campus; the administration probably thinks about it only when parents complain that their kids can't get into the general education writing classes. So you don't normally need to worry about interference from outside your building.

But within your building, you need to know who has what kind of power, both nominal and real. Control over the writing program may be spread among many different people: the department's chair, other administrators, and executive secretary; the writing program's own administrator(s); departmental committees that deal with composition issues; and veteran writing teachers. In some English departments, tenure-track faculty would prefer not to expend any energy on composition and leave most decisions to the people in the trenches, the veteran instructors. (Be careful not to catch a condescending attitude toward composition; even if you're headed for a lit Ph.D. or publication in *The New Yorker*, you need to respect the work you're doing or both you and your students will suffer.) Other English departments recognize that the composition program justifies the department's existence, and they take writing decisions as seriously as they would those of lit faculty.

You may deal with one person to get an office, another to resolve grade disputes, another to determine your salary, another if you have teaching questions. So who's "in charge"? Perhaps most importantly, who makes decisions about future hiring? Most administrators are used to new instructors making impolitic mistakes as they learn the ropes at a new school, but it pays to be as savvy as possible as soon as possible. And if the major players don't get along, as is common, you're smart to learn quickly what the issues are, who can't stand whom, and how the struggle affects comp teachers. Veterans and secretaries can help you.

COME TO YOUR OWN TERMS WITH TIME

No one ever has enough of it, students often want more of yours, and most people need plenty of it to get over their first-year fears and begin to see how they're building a career. Any advice about time sounds obvious, too easy, and therefore not helpful. Two warnings:

1. The time crunch doesn't get any better—you'll get more efficient at your teaching tasks, but you'll also start spending time on committees or job applications or something endless and frustrating.

2. Other people's time management techniques may not work for you. You can pick up professional tips, like marking up and commenting on only one or two things in each student paper, because that saves time *and* makes pedagogical sense. But in terms of how you arrange your life, what periods you reserve for yourself and how you get everything done that needs to get done, you will evolve a system over time that is as unique to you, and as much a product of your family, background, and experiences, as your eating habits. Some people don't work after dinner; some keep weekends free. Some appear never to sleep. Some procrastinate and then do marathon grading sessions. I tend to do everything the moment I get it and to take off at least half a day every week—but I didn't reach that resolve until I was in my forties. One problem is that our work has no natural limit—we could always dig up a little more background information about tomorrow's reading or spend another hour on that essay we promised to finish a month ago.

Working nonstop is not the key—then you'll just burn out or become so disgruntled that you'll quit. And doing just enough to get by doesn't work either—you'll never give yourself a chance to become really invested in the work. People can change, or at least modify, their time habits, but it takes a lot of willpower and effort. For starters, when you feel you're taking on a mountain of work larger than you ever have before, look back at the time habits of the past and ask yourself how they can accommodate this new influx.

That said, most successful people I know are list makers, and all good teachers develop their own lesson planning approach into something that's flexible and thorough. If I were about to start my first year of teaching, I'd do what I *will* do starting my thirtieth: make lists of everything.

- things to do in the first class
- things to bring to the first class
- classroom features to check out before the first class

- copies to make before the first day
- nonschool things I need to check on

USE CONFERENCES

It may seem ironic—or cynical—to suggest, right after a section on time management, that you engage in what is surely the most time-consuming way to teach—conferences, one-to-one meetings with students. You *can* meet with more than one student at once and conduct productive conferences in five or ten minutes rather than half an hour, but if you have fifty students, even a ten-minute conference with each will take nine hours and leave you reeling.

So you need to see conferences as an investment. Much has been written about conferences—how to conduct them, their benefits for student writers—and after you've had a few yourself, you'll see why most writing teachers consider them "so rewarding" (Corbett 6), the ultimate tool for teaching writing. But my concern here is, what's in it for you? Why should you hold conferences if your program doesn't require them?

1. It makes us feel efficacious: we're doing something valuable. In class, we're seldom sure we're getting through, but after a conference, you can see on a student's face the relief at finally having found a focus for a paper or finally having learned the difference between a colon and a semicolon. Difficult conferences make us want to tear our hair, but you'll almost certainly leave a string of conferences feeling, "I got somewhere today."

2. It's the best way to learn students' names, identities, and interests. Once I can connect a face, a name, and a paper, I usually remember the student's name for the rest of the semester. And after I've met all the students once in my office, the class has a palpably different feel, more relaxed and friendly.

3. It can head off behavioral problems. Once you've met individually with a student and talked a bit about the student's musical interests or dictatorial history professor, the student has a harder time seeing you as anonymous "teacher," butt of backrow snickers. That's why I put conferences in the chapter about stress—I think using conferences trades time for stress reduction. Just having a ten minute conference the first week with each student so impresses some students that they note it on the evaluation form fourteen weeks later.

4. It makes our classes better. When you know you're soon going to meet all your students individually, you don't have to take class time to try to deal with their individual grammar foibles. Reading students' papers and talking about them in conference gives you a good idea of students' common problems, knowledge that can determine your class emphasis.

5. We learn a lot from conferences. I find that I monitor myself more closely in conference than in class, and almost every day of conferences leaves me making a resolution to follow my own advice, do the things I've been telling students all morning. But that's just the tip of the iceberg. Conferences teach us everything from how to revise tangled sentences—our students' and our own—to how to praise and critique in the same breath.

So how do you conduct conferences? Much has been written to answer that question, too. Don Murray's "The Listening Eye: Reflections on the Writing Conference" is perhaps the most often-cited piece on the subject. Rebecca Rule's chapter in *Nuts and Bolts* presents some of the refinements she worked out in the every-week, every-student system I cut my teeth on at UNH. Kate Freeland's chapter in *Practice in Context* records her conversion from "teacher-centered conferences" to "collaborative" ones.

Here are a few quick tips:

- The student should talk first, explaining what works and what doesn't, ideally suggesting what should happen next. As much as possible, we listen.

- You'll save a lot of time if you use "cold" conferences: the student arrives with a draft, you read it while the student waits, and then you discuss it. That system may seem scary at first, but if you gather papers beforehand, read them on your own, and start thinking about or writing down how to approach them, the papers will take over your life.

- Schedule conferences for ten or fifteen minutes. That gives you enough time to read a five- or six-page paper and discuss two or three key elements in it. Five-minute conferences are possible, especially in class, but I hate feeling rushed all the time. Many students would love twenty- to thirty-minute conferences, but just do the math to figure out how much of your week that would absorb.

- Though even the laziest students generally appreciate the value of conferences, few students will come if you just say "I'll be there."

> You need to require the conferences. I always pass around a
> signup sheet to get students committed, and I treat missed confer-
> ences as missed classes.

Lad Tobin reminds us that "Like writing, the writing conference is a
process—not static, not a noun, not a thing, but rather dynamic, organic.
It changes with each student and each teacher and each second" (43). It's
certainly valuable to have some stock questions ready—"What surprised
you when you were writing? What was most fun? Is there anything you
want to build or expand on?" But there's always an element of spontane-
ity in conferences, and no two are exactly alike. That's what makes them
so interesting.

ACCEPT THAT YOU'RE EVOLVING

Jody D. Nyquist and Jo Sprague argue that most teaching assistants (TAs)
evolve developmentally in reasonably predictable ways; although they
focus on TAs, the evolution they describe no doubt occurs, perhaps at
different rates, for many non-tenure-track teachers taking on new positions. (See Figure 9, which reproduces their figure 4.1, p. 67.) They
worry that TAs "run the risk of freezing . . . prematurely" if they become
convinced that they deserve certain labels or feel they have an immutable
teaching style (61).

> Movement through [the steps in the model, from "Senior Learner" to
> "Colleague-in-Training" to "Junior Colleague"] is a cumulative process. Even
> if it were possible, it would not be desirable to skip steps in a developmen-
> tal process because each phase plays an essential role. The behaviors and
> attitudes of the novice phase are not to be shed, but transformed as growth
> continues. (77)

So if you find yourself feeling guilty for challenging your supervisor
for the first time, or for pulling back from your students because your
first case of plagiarism makes you so angry, don't worry. You may have
to experience such feelings on your road to being a happy, effective,
confident writing teacher. You may even go through a period when
your increased interest and confidence in your scholarly studies means
that your "teaching effectiveness . . . may temporarily seem to regress .
. . as [you] lose sight of what will be meaningful to beginning students"
(70). At the least, Nyquist & Sprague's table might form the basis of
an apology to supervisors or students: "I must be in a developmental
transition."

Figure 9

Indicators of TA Development

	Senior Learner	Colleague-In-Training	Junior Colleague
Concerns	Self/Survival *How will students like me?*	Skills *How do I lecture, discuss?*	Outcomes *Are students getting it?*
Discourse Level	Presocialized *Give simplistic explanations*	Socialized *Talk like insiders, use technical language*	Postsocialized *Make complex ideas clear without use of jargon*
Approach to Authority	Dependent *Rely on supervisor*	Independent or Counterdependent *Stand on own ideas—defiant at times*	Interdependent/ collegial *Begin to relate to faculty as partners in meeting instructional challenges*
Approach to Students	Engaged/vulnerable; student as friend, victim, or enemy *"Love" students, want to be friends, expect admiration, or are hurt, angry in response, and personalize interactions*	Detached; student as experimental subject *Disengage or distance themselves from students—becoming analytical about learning relationships*	Engaged/ professional; student as client *Understand student/ instructor relationships & the collaborative effort required for student learning to occur*

Adapted from Sprague & Nyquist 1991. Used by permission.

GET YOUR OWN ATTITUDE

It's a common experience for comp teachers—you teach two good classes; your students are excited and obviously learning; they appreciate how much you know and how much effort you put into helping them; you wander back to your building exhausted but feeling that maybe it is all worthwhile . . . and then the real world intrudes. The department chair ignores you in the hall; you get turned down for a parking permit because the computer can't make sense of your in-between status; you overhear a couple of literature professors saying they'd rather lay asphalt than teach comp. And suddenly you feel very small.

It doesn't help that much of what we hear about our jobs is clichéd and clueless—non-academics griping that we're overpaid because we only work a few hours per week and no one knows how to spell anymore anyway, professors outside English assuming that anyone who can write can teach writing, people within English implying that in the hierarchy of status and value within our discipline, we're on the bottom.

Worse, perhaps, few people appreciate the intrinsic benefits of the job that we *must* value to stay sane: the interactions with young people, the insights into their lives and minds, the thrill of seeing some tangible improvement, the in-the-trenches camaraderie of the comp instructor ghetto.

In part because the world around us finds it hard to imagine why we do what we do, we often internalize those doubts. We have trouble believing that what we do is meaningful or has any effect. We're not sure we're cut out for the job, even if we do believe in it. We may buy into the widely accepted notion that teaching composition is a transitional, temporary job, something to keep food on the table while we move onto something better, presumably involving literature.

A main goal of this book and my earlier *Composition Instructor's Survival Guide* is to help teachers combat such feelings, answer such interrogations, feel good about what they do. You may find it difficult at first to get the veterans around you to talk about such things, answer such questions, be positive about their experiences. It's part of the ethos of many writing programs to complain, to emphasize the difficulties. And yet people come back year after year. Talk to one of those always-returning vets alone; get them to tell you why they keep coming back. And if you watch them interact with administrators, lit people, "real" people, you may see that they have a comp trenches attitude, and they genuflect to nobody.

•   •   •

If this is your first job with full responsibility, you might want to do some thinking about the whole issue of stress—what does it mean to you, and how can you differentiate it from excitement, enthusiasm, being "psyched"? It's possible to read the adrenaline rush that comes with the first day of a new class as stressful nerves or as part of the excitement that makes teachers come back each fall. Jobs with no stress at all may become boring. So I end where I began this chapter—know yourself and what bothers you. I'm not trying to keep your heartbeat slow all semester, but to avoid the migraines or whatever body symptom tells you, "this is too much."

9
NIGHTMARES

What's amazing . . . is how many survive it: how quickly they learn and how capably they manage.

Elizabeth Rankin

Think twice before reading this chapter. I'll probably bring up some frightening scenarios that you haven't imagined yet. And I can tell you right now that I don't have fast, sure solutions to any of these nightmares—they wouldn't be nightmares if they were easy to solve or avoid. You might want to skip this chapter and return only when you actually face one of the problems identified in the sub-heads. But if you're feeling courageous, plunge ahead for some combination of these reasons:

1. If you ponder these scenes, you'll be in a better position to avoid them or to deal with them if they do happen. That's one of the assumptions of this whole book, and it applies here—though with luck you may never have to grapple with these nightmares, unlike most of the issues discussed in other chapters.

2. If you're like me, when you're first stepping foot into unknown territory, you have a vague sense of dread that can produce almost overwhelming anxiety. It's healthier to exchange that amorphous dread for specific worries. I'm hoping that you will read this chapter and say, "Gee, if that's the worst that can happen, I can deal with it!"

3. It cheers up most people to realize that everyone's in the same boat, dealing with the same fears, and that even grizzled old geezers like me lose sleep over those fears—not just first-timers.

4. Thinking about these issues one after another might help you formulate a general stance or philosophy—to be tough and unbending, for instance, or to be accepting whenever possible, or to refer all nightmares to the program director.

One point relevant to almost all these nightmares: most students' views of the world change radically when they're in college, and the anger or frustration that students vent at you may well be an expression of the way they're feeling about their whole lives, confused and uneasy. Students often look back on their first college year with embarrassment; many have come to see me in junior or senior year to apologize and thank me for putting up with them. College students' perspectives evolve in fairly predictable ways, and it may help you to read about those ways and see that you may have little to do with students' feelings. Wilhoit provides an excellent summary of the studies done by researchers like William Perry and Mary Belenky et al, fascinating work on the ways that students learn and view the world (166-169).

So, here we go. If I don't include your own personal nightmare, that gives you one more thing to talk to veterans or mentors about. And if you're a glutton for this kind of punishment, check out Power and Hubbard's *Oops: What We Learn When Our Teaching Fails.*

NO ONE DOES THE READING

It would be rare if *no one* did the reading, but you're almost certain to have a day when you ask the first question about the day's homework and look out to see all eyes on the floor. The big questions then are, "What do you do at the moment?" and "How can you prevent it from happening again?"

At the moment. We normally try not to react emotionally, but sometimes it may not be a bad thing. At least some of your students will probably respond to your emotion—when you break out of your role as unflappable, distant teacher, they may break out of their roles as "You can't make me learn!" students.

For me, getting emotional at such a moment would mean having a little "time out" in which I empathize with their overwork and their resistance to the reading, but explain that any future lapses will produce consequences. I've known teachers who said, "If you don't want to do the work, there's no point in my being here," and just walked out. I don't think you can do that more than once a semester, but it certainly gets students' attention. Or ask those who didn't do the work to leave. Getting the day off may seem like a reward, but no one wants to file out past more conscientious classmates.

If you're really pissed off, don't rule out forms of punishment—give a quiz or a short essay about the reading, or arrange the class into a circle and ask everyone to talk about a favorite detail and explain how it contributes to the point of the piece assigned. A student who has to admit, "I didn't do the reading"—or who tries to bullshit until everyone realizes that's the case—will probably work to avoid such humiliation again. Or you can reward those who did the reading by having everyone write an extra credit essay about it, or by holding a discussion in which the diligent students can shine.

Me? I roll my eyes and sigh and go on, filling in the details or whatever was necessary.

For the future. All but the best students need to be held personally accountable for anything you assign them. So let students know there will be a quiz about the reading every day, or a short essay or an "everyone contributes" round-the-circle discussion, and they will be graded in some fashion. You can't influence a student who'd rather get a D for the course than do the reading. Try to make the "checking up" educational, not punitive: avoid fact-and-date quizzes; ask questions that require thought as well as memory and upon which you can build a class discussion or an essay.

And ask yourself some tough questions, too. Are your readings too long, too difficult, too alien to your students? Did you ask them to do too much in one day? Are they overwhelmed by exams or by something extracurricular like a big concert or an upcoming holiday? Have your past questions been so difficult that some students have concluded there's no hope even if they have done the reading? Do you answer your own questions too quickly? Always consider the possibility that student reactions tell you something you need to hear.

STUDENTS CHALLENGE YOUR AUTHORITY

This happens much less often than you might imagine. Most college students have spent almost their entire lives in school. They know appropriate teacher-student roles, and very few work up the energy or the animosity to violate them. Real troublemakers generally don't make it out of high school and very seldom go to college.

But it does occur occasionally. It probably has almost nothing to do with you and everything to do with the student. Although few students are outright hostile, most teachers have at least one student per class who accuses the teacher of being unfair, having favorites, or not liking students because of their ideas or writing styles. Some are, in the words of one of Elizabeth Rankin's study subjects, "aggressively apathetic" (1). Some students whine because they can no longer get an easy A in English, and they vent their frustrations on us. Others assert that they can do whatever they want in class because they "paid for it."

You can head off challenges by being approachable, caring, and interested in students, developing a personal relationship with each one. It's much easier to be rude to a role than to a real, emotional person. As Lad Tobin says, "writing students succeed when teachers establish productive relationships with—and between—their students" (6). Meeting them one-to-one in conference is the best way to establish a respectful relationship. (See Chapter 8). Quickly learning names helps, as does playing music or doing something else every day that the disgruntled will enjoy. And while you don't need to make a show of recounting your qualifications to teach, I always give my students a summary of at least part of my background because a student in any class deserves to know what right someone has standing in front of them and claiming expertise.

Your personality should dictate which of the many possible strategies you use to deal with student challenges. Choose the one that feels most natural.

Get the class involved. "Ok, time out for a second. The word that Richard just used bothers me. Does anyone have anything to say about whether that word should be used in a class like this?" This strategy almost always works. My wife still remembers what the rest of the class had to say when one of her students complained that Frederick Douglass was biased in his portrayal of slave-holders.

Give yourself time to think. If possible, postpone acting on the issue until the next class period. Although the student may sound hostile, and you may feel that the student is trying to make you look foolish, perhaps the student's challenge is really a badly worded request for information. When *is* the paper due? How *do* you deal with the subjectivity of grading? Even if you doubt the student's intent, acting as though you're having a civil discussion about information may defuse the situation: "I shall certainly look into removing my head from my ass, Richard."

Use humor. Some people can joke, cajole, and tease their way out of any situation and into anyone's heart. Your acting as though the trouble-maker was just kidding gives the student a chance to have second thoughts and to retreat from the confrontation.

Be firm. I debated the best way to label this approach—"be tough?" "pull rank?" "show who's boss"? I chose "be firm" because it implies or assumes that you have the right and the power to assert yourself; you don't need to try to look big and tough or assert that you're the teacher. A simple statement that leaves no room for debate—"Shanan, you need to stop talking now" or "Billy, put the newspaper away please"—will usually achieve the intended result.

Confront the student one-to-one. Many students lose their bravado when they don't have an audience egging them on. And a tete-a-tete erases any doubt about your seriousness. Usually a meeting after class or during a normal conference will suffice. A couple of times during my career I've asked a student to step outside for a quick consultation during class time.

Email. Like most people who hate confrontations and telephones, I love email. When you're dealing with an unruly student, email has the advantage of giving you a permanent copy, useful if you decide to initiate formal disciplinary procedures against the student. Many disciplinary codes require written notification of the student as a first step. Using email also gives the student a chance to calm down after class and perhaps think about the seriousness of his or her actions and then respond to you without the bluster that he or she may carry into an after-class meeting. On the down side, email may not reach the student quickly, the student may claim never to have gotten it (though you can avoid that problem by choosing the "sender requires return receipt" option), you might write too hastily and with too much anger, and it may feel to both you and the student like a copout: you didn't have the guts for High Noon.

Stare silently. Students who are being disruptive often wither under almost any kind of attention except the sly high school laughs that they trained for. Silence can be very effective. Or asking the talkers to share their ideas with the class. But I try not to be sarcastic; no point in losing the student for the semester.

Ask someone to observe the dynamic in the class. Maybe the student you view as surly or belligerent will seem shy or defensive to an observer—our assumptions about student attitudes and motivations are often wrong. Is it possible you've gotten in the habit of asking rhetorical questions that might drive a student to rebellion? Perhaps in your attempt to solidify your authority in the class, you have unwittingly placed yourself on the English Teacher Pedestal and become the latest symbol of something that students may despise. Maybe what you need is not more authority but less. Try asking the offending student to your office and talking about the music he or she likes.

Get your supervisor involved. You'll have to tune in to the department gossip to learn whether your supervisors hate to be bothered. Most writing program administrators like to know when trouble is brewing—before an out-of-control situation walks in the door. And your supervisor may suggest strategies you hadn't thought of. If you envision the situation escalating, you should certainly talk to a supervisor, because any action like removing the student from the class will almost certainly require the supervisor's cooperation. Just having the supervisor visit your class may be enough to get the problem student to shape up.

Don't ignore it. Sure, a rude word or nasty tone every now and then doesn't require United Nations intervention, but ignoring an obnoxious person repeatedly may affect the morale of the whole class. You may be able to ignore the troublemaker, but your students won't.

Read. Since fear of the unruly student is almost universal, much has been written about dealing with such challenges. You might start with Jennifer Meta Robinson's chapter, "A Question of Authority: Dealing with Disruptive Students." And see if your institution has a classroom civility policy that can scare some manners into students.

In your elusive quiet moments of reflection, analyze why certain students bug you so. A colleague of Elizabeth Rankin's noticed that "The students who give me the most trouble are often the students who are like me in some way" (2). Does the student remind you of one of your parents, or bring out the parent in you? I'm not suggesting you need to hit the psychiatrist's couch to figure out why you're irritated by someone in the back of the room making farting noises, but if you realize, "She bugs me so much because she reminds me of my bossy older sister," you may be able to undermine the power the student seems to have over you. And never dismiss the possibility that one of the Big Factors—race, gender, class—influences your reactions.

If you feel that you can't start to deal with a student's behavior until you can make more sense of it, read Susan H. McLeod's *Notes on the Heart: Affective Issues in the Writing Classroom,* which offers a variety of different ways to understand our students' behavior and our reactions to it. For instance, she says, "of interest to writing teachers" is the "theory of learned helplessness, where students who feel they have no control over their success or failure simply give up at the first sign of difficulty" (13). She relates a study that concluded that most students believe "the most important purpose of writing is self-knowledge and self-expression" (14) and worries about students with those beliefs resenting teachers who emphasize something less personal like persuasion. And she reviews studies that conclude that

extrinsic reward, when added to an ongoing intrinsically motivated activity, reduced the subject's interest in the activity for its own sake. . . . Researchers suggested that situations enhancing intrinsic motivation include self-determined behavior or choice, positive feedback, and optimally challenging activities; those that decrease intrinsic motivation include external rewards or pressures to act in particular ways, feedback that implies external rather than internal reasons for success, and ego-involving task conditions that might challenge self-esteem. (50–51)

McLeod's chapter, "Motivation and Writing," offers a wealth of possible interpretations of students' behavior and suggestions for improving motivation (43-66).

Although it's difficult to take this perspective when dealing with an unruly student, try to keep in mind that rebellion and resistance to authority may be positive, healthy signs, especially for young people who have done nothing but obey all their lives. As Peter Elbow says, "An important goal for teachers is to help students find fruitful or healthy ways to resist" (1998, 103). If we're lucky or clever, we can unearth the student's real beef and help the student express anger or resistance in writing.

DIVERSITY SCARES YOU

It's all well and good to support diversity theoretically, but living with a diverse student body keeps you on your toes. If you imply that all romances are heterosexual, will that offend a gay student? Should you mark the nonstandard verb inflections on the African American student's paper? Should you go easy on the student from the Middle East who defends his plagiarism by saying that everybody does it that way in his country?

Ask. Students appreciate that you're aware of and trying to deal with their particular issue. The African American student probably wants lots of "correctness" feedback, but discussing the issue can give you a chance to support the student's home language before you start critiquing the student's writing.

In the plagiarism example, you may want to ask your colleagues. Whether the student's claims are valid—whether his culture really does encourage what we call "plagiarism"—might affect how you handle the student's consequences, but it should not lead you to bend your standards. Because universities require composition classes in part to familiarize students with the peculiarities of writing in different discourses, particularly "standard" and "academic" English, your student needs to learn the traditions of English, whatever he may have been taught at home.

Just being sensitive to the issues will put you a step ahead. And if you blow it, you can always make your mistakes into teachable moments. A couple of years ago, a member of my tenure committee who teaches communication disorders as well as English observed one of my classes in which there was a deaf student, Craig. In her observation write-up, the observer detailed how the students and I could make things easier for Craig. When I discussed the letter in class, my students could see I was chagrined, and I think that meant they took the lesson seriously. And that we'll all remember it.

TOO MUCH—OR TOO LITTLE—TIME

I remember during my first semester of teaching I often worried that I didn't have enough material to fill up the day or the week, and I would trade with other novices for filler ideas to get me through the fifty minutes.

I don't know if anyone feels that way any more—it's kind of hard to imagine, since the handful of composition books available when I started has now become an overwhelming library, and many of them can be opened randomly for an instant activity. But I don't think it was the lack of books that left me with dead time—I lacked a sense of how class time could and should be used. I had the vague idea that I could focus on anything concerning writing, but having so many possibilities was almost as paralyzing as having no possibilities at all.

Two thoughts for anyone in that position today. First, it's always a good time to write. Students need to know that you consider the act of writing important enough to devote class time to it. If you write with your students, you'll have endless opportunities to make points about writing processes and goals as you write. Students like using class time and class activities to provide momentum for the writing process that will follow the class session. I particularly like having students brainstorm leads in class, because the opening paragraph hangs people up more than any other part of the paper, and a good lead can point the writer to the organization the paper needs.

Which brings me to the second point—always work toward an assignment. Both teachers and students get bored and antsy if writing class activities seem like drills, without any perceptible link to the real world or the requirements of the class. Always try to connect the day's writing to a paper that students are or will be working on—brainstorming for paper ideas, freewriting about the best of those ideas, focusing or ordering material they already have, revising sentences, critiquing drafts with peers. There's no end to the valuable, paper-directed work you can do in class, and as long as students see how the activities help them get their "homework" done, they'll be happy to do them. I always jot down one or two such activities at the end of my day's lesson plan, thinking of them as extras that I probably won't get to. But when the group doesn't show up for its presentation or the reading discussion falls dead fifteen minutes early, I'm always glad to know I have something useful ready to go.

The opposite problem—too much to do, not enough time—plagues experienced teachers or novices who have collected ideas from everywhere. It's not a problem on the same scale with most in this chapter, but it can be a frustrating surprise the first few times you realize it's almost Thanksgiving and you still haven't done about half of what you planned for the semester. Three thoughts:

1. Keep yourself more or less on track by setting paper due dates before the semester begins, sticking to them, and making sure that the class can complete them on time. For me, "making sure" means counting the activities I want to do before the next paper and apportioning them over the days remaining.

2. With four or five weeks left in the semester, make a list of everything you *have* to do and everything you would *like* to do in the remaining time, and plan each day. I find I often have in the back of my mind a category, "slip in when possible," that keeps growing all semester, and "when possible" never appears. So at some point I need to face that category squarely and figure out what I can realistically do.

3. Plan out every day of the semester before it begins and/or leave yourself two or three blank days for makeup and fitting in those leftovers. I like to make my schedule flexible enough to be able to respond to the particular needs of the class, so I'm hesitant to commit myself to a set agenda. But the more you plan each day before the semester, the less trauma each day will bring during the semester.

THE CLASS IS DEAD

It happens to everyone. Everyone. Sometimes it's just a bad day—late on Friday, mid-semester blahs, a vacation or a big concert is coming up or has just occurred. You probably won't be able to do better than guess at the reason, and unless it can turn into a writing prompt ("Why is it worth a night's sleep to go to a Radiohead concert?"), it doesn't matter. Much more disconcerting is the perpetually silent class, the class that stares fixedly at notes whenever you ask a question. Seconds click into eternities as you wait.

Chances are you won't have such a class, at least not right away. The Good Fairy that keeps an eye on teachers usually allots one talkative person to each group, which leaves you with a different problem—how to keep yourself from giving an automatic A to someone who makes your life so much easier. But what can you do the first time it *does* happen? How do you avoid panicking?

1. Write first. You may have read the day's essay three times in the past twenty-four hours, but your students probably read it only once, very quickly, thirty-six hours ago, and have read material for four other classes in the intervening time. Even well-intentioned, bright students need considerable time to think: "Yeah, okay, English class. That little green book. We were supposed to read something . . . yeah, that E.B. White essay. Something about a lake? Where's my damn pencil? Okay, now what was the question?"

    Writing for ten minutes before a class discussion allows students to go through that kind of thinking on their own, not while you're holding your breath. And once they've finally collected all the necessary materials, found the right page, and repeated the question a couple of times in their own heads, they'll actually be ready to think about it. In the remaining minutes, as they try to write a coherent sentence or two, they may actually come up with something to say.

2. Wait. When you're on the spot, every second of silence tortures; the few seconds that you actually wait seem to take up the whole class period. It's a fascinating phenomenon—when you're an observer. I've watched teachers wait resolutely, gradually use up their patience as the silence gets to them, give in, and provide an answer, all while my watch ticked off five seconds.

    If we wait long enough, someone will eventually talk—a student will feel the weight of the silence almost as much as we do and come to our rescue. Since I was that kind of student, it's difficult for me to imagine what other students feel at that moment, but I know that some will eventually give in—out of boredom, empathy, or the slow gelling of a vague idea. If you've been in the habit of answering your own questions, it may take a number of long silences before the class realizes the old pattern has died and they need to deal with a new one. Classes stay mute when they've learned that the teacher will answer the question in a few seconds, so there's no point in trying to answer it themselves. With practice and an iron will, you can outlast them.

3. Go around the room. Give the class a specific assignment and a few minutes to prepare: "Find a detail in the essay that you think is important and be ready to explain why." Get them in a circle, then start somewhere and go around the circle. You can keep to a strict order without much discussion or encourage everyone to respond and add their two cents when someone brings up a subject close to their own. Any approach that includes everyone but singles out no one has great advantages—no one feels picked on, so students tend to be resigned rather than outraged when it's their turn. Among the many other ways to get everyone to contribute: go through the role alphabetically; ask everyone to speak only once until everyone has said something; divide the subject into different sections (perhaps "thesis," "assumptions," and "evidence" if you're discussing a persuasive essay) and then have everyone who focused on each section talk.

4. Use small groups. Groups have become the remedy for almost any class problem, and with good reason. Often students who won't say a word to the whole class will find plenty of energy in small groups. And even students who aren't sympathetic to the teacher's plight have trouble ignoring the interpersonal pressures to talk when two or three people rely on them and the group needs to get a job done. Using groups can also encourage more students to do the reading: some students feel more embarrassed to admit to peers than to teachers that they didn't do the work and don't know what they're talking about. Small groups can be an end in themselves, working for the same amount of time that the whole class would have talked, or the groups can tackle a particular task and then choose a spokesperson who reports to the whole class. Sometimes if the class just won't seem to talk as a whole, I'll hold most class discussions in small groups.

   Much has been written about group work, and once you've used groups a few times, you might want to read what the experts say and experiment with different kinds of small group tasks. Kenneth Bruffee says that a three-person group is the optimal size for a "working group" that will meet more than once and perhaps produce a paper or presentation together, while five is the best size for a decision-making group (89-90). More controversial is his recommendation that teachers should stay out of small groups once they're set up: "Emphatically, the teacher does not 'sit in' on consensus groups, hover over them, or otherwise monitor them" (87). Meeks and Austin, on the other hand, encourage teachers to "monitor each group" (48). I tend to stay at my desk, not intervening in group work, but listening to the conversational scraps that come my way and visiting groups that ask for help or seem to be straying from the task. There *should* be a task, generally one that requires discussion and a variety of opinions, not one that can be solved or answered quickly. Usually groups should have a scribe or recorder who reports back to the whole class after the group session. See Milner and Milner for a summary of group designs (359-360). But you don't need elaborate role-playing for groups to succeed.

5. Call on individuals. I must admit, I suck at this. I hate embarrassing people, and I know when I call on a normally quiet person that I'm embarrassing that person, even if he or she has an answer. But I've witnessed many classes in which the teacher routinely calls out a name whenever waiting a few seconds doesn't produce a volunteer, and I've never witnessed a classwide revolt or a student walkout. In fact, the radical act produces no sensation at all, since students have been singled out by teachers since kindergarten. The teacher just needs to act as though calling on individuals is as natural as asking for raised hands.

6. Use alternative modes of expression. I've had students who can't say a word in class beg to be able to exchange daily class journals with like-minded classmates. One of the best responses to literature I've ever seen was the painting that my house-mate did about Joyce's *Ulysses;* he never said a word in class, but as an art major, he did his thinking in oil. A student who shied away from political subjects in class produced long, well-reasoned diatribes when encouraged to write whole-class emails. Could students respond with songs, limericks, video clips?

THEIR PAPERS ARE HORRIBLE

If reading spiteful course evaluations is the worst moment in a teacher's year, getting a stack of really bad papers may come in second. You agonize through the weekend reading them, wondering, "Is my teaching that bad? Have they really learned nothing?" It's possible that your students really are numb as posts and will never improve. But it's self-defeating to think that way; better to focus on the things we can do that might improve the papers or at least improve our attitude toward them.

Remember Tom Carnicelli's twelfth week rule: no matter how good the teacher, no matter how smart the students, most student writing doesn't start to show substantial change until the twelfth week of a fifteen-week semester. Student improvement that seems glacial probably is, but don't worry about it.

Examine the prompt. Students write weak papers in response to weak questions. Is your prompt specific and clear? Did you leave room for students to focus on their own subjects or write from their own perspectives? Are your questions likely to interest students? Are there relatively easy and obvious ways of constructing a response? I'm not calling for ritual self-flagellation and burning of the question. But if you can find significant shortcomings in your question, you might improve the next batch of papers drastically by improving your question, and wouldn't that feel good?

Change your focus. As I see it, three very broad focuses compete for our attention in the comp classroom—product, process, and attitude. Traditionally, as I discussed in Chapter 5, English teachers focused on product, urging students to clean up mistakes so that the paper looked tidy, even if it said nothing. A process focus looks at what we do more than what we produce. But both focuses may fail if we ignore students' attitudes, so many comp teachers specifically design activities to improve attitude. It's easy to go too far in any of the three directions—to focus on correctness and clarity but ignore how to produce it, to look only at process and forget that the measure of any process is its product, to worry only about attitude and forget about good writing.

To improve the caliber of your students' papers, consider shifting your emphasis. But don't think "I've got to spend more time on the picky stuff" just because the papers are sloppy. Maybe the sloppiness says more about students' "who cares?" attitudes or their procrastination than about how you've taught or how much you've emphasized grammar and editing.

Read a colleague's papers. Ask for some bad ones. It may comfort you to learn that even the teachers we look up to, the veterans with years of experience, still get wretched papers. Do whatever it takes to convince yourself that it might not be your fault.

Separate the weak from the terrible. Sometimes if I read two really bad papers first, they color my impression of the whole stack. If they're all bad, either your expectations are unrealistic, your luck is bad, or your assignment is faulty. More likely, you'll find that most papers are just sloppy and rushed, the result of procrastination or an ineffective writing process, not of inability or illiteracy.

But what do you do about the student who can't seem to form a complete sentence and who assures you that the paper *is* the best he or she can make it? First, although the job of improving the writing may seem overwhelming, don't panic. Your school probably has some system for dealing with such students—"remedial" or "basic" writing courses, a writing center or tutors. If you don't have, or are not sure you want to use such resources, it might help you to see how experts in basic writing approach such a paper. Mina Shaughnessy's *Errors and Expectations,* the classic work in that field, insists that even the worst student writing has its own logic and that we need to understand that logic in order to help the student. A short, helpful, more recent piece consistent with Shaughnessy's philosophy is Glynda Hull and Mike Rose's "Toward a Social-Cognitive Understanding of Reading and Writing." We need to see that even experts are often overwhelmed when they first see poor student writing and that we can take steps to help weak writers, even if we don't have training in basic writing.

A STUDENT ACCUSES YOU . . .

of sexual harassment, of racism, of being unfair or unprofessional. The nasty student accusations that I've witnessed have resulted most often from a clash of personalities or from a student's going through a bad life period and taking it out on the teacher. A distant third cause has been real teacher error. So, as awful as it feels to have someone accuse you of a serious offense, you probably haven't done anything wrong and you won't, in the long run, have anything to worry about. But you do need to handle the situation with care.

Take notes and date them. Keep track of everything you and the student say and do. There's nothing more frustrating than getting into an "I said . . ." / "No you didn't" argument.

Get help. Talk to a veteran or supervisor. Find out what channels the student has to pursue to file a grievance against you. Consider asking a third party to join a meeting with you and the student. At the least you should get some advice. At best, you might find that the student has a history of making groundless accusations. Supervisors respect teachers who deal with student nastiness with grace and equanimity.

Realize that it's part of the job. It happens to everyone. A couple of years ago my supervisor was accused of being racist for not overturning university rules to favor a particular Asian student. My nastiest student accuser was pregnant and had to wear a fetal heart-rate monitor everywhere. I guess yelling at me helped relieve her stress. Even in the one legitimate sexual harassment case I've adjudicated, the student complained only months after the harassment, when it was clear she wasn't going to get the grade she wanted. I'm not dismissing all student complaints or holding teachers blameless, just trying to ease the paranoia. You've no doubt heard of made-up stories ruining the lives of teachers and daycare workers. But that particular hysteria seems to have run its course, and if you feel innocent of the charges, you'll probably be fine.

PLAGIARISM

probably deserves a chapter of its own, and I have devoted a lengthy appendix to it, but I don't want to give it that big a place in your imagination. It's rampant, everyone says. But in my own classes I've caught only two people— one copied an Ann Landers column verbatim, the other badly erased the page numbers from a high school paper and wrote in new ones. I'm sure other plagiarists have avoided my detection. But I don't lose sleep over it.

Plagiarism upsets many of us because it feels like such a betrayal of the relationship we've built with our students, of the mutual trust that we pride ourselves on. It is often its own punishment: the bought paper that doesn't fit the assignment earns the student a lower grade than the uneven draft that it replaces. The page lifted from the textbook doesn't support the badly conceived thesis.

Sometimes plagiarism is not what it seems. We tend to get so outraged by plagiarism—with justification, I think—that we may overlook circumstances that would, in other situations, elicit our sympathy or understanding. The plagiarism policy adopted by the Council of Writing Program Administrators makes a crucial distinction between plagiarism—usually conscious and willful—and "misuse of sources": "carelessly or inadequately citing ideas and words borrowed from another source" (2). Raking a student over the plagiarism coals for carelessness wastes your time and energy and will probably damage both of you. Maybe the plagiarist is undergoing a personal crisis, strung out and sleepless, and in a time of diminished capacity for judgment decides that plagiarism is less shameful than asking for an incomplete or dropping the course. Maybe the student has misunderstood something that you're promoting—as did the two students on the same soccer team who knew that their teachers prized "collaboration" and turned in identical papers about their big soccer game. Maybe the student grew up in a culture—there are quite a few—which has no concept of "plagiarism," and in which borrowing without attribution is an important part of the erudite writer's art. And while ignorance may be no excuse, it certainly explains the large percentage of students who say that anything on the Internet is common knowledge and therefore public domain (McCormick 68). Wilhoit's students say they were told in high school they didn't need to quote passages lifted from encyclopedias (163).

Don't chastise yourself for being a softie if you don't punish a student who borrowed badly. Most cases of "plagiarism" rightly end up as slightly scary learning situations for naive students.

There are ways to prevent plagiarism and ways to catch plagiarists, and I'll list a few of each. Standard operating procedure about plagiarism varies from school to school, department to department. So when you suspect plagiarism, ask around, find out about procedures and normal punishments. Get plagiarism statements and definitions from the writing program, the department, or the university.

Prevention

It may seem like a pain to spend your time on these strategies, but if you've ever pursued a full-fledged plagiarism case up the administrative chain, you know that prevention is much more efficient than punishment. Suggestions to head off plagiarism:

1. Monitor student papers. If possible, require multiple drafts and teach with conferences and/or frequent email exchanges, so you know what subjects students begin pondering and you can track how papers develop. Because we *can* spot things in papers that the authors themselves aren't aware of, students often get an exaggerated sense of our memories and develop an exaggerated respect for our ability to sniff out any hint of ethical infraction. So our familiarity with their papers may provoke a healthy paranoia in our students. If you can catch plagiarism problems early in the writing process, you can use the transgressions as learning moments rather than treat them as crimes that require punishment.

2. Collect preliminary work on important papers: annotated bibliographies, summaries, freewrites, overviews, discovery drafts, maybe even outlines. Insist that students show you a draft of any paper turned in for a final grade or as part of a final portfolio. You don't want to get a totally new paper in the portfolio and have to guess whether it is the student's own work.

I don't favor the traditional approach—"turn in the Roman numeral outline two weeks before the paper"—although even that can be generative for the student if it's taken as a starting block, not a lane you can't change. Collecting preliminary pieces helps you get to know the paper, the evolving idea, without directly checking up on students, and the pieces themselves have value as process steps for the writer.

3. Discuss plagiarism. Use some of the activities in Appendix E, the academic integrity appendix: define plagiarism, orchestrate role-playing skits about it, lead students through plagiarism practice. Let students know that plagiarism is

- important. Recalling high-profile cases and reciting plagiarism penalties may be effective.

- personal. That is, we as teachers take plagiarism in our classes as a personal betrayal. It hurts our feelings, it makes us mad, and it provokes us to punish.

- easy to slip into. In seconds, students can plug into their paper a great quote found on the Internet, and the source may include no reference information even if the student looks for it. So why waste time flipping through books? Most students can figure out for themselves that buying a paper on the Internet or pulling one from the frat's file is wrong. So we need to devote our time to helping them understand and become alert to the subtler forms of sometimes-unintentional plagiarism.

4. Develop a personal relationship with each student. Of the many ways to do that, the most effective is the conference. Just one ten-minute session of swapping musical favorites or talking about hometowns changes my relationship with my students forever. Students have a much harder time cheating on someone they've traded stories with than on a distant "professor."

5. Show them some of your aces: tell them about the things in the next list.

Catching Cheats

1. Get a second opinion—ask a colleague to read the sections of the paper that you suspect.

2. Use your department's communication network—send out a query: "Has anyone else received a paper about bulimia as a free speech issue?" Be careful, however, not to provide information that would lead to the identification of a particular student as a possible plagiarist. We can't ignore the student's rights.

3. Find the sources. Often the plagiarism is direct and easy to spot in the original.

4. Google it. You may find the original source for a key phrase in one quick Google search.

5. Use Internet sites.

   The following plagiarism detection sites charge a fee, and they don't always catch papermill papers.

   plagiarism.org

   plagiarism.com

   integriguard.com

   turnitin.com

   Paper mills themselves offer large databases of papers. You must search through a catalog of topics to find papers and compare for possible plagiarism on these sites.

   www.123helpme.com

   www.123student.com

   www.schoolsucks.com

   www.bignerds.com

   See Robert A. Harris's The Plagiarism Handbook.

Punishments

1. Get help. Administrators don't mind being asked for advice; what they hate is cleaning up after teachers trying to do everything themselves.

2. Don't feel like a failure if you're conflicted and end up letting the plagiarist "off easy." Plagiarism makes me angry, and I'm happy when a school summons the courage to expel habitual or flagrant offenders; a student given one break may be prone to repeat the offense. But when I'm in my office listening to the plagiarist's story—which usually involves bad judgment piled on bad judgment, not intent

to defraud—my tough-guy resolve often dissolves. It's never an easy issue; try to make the punishment a committee decision.

3. Follow the book. Your university may have very specific requirements about what gets reported to whom—advisors, deans, university counsel etc. You don't want to spend hours on a case and then have it blow up in your face because of a technical issue.

In plagiarism cases, as in most other quasi-legal aspects of the teacher's job, you need to keep notes on everything. If a student contests your handling of a case, a paper trail is crucial.

YOU'RE THE STUDENT'S ONLY FRIEND

At 2:00 a.m., a desperate first-year student feels suicidal, starts swallowing pills, and with her last sane thought calls . . . her composition teacher, you! Yes, it happens. A student's comp teacher is often the only friendly adult face that a student sees during the week, the only "professor" that knows the lonely student's name, the person who teaches the only small class the student takes.

It's a compliment to be the most trusted adult that some eighteen-year-old knows. But do you want the 2:00 a.m. phone call or the string of emails as a student negotiates a first college romance? That's not a rhetorical question—if it's a choice of the student's calling me or finishing the bottle of pills, I'd rather get the call. And I have been lovelife advisor for more than one student.

The issue is boundaries. You need to decide where yours are and make them clear to students. That's a relatively easy task, once you're aware of it, except for those of us who are flattered by any attention and never learned to say no. I've never heard of a student latching onto a teacher out of the blue. The process is almost always slow, and you can head it off if you redirect the conversation to the merits of the paper rather than the heartbreak at its core, or you respond to the first pleading email by sending the number of the counseling center, or you make it clear that you *don't* have forty-five minutes after class to talk.

There's no right way to manage individual relationships with students. I like getting to know my students as individuals; it's one of the joys of teaching. Many of my current friends started out as my students, and I've almost never run into problems with students wanting to be too close. But the time and energy I expend on students appalls many of my colleagues who keep students at arm's length, the boundaries clear. Every teacher needs to work out the balance between professional and personal. And we all need to learn to say "when" if a relationship with a student gets too intense.

A STUDENT DISAPPEARS

You see a student every Monday, Wednesday, and Friday for twelve weeks, then she disappears without a word. You email her to ask what's up but get no reply. Then at the grade deadline you give her an F because you have no choice, though in general you like her as a student and think she could have earned a B if she had finished the work. You worry. Should you have called? It's not your business and not your responsibility, but still . . . maybe all she needs is a little push from an adult. What if she's suicidal?

I hate it when students just drop out of sight. As my courses get to the home stretch, I repeat the refrain, "keep in touch, let me know what's happening especially if you can't meet the deadlines." But at least once a year a student vanishes and I'm left wondering.

I've learned not to assume I have a clue about what has happened to the student. I hear stories all the time that include the "leaving school without notice" phase, and the reasons range from a mental breakdown to a decision to become a ski bum. Most commonly, students need to deal with family problems: mother's in the hospital and needs older sister to take care of the young ones; someone has to stay with Grandpa 24/7, and there's no money for a nurse.

A one-email query is, I think, the perfect way to handle the situation. We certainly don't "owe" students such a note; it's up to them to get to class. But often students seem immensely grateful that someone had an eye on them and cared enough to write a thirty-second email. (The sense of being a faceless number that no one cares for contributes to much undergraduate despair.) After one email, if I have particular reason to be concerned about a student—because of what I know about the student's background or what she has written—I might take one more step, probably trying to figure out through semi-official channels if she's been attending other classes. At that point, I just want to make sure she hasn't fallen into a well.

But if you lose sleep over vanishing students, you'll be tired all year. You'll have plenty of opportunity to invest your time and energy in people who clearly need it and will get something out of it. Think of how small a percentage of your consciousness classes occupied at some points in your undergraduate career. At times of stress, when we need to jettison something to keep our sanity, academics are sometimes a logical thing to throw overboard.

•   •   •

Unfortunately, this chapter could be twice as long without even mentioning the particular scenario that gives you nightmares. But I hope thinking through some of these issues will help you improvise when your own nightmare looms.

10

OUTSIDE THE CLASSROOM

At first, most novice teachers focus on their hours in the classroom; they're the newest, most intense aspect of teaching, the part that may resemble nothing else in the young teacher's life. But as the teacher gains experience and the hours in the classroom become more routine, life outside the classroom becomes more important until, for long-term veterans and tenure-track faculty, the classroom comes to feel like a sanctuary from endless meetings, conferences, and non-teaching paperwork.

You won't spend much time outside the classroom soon, but decisions made and habits formed early in a teaching career may set a pattern for years to come, so make informed choices from the start.

COMMITTEES

Committee work, the gold plating on the balloon of academic status, shows you're moving up in the world, but also brings people down. A cartoon on my door sums up my feelings about committees: one of the participants in a round-table meeting wears a sign saying "I'd rather be grading papers," and the caption is "Higgins was not a committee kind of guy."

But as I've warned my own busy staff members who couldn't find the time to come to staff meetings, committees may not accomplish much, but they can make or break careers. You get nothing for participating in the university-wide committee on writing improvement except the aggravation of having to listen to bozos from sociology and political science proclaim that anyone can teach writing. Yet during one of those interminable meetings, you may exchange rolled eyeballs with the person next to you who turns out to be chair of the Internal Grants committee currently considering your proposal. Writing assessment reports may be the most unpleasant work you've ever done, but because everyone hates it so, the chair takes note of those who make the sacrifice and gives them a break in the next round of assignments.

Being on committees also gives you a peephole into the way your institution works, and that kind of insight can help ensure that the institution works for you. At some schools, the whole department votes on hiring and promotion decisions, making it imperative for every candidate to know a little about even the most arcane, musty corner of the department and the people who work there. In my current school, a stable committee monitors my tenure progress and makes the crucial vote, so the only person I need to impress who's not on the committee is the department chair.

My colleague, Writing Director Lynn Meeks, asks each new group of graduate instructors for volunteers to staff committees that make decisions about such things as textbooks, social functions, and curricula. Participation is voluntary, but the assistant directors that Lynn hires for the following year have always done their time in such committees.

That said, you have every right and reason to follow your instincts and avoid committee participation whenever possible. Unless you're in an unusual situation, you probably won't get any pay or official credit for serving on committees, and "service" probably isn't a key category in your work evaluation. In the worst situations, administrators may pressure you to do the department's work, knowing you're "free" and not likely to feel powerful enough to turn the department down. So you should always have your exploitation sensors on when someone asks you to join a committee. And hope that the committee miraculously has some intrinsic value.

Default: Do your homework on committee makeup and accept a committee position only if the group includes people you need to impress. Always ask for time to think over a committee invitation, then ask a veteran or supervisor for advice.

STAFF MEETINGS

Staff meetings are, I suppose, a special kind of committee meeting, but I think they should be approached very differently. Staff meetings have their drawbacks—doing a grade calibration exercise can be really disturbing—but I always used to judge the quality of a staff meeting by how depressed it made me, how much I felt, "Gee, I should be doing that." So if you leave a staff meeting feeling that way, it's a good thing. Or at least it tells you that the meeting had substance, though it may take you weeks to get over the self-criticism and make use of the ideas from the meeting.

Although staff meetings may not be the highlight of your day, you'd be crazy not to go, unless whoever runs the staff meetings uses them to browbeat the already overworked staff. A good staff meeting is the best place to learn about teaching comp in general and how your school does it in particular. Perhaps more importantly, it is where people make decisions, form alliances, exchange gossip. Talking to people in staff meetings is the first step in networking, something you need to do if you have any thought of moving up and out of your current position. Staff meetings provide the opportunity to hear that others, too, have had trouble keeping their classes awake this week, to connect with staff members who don't have offices in your hall, to ask veterans what classrooms to avoid.

Default: Go if you can.

WORKING AT THE WRITING CENTER

You'll rarely run into a veteran composition teacher who has not worked in a writing center or writing lab. The short, intensive sessions helping student writers in a lab setting prepare teachers for the work they need to do in their own writing courses. Muriel Harris quotes from a fistful of others who praise the teaching preparation they received as tutors, and she lists the main benefits for the tutor as learning about "writing processes," "individual differences among writers," "response to student writing," "difficulties with assignments," and "instructional strategies" (197-201).

Your program may well insist that you work in the writing center, or it may reserve that honor for veterans. But if working in the center is an option, take it seriously. The kind of experience you have will depend to a large degree on the philosophy of the center, its administrators, how it is perceived in the program and the institution in general, and especially students' attitudes and expectations. Unless they've been well prepared and coached about what to expect from a writing tutor, some students will come wanting you to "fix" their papers, or proofread, or give them an idea or sources. It's often tempting in such situations just to be a good editor instead of a good teacher.

Default: If department gossip says the writing center is well run, sign up. You'll learn—probably better than you could in a class you teach—what students think about their writing courses, what kinds of problems they have with assignments, what they think they need help with (often more superficial issues than you might want to focus on), and how grateful they can be when, after fifteen minutes, they leave with a better sense of how they can improve their paper. As Irene Lurkis Clark says, working in a writing center "provides opportunities to learn through firsthand observation how the writing process actually works" (347). It can be a gratifying experience, it will almost certainly teach you important things about your craft, and it might even earn you a dollar or two.

PROFESSIONAL CONFERENCES

If you're lucky, a faculty mentor has already gotten you hooked on the conference habit. Conferences give the people you know a chance to introduce you to the people you *need* to know. You can meet people at conferences who will mentor you long distance, give you feedback on your ideas, inspire you to send out your poetry or finish your Ph.D. People build careers out of the connections they make at conferences, and the ideas, approaches, and techniques they pick up in conference sessions revitalize their teaching. It's hard *not* to learn something at a place where thousands of people who share your interests talk nonstop for days. And if you fantasize about a stranger recognizing your brilliance and rescuing you from oblivion, conferences provide the dream setting.

Although few conferences accept all proposals and some are quite competitive, they're not usually as selective as journals, and they generally require only a summary of one good idea, not brilliance fleshed out in stellar prose. So you have a better chance of breaking into the comp world in a conference than with a publication.

Since most colleges consider conference attendance an important way for professors to stay on top of their subjects, some departments' travel funds send professors around the world, as long as the professor presents a paper at the conference. But few schools provide travel support for graduate students and instructors, so before you get your heart set on going to CCCC, check your department's policies and see whether your school will help pay for trips for people of your status. If your department won't send you, maybe the humanities program or the women's studies office or the faculty retention task force has some money. And don't give up if you can't afford to go to CCCC or NCTE, the big national conferences held in expensive hotels far from your campus. Much smaller, friendlier, and less competitive state and regional conferences offer many of the same benefits as the biggies, and they're not as likely to leave you feeling lost and small.

I must confess that while I believe what I just wrote, I don't like going to conferences. I get nervous months before my presentation, and those butterflies keep me from appreciating everything the conference has to offer. I'm living proof that you don't *need* to go to conferences: I hope to be getting tenure the year this book is published, having presented at only one national conference. But most people who want to climb the tenure ladder would prefer to do it in less than the twenty-five years it has taken me.

Default: Try to go to at least one conference per year, and be as gregarious as possible.

PROFESSIONAL ASSOCIATIONS

Every composition teacher should join the National Council of Teachers of English (NCTE) and its subgroup, the Conference on College Composition and Communication (CCCC). They're the premier organizations representing your views on a national level. They fight for small classes, for recognition of students' own voices, for nonsexist language. NCTE, one of the most consistent and prolific publishers of books about composition, also produces newsletters, both paper and electronic, and publishes journals for "the college scholar-teacher" (*College English*), and for instructors in college composition (*College Composition and Composition*), in two-year colleges (*Teaching English in the Two-Year College*), in high school (*English Journal*), and on down the line. Conferences, publications, networking, job lists, political representation . . . NCTE and allied organizations do it all. So why not join, and at least start building a collection of *CCC*s that you might read some day? NCTE's electronic newsletter, *Inbox,* may be the single best way to keep up with the field. It appears weekly via email with summaries and links to news items and scholarly articles.

Keeping abreast of a professional association lets you know what topics are hot, whose work you should read, what the job situation is, what subjects researchers are just beginning to probe. It can make you feel at home, part of a larger whole.

Default: If you have no desire to make even a short-term career out of teaching composition, skim the library's copies of the NCTE publications a few times each year to see if anyone has addressed your most pressing teaching problems. But if you think it's possible that your future will include teaching writing, join as soon as you can afford it.

DOING YOUR OWN WRITING

Although most composition jobs, even "part-time" ones, keep us working long into the nights, weekends, and "vacations," many comp teachers persist in pursuing goals that usually predated their teaching experience. They want to write something besides class handouts, notes to students, and required papers. We cling to such writing—or at least the possibility of it—as our hope for recognition, the focus for our creativity and expression, the reason we have this teaching "day job" in the first place. We want to write. We want to be writers. We want to tell the world our story or our opinions.

Yet it seems that every word we write, every minute we spend on a poem or essay or story of our own, we have to steal from our students, from our class preparation, or from the courses we're taking, and the theft makes us feel conflicted and guilty. Teachers who clearly put students second to their own work make students feel uncomfortable. It's an unpleasant feeling; anything you ask of the teacher is an interruption, an imposition. We never want to make our own students feel that way.

I solve this competition for my time and attention by doing what can be loosely defined as "teacher research"—I write about my teaching, so anything interesting I'm doing in my classes may also wind up in a book or article. I'm certainly not the only teacher to mix day job with writing avocation—we can use our teaching to write essays, poems, op-ed pieces, creative nonfiction, conference presentations, screenplays and teleplays, as well as scholarly articles and books. I suppose only a finite number of books like this one can be written largely about teaching experiences, and I should defend my territory and not even mention that, after a quarter-century of experience, you too could write this book. But I think experience—our own and others'—is our best teacher, so I'm not concerned about being edged out of the market.

Even if your teaching doesn't provide the material for your writing, it *is* possible to teach well and keep your writing aspirations alive—thousands of people do it. They learn to use every eight-minute bus ride. They store ideas during the school year and then write like crazy in the summer. They get by with less and less sleep.

Having your ability to write curtailed by endless time constraints can teach you an important lesson about yourself and your own motivation. Many people who once imagined themselves the next Toni Morrison or John Updike never quite find the time. "Next weekend" never comes. Lord knows it's enough to "just" be a teacher, and being a great teacher may well be more important than being a great poet. But always having too much to do will reveal to you what's really important, what corners you can cut, and what you're willing to stay up late doing.

If you're really lucky or talented, you might find someone willing to fund your writing habit. Ironically, the less you need money in academia, the easier it is to get—you probably won't qualify for nearly as many research, travel, and teaching improvement grants as a professor would. But ask around and visit websites. You might be surprised at the number of awards, fellowships, grants, and prizes that target people in precisely your position.

People who really want to write find a way to do it on top of their grad student responsibilities or full-time job . . . or they feel so frustrated at the lack of time for writing that they find ways to cut back or change their day job.

Default: Do the writing that keeps you sane, and keep track of some of the momentous changes you're undergoing. But don't worry about trying to get the next chapter written this semester.

IN THE COMMUNITY

The movement to extend writing instruction, students, and teachers into the community beyond the university is, to my mind, one of the healthiest and most exciting trends in composition. If your school has a community outreach program, or one of your colleagues has developed the necessary contacts, teaching in a community program, or having your composition classes work in the community, may be an easy and accepted part of your role. Lucky you! The rest of us, though, need to remember that our schools are not likely to reward us for work done in the community and may even be skeptical of our desire to send students off campus as part of their coursework. Work in the community because it makes you sane, because it may be your future, because it's a good thing to do . . . not because it's likely to get approbation from your institution. But if you're interested, start doing some reading—try an article like Hildy Miller's "Writing beyond the Academy: Using Service-Learning for Professional Preparation" or Laura Julier's, "Community-Service Pedagogy."

Default: Go with the flow. Unless many others are involved in their communities, wait a semester or two before you take the initiative.

11
BUILDING YOUR FUTURE

There are some real advantages in not being cocksure, from the moment
one goes to college, declares an English major, or even gets his or her
Ph.D., about what one is going to do.

Donald C. Stewart

Immersed in a semester of teaching composition, you'll find it almost
impossible to think about the future, especially a future beyond turning in
your last grades of the semester. And that's not necessarily a bad thing. I'm
not going to urge you to raise your periscope every few days, look at the Big
Picture, and adjust your daily activities. In this chapter, I want to get you to
see how you *are* building your future just by doing your job. Teaching composition may seem like a professional dead end, but as you do it, you learn
a wide variety of skills that can prepare you for professions from librarian
to corporate manager to, well, English professor. I will list some of those
skills that you're practicing as you teach, then encourage you to tear down
the barriers that separate teaching from the rest of your life.

BECOME CONSCIOUS OF THE SKILLS YOU'RE PERFECTING

It's never too early to start collecting materials for a teaching portfolio.
(See Chapter 12, "Constructing a Teaching Portfolio," in Roen.)

Writing

You probably thought of yourself as a pretty good writer before you ever
dreamed of teaching writing, but I can almost guarantee you that your
writing will improve as you teach. All writers need to hone the ability to
see their own writing, read what's really there, not what they had in mind
when they wrote it. As you read hundreds of pages of students' writing,
you get better and better at spotting passive verbs, redundancies, strong
verbs hidden in nominalizations, the real emphasis in a passage, and you
carry those skills over to your own writing.

The same holds true for a myriad of other writing skills—if you help
your students focus, organize, edit, proofread, format, you can use the

same approaches on your own writing. It doesn't happen automatically—many of us have to apologize to our students, "Do as I say, not as I do." But at least we have the tools, and it shouldn't be too great a leap to apply to our own writing what you've helped student writers apply to theirs.

You don't think about this as you're hurriedly scanning a student paper trying to find something to praise, working to trim the endless possible criticisms to one "thing to work on," but each of the writing skills you're practicing is a profession in itself. In the outside world, you can make a living performing just one of the many functions you now take on each day.

You could become a writing *coach* who encourages other writers, helps them find ideas and get started, suggests ways they can organize and focus their writing. Some newspapers hire such coaches to work with their staffs. Rich and/or desperate grad students find coaches to help them over a writing block and finish dissertations. Any university has a vast and largely untapped market for writing coach services, and I've often thought if I got tired of teaching I would hang out a shingle as someone who would help professors and grad students write the proposal that would bring them the big grant or finish the paper that would be the ticket to a better job. Think of the advantages of being such a coach, working with motivated writers—you're unlikely to run into a grad student or fledgling reporter who's as reactionary, uninterested, and unmotivated as some comp students. It's fun to work with people who appreciate your expertise and want your help.

You're also busily practicing the skills needed by the many different kinds of *editors*. Acquisition editors read proposals and manuscripts to find those that have the most promise. Development editors nurse a project (and a writer) along from initial idea to completed draft. Copy editors mark up manuscripts and suggest changes, deletions, and additions; they find and fix the tiniest things that writers have overlooked. Production editors oversee the steps from disk to marketable published product. Specialized indexers and proofreaders complete the final steps. Writers with computer expertise create and update websites. And all such editors work not just in publishing houses but in almost any institution large enough to have a website or an in-house newsletter. Some of your more experienced colleagues no doubt already work as editors. It's a good day job for those of us who like to teach.

You may already be conscious of trying not to do student writers' work for them, not taking over their papers. Yet unless you're a completely hands-off teacher, you're getting valuable practice in being a *ghost writer* or *technical writer*—you're helping to shape someone else's ideas and words into the best, most readable form. And if that interests you, if puzzling over an awkward phrase and finding a way to make it short and sweet intrigues you, you may be able to earn good money if you decide to give up the academic world. Contrary to some expectations, the computer revolution made the ability to convey technical information in clear English more, not less, crucial. And anyone who has read a computer manual or looked for assistance in a help file knows that there's plenty of room for improvement in writing digital-age texts. So while spending ten minutes trying to get a student's paragraph to make sense may seem like a frustrating, pointless exercise, if you get a little burst of satisfaction when you finally succeed, you may have the makings of a technical writer. And all the practice you get writing handouts, memos, and exercises doesn't hurt.

Depending on the content of your courses, you may also be picking up skills in specialized varieties of *business writing*. Some people make a living writing, or helping others to write, business letters, resumés, proposals, business plans, annual reports, CEO speeches. Many people who teach composition think of business as the dark (and perhaps evil) side of the moon, but if you can teach a good freshman comp class, you can teach business writing, as I discovered when, without any prior training, I taught Advanced Business Writing for MBA students early in my career. If you understand and apply basic principles like purpose and audience and get a book that tells you a little about specialized business formats, you're all set. And you might be amazed at how well businesses will pay you to teach the same kinds of skills that you now teach essentially for free in freshman comp. I taught "Effective Writing" for years to small groups in an insurance company, making roughly twenty times as much per hour as the university paid me.

Managing

As my last example illustrates, teaching isn't just for schools any more. In fact, as the gap grows between what employers need and the skills employees possess, non-educational institutions spend more and more on in-house training. While employers may be impressed by the specific, "Englishy" aspects of your teaching experience, they may be more intrigued by the nonspecific aspects of your training and experience— your ability to plan and organize your own work and that of a large number of other people, to manage meetings, lead productive discussions, solve problems, create effective small groups, praise and criticize in one breath, plan and evaluate, read and write. You can even build teams and help disparate factions reach a consensus—skills for which companies pay management consultants big bucks. Businesses pay well, too, for teachers of time management, listening, and public speaking.

Do you meet deadlines? Get a lot of writing or reading done in a short period of time? Many teachers, and even serious undergraduates, would answer "Of course!," believing that's what "professional" means. Yet because non-procrastinators constitute a small minority in our culture, businesses prize employees who can turn out good work on time. I was a top freelancer in a major publisher's "stable" for years partly because they liked my writing but I think more because they knew they could give me an assignment with an absurdly short deadline and I would get it done.

Even your experience doing the parts of your job you may hate most looks good on a resumé. Can you negotiate the minefield of departmental politics, make peace between warring factions, find common ground? A career in administration may be calling. Do you have a knack for dealing with red tape, getting what you want from bureaucracies set up to deny your every request? You might consider working as an academic advisor or ombudsperson. You may be young and feel that you're relatively untested, but how many people your age are responsible for twenty-five or fifty or a hundred college students? Taking on that responsibility is no mean feat.

When I worked as a ghost writer for a business management guru, I was impressed by how similar the "new, revolutionary, Japanese" management techniques were to the process approach to teaching writing. (See my "The Other Process Revolution.") Without realizing it, you've probably been "studying the causes," "focusing on the system," and working for "continuous improvement"—all management buzzwords explained in high-priced seminars to which companies send their managers. You know that "workers are the experts" and you focus on "value-added work." To succeed in the corporate world, just don a dress-for-success outfit and work up the chutzpah to say, "I can do that."

Working Collaboratively

Americans are supposed to learn to work together on sports teams or in Scouts, but I became a team player largely by teaching comp as part of a large staff trying to enjoy endless underpaid effort. The urge to support and share came almost automatically. We were close enough so that I could see most people's weaknesses, but that didn't get in the way of my developing an abiding respect for them.

It may never have occurred to you how unusual it is to be one of ten, thirty, or fifty people working independently but collaboratively, setting their own goals but also pursuing goals set by the writing program, the department, the college, and the university. As English department chair and writing program administrator Roger Gilles puts it, teachers "who know how to work with and contribute to programmatic—rather than simply personal—teaching goals are invaluable to any department (and department chair)" (9). "I might . . . suggest to job-seeking graduates that they include a description on the c.v. of their program-related experiences and contributions" (10). Your administrators probably appreciate your team-player ability, as will business leaders if you should ever stray from the teaching fold. Your finesse in dealing with the mixture of autonomy and cooperation, innovation and tradition, individual and group identities is a skill that will serve you well wherever you go.

Reading and Researching

You've spent your academic life with books, in libraries, and on the Internet, so you may have to emerge from the academic bubble to realize that non-academics value those skills too. People who start out with degrees in English often end up in libraries, or doing government or corporate research, working for museums or historical preservation groups, teaching speed reading or running adult literacy programs, writing book reviews or summarizing books for people too busy to read them, developing questions and finding answers for trivia games and quiz shows. You may laugh cynically about having degrees in English, but don't assume prospective employers will laugh with you.

Working One-to-One

Even if you don't hold regular conferences, you work with students in office hours and in the intense mini-meetings before and after class, you read and respond to students' sometimes very personal writing, and in every interaction you strike a balance between supportive and critical, personal and professional.

Many "helping" professions, particularly therapies, require such ability to handle intimate circumstances in a professional way. I'm sure I'm not the only writing teacher who has fantasized getting a counseling degree and becoming a writing therapist. When you deal with divorce, alcoholism, sexual abuse daily in students' papers, it's only logical to think that instead of always bringing the focus back to the writing, to the paper, perhaps you could help the writer deal with the subject of the paper. At the University of New Hampshire, where the writing program revolves around conferences, the counseling service comes to writing program staff meetings every year, knowing that comp teachers learn more about students' lives than anyone else on campus and hoping to use that intimacy to identify and help students at risk.

So if you've had the desire to help the student rather than the paper, know that you already have experience on which you could build a career as a psychotherapist, a school counselor, an academic advisor, a personnel manager.

Knowing Young People

If you teach three or four sections of college composition each year, and you sometimes let your students write on their own interests, you qualify as one of the country's experts on the tastes and interests of nineteen-year-olds. You read several hundred essays each year, hear the chatter before and after class, see the stickers on their notebooks and the graffiti they leave on desks. You know which rock bands are hot, which actresses the boys yearn for, the latest styles in footwear and makeup. I knew about the Rainbow gatherings, windsurfing, and aerobics years before my peers did, simply because students would bring their new passions to their essays. Yet we have enough distance to be able to put their current desires into perspective and see how they resemble our own tastes at that age, how they fit with the national adult mood. So in some ways we know them better than they know themselves.

So what? When TV commentators make sweeping generalizations about the current college generation, you can yell "bullshit" at the screen, but what other advantage do you gain from your vast knowledge of a particular demographic group? You have to think in marketing terms. The group you know so well may not rival baby-boomers in terms of demographic bulge, but think of the kinds of companies to whom the tastes of current nineteen-year-olds matter—designers, record companies, credit card companies, media companies, advertisers of all kinds.

Such knowledge led to one of the great breakthroughs of my career. A publisher's rep came to our journalism program, wanting to hire a journalism class to write a *Time*-style glossy magazine to be given away as an ancillary lure with undergraduate business texts. Don Murray persuaded them that having twenty-five different authors was not a good idea; what they needed was someone who had his fingers on the nineteen-year-old pulse and the energy to write fifty stories in six weeks. Me. The relationship I started that summer with the publisher lasted almost ten years and allowed me to support my teaching habit in style.

I can't say with certainty that such knowledge has helped anyone else land a job, but I know that American businesses need to be able to "think young," and with our unique, long-term exposure to young people, we know what that means. So don't sell that kind of knowledge short.

Computer Skills

The degree to which current composition courses rely on computers and other technology varies tremendously. Some courses are taught very much as they were in the 1970s, except that the copy machine has almost universally replaced the ditto machine. I'm old fashioned enough to think that the basics of writing training haven't changed much, and I am not advocating that you start teaching online or in a computer lab just to get more high-tech experience. But if you do have that experience, you can do a lot with it.

I have seen a number of English department people—writing teachers with a side interest in some form of technology—build slowly on their technological side until it became their career. At the moment, there seem to be plenty of programmers and focused computer people in the country, but never enough people straddle the line between worlds, between the online environment and the blackboard. Anyone who can follow a conversation among computer gurus and then explain it to people in the humanities might consider going into instructional technology (the hottest educational field at the moment) or administration in computer services. The need for technology experts has been less consistent than the need for writing teachers, but having a foot in both worlds allows you to go with the latest wave and not worry about changes in demographics or technology patterns.

Survival Skills

Touting the skills you develop by working an underpaid, underappreciated job may sound like a coal miner bragging about the ability to bend over. But if you're going to do something degrading and repetitive, you might as well make use of any benefits it offers.

After teaching for a while, you become comfortable with a teaching persona and realize that you could develop other personas. I like the teacherly me, just as I liked my father when he was teaching. I hope that the at-home me has learned some lessons—in tolerance, acceptance, patience—from the teacher. I'm not consciously different in class than outside of it; I don't create two identities as much as I stretch the one I have to accommodate the sides of myself that appear in class.

You may also become comfortable with new aspects of your life, even some that you wish you could change—like commuting long distances between jobs and not getting any sleep. I can't see any silver lining to commuting, unless you view it as a boost to the American economy. I don't advocate sleeplessness, but I liked discovering that I could get by with significantly less sleep than I had always thought necessary. (I learned that lesson from caring for babies rather than from holding down three part-time jobs, but the principle applies.)

You learn how much you can get done if you really need to. Some graduate students have so many balls in the air they can't even remember them all, much less keep track of them. After being jobless the semester after graduate school, I ended up with six courses for a short time the following semester. I suppose each of us has a different way of realizing "I can cope" when we get to adult life. Teaching a lot of writing taught me.

Teaching composition as many do—different classes in different schools with different rules—we inevitably learn to be flexible, put on different hats, develop different emphases, to meet the different needs of our schedule. Such variety can keep things interesting, and it dispels forever the idea that there's only one thing we can do, one way; it prepares us for the huge variety of job possibilities that open before us.

BRING YOUR REAL LIFE INTO THE CLASSROOM

We tend to separate our professional lives from our "real" lives and miss some of the ways they can and should build on each other. I've written most of my professional composition work on subjects that come from outside the composition classroom—music, poetry, business, comp survivalists hiding out in the Idaho mountains.

And I don't think I'm alone. Much good writing and good teaching springs from the intersection of a variety of interests. (See Chapter 4.) So as you're building your career, trying to pick from the scores of directions you *might* go, or just trying to resist the slurping rotation that seems to be carrying you in one particular direction, keep examining the things you do in your "off" time and how you might bring them into your classrooms and your career.

USE YOUR FAVORITE METAPHORS

Bruce Ballenger, author of the "Curious" writing book series, used to build writing classes around the camera and its metaphors. I've made a small personal industry out of playing music in my classes, which I started doing almost solely for enjoyment. Many other people use film or TV clips or art to get themselves and their students thinking.

No matter what your outside-the-classroom hobby or obsession—from dance to cooking to martial arts—you can productively bring it into the classroom. It's a process with a product, right? Do the maxims of your hobby apply to writing? Can you introduce writing topics by demonstrating the martial arts equivalent of a free write?

Bronwyn Williams's book on TV, like mine on music, can help you use non-text media in your classes. William DeGenaro's chapter about using film in a basic writing course might give you a good starting point if you're a movie buff. But my point is not to promote those resources or try to convince you to bring anyone else's hobby into your classroom. I want you to look at *your* life and at the things that try to sneak their way into your classroom, and ask yourself how you could integrate them in your classes in a pedagogically productive way. If you're clever enough, like my colleague, folklorist Jeannie Thomas, you can teach about Barbies.

LEARN FROM OTHER GENRES, OTHER GROUPS

Many of us spend a significant amount of (as yet) uncompensated time doing other kinds of writing and talking about writing with various voluntary groups. Why not bring that writing and those conversations into your classes? Nothing revitalizes your own teaching of writing better than to take up a new genre yourself and see what it feels like to be a novice. (See my "Becoming a Beginner Again.") Do you know something about screenplays, haiku, grant proposals? Almost certainly that knowledge is relevant to your work in composition, and an interest can easily develop into an expertise, which is only one break away from a job. If you end up talking with your students about screenplays once a week, before you know it you may be writing one.

Any writing group you belong to—friends, colleagues, strangers—also provides endless insight into the peer groups that have become the heart of most composition classes. We develop our sense of what works in small groups by being in our own small groups and experiencing different kinds of feedback, different mixtures of support and critique. And you can really *study* small writing groups, as my group-mate Andrea Luna did in her dissertation. Early in your career, you don't need to be thinking about doing teacher research on a subject that interests you, but at least record it as an interest. If an itch like that grows for a few years, you'll find some productive way to scratch it.

VIEW YOUR DAY JOB AS MATERIAL

I've almost always made my living with words; my non-teaching jobs have overlapped with composition work more than have many comp teachers' day jobs. But the day I wrote the first draft of this chapter, I was also working on a poem about the one seven-month period between college and grad school when I worked an eight-to-five job cutting brush and holding plumb bobs. For a writer, every experience offers potential material; a lead might prove to be a dead end or might become a focus for years of investigation.

•   •   •

By highlighting the skills you're gaining and suggesting ways that the world beyond composition might value them, I don't mean to imply that success and happiness lie only outside the walls of the composition classroom. I've done most of the jobs I've mentioned in this chapter, yet here I am, thirty years after teaching my first writing class, eagerly awaiting the next one. To appreciate what we do, we must not feel that we're trapped in it; composition isn't a dead end but a path that can lead to a thousand places, including more composition. If you see some of these future possibilities, you're likely to be happier now in what you do and perhaps to make teaching decisions that will broaden your career possibilities. I'm not at all saying "leave this profession." I'm saying, "Think big. And build on what you already know how to do."

THE LAST WORD

Ok, this is not a game show. You don't have to guess: the word is *professional.*

Stinging put-down on a student evaluation: "The teacher was unprofessional." Worse than wrong. Below boring. Violator of the quasi-legal contract between teacher and student.

You can write great stuff without being professional. You can fascinate and inspire students, win the respect of colleagues, teach and learn in exciting and satisfying ways. But you won't be a favorite with the powers-that-control-your-future.

If you're unprofessional, I can enjoy your writing, your teaching, your ideas, your friendship. But I won't rehire you.

When asked what English teachers need, veteran Jane Adams replies, "A good work ethic. You've got to know the job doesn't start at 8:00 and end at 3:30 every day."

Professionals don't have fewer accidents than amateurs, or suffer fewer debilitating illnesses, but the earthquakes in their own lives don't rock the lives around them. They get someone to teach their classes, collect their papers, negotiate deadlines, finish the job. They squeeze insight from disaster. Their students don't suffer.

Professionals are organized enough to be able to find student papers on their desks. They make it to class despite hangovers and disappointed lovers. Their syllabi are ready on the first day of classes. They return student papers before the staples rust. They don't ask for special treatment. Their enthusiasm animates their work and their students.

If you're professional, you make the VCR work, learn names and routines, respond quickly, and write and talk effectively, so you can dress all pink, or spike your hair, or discuss Karl Marx or Robert Mapplethorpe. By being responsible, doing the job, you earn the freedoms that make teaching fun.

Professionalism gains you career investment capital. Three or four years of impeccably professional behavior can solidify a reputation to coast on while you have a baby or write a novel.

You can practice professionalism at any level, in any job. You can wash dishes professionally, or shovel snow. It's not an avocation, it's attitude turned to action.

Don Murray says, "There is satisfaction in being a pro, like meeting the challenge of writing something good despite ludicrous editorial edicts." At age twelve, he learned "If you do the work, you make yourself necessary." The fifty-cents-a-day worker made himself indispensable by inventing a clever system for stacking cans at Miller's Market.

With Don in mind, I want to close with these snapshots of young pros—the kinds of scenes that keep me in this business.

In the final stretch of compiling the student reader, Shanan asks other instructors for help and lobbies for a deadline extension. But the editor wants the disk Friday, so Shanan does the work herself, does it well, and gets the disk to headquarters before they start beefing, fully aware that they won't even open it for a week.

Denice spends the first day of her break doing the paperwork to make sure that if her three plagiarists ever come to the university computer's attention again, their sorry asses will get expelled. She sacrifices a morning to do a job that would be easy to ignore, putting in time so others won't have to.

Karmen, an undergraduate, falls apart near the end of the semester, stops coming to class, no communication. I email her and she shows up the last day, but no portfolio. It's been a rough semester, and many in her position would give up and take an F. But Karmen finishes her portfolio a few days late, and she does a good job with it. I like the challenge, the warmth, the precision in her final papers. She's too late to get an A, but she's taken a step toward becoming a professional.

•   •   •

These are the kinds of scenes that keep me in this business . . . and that make me eager to be involved when others experience their first time up.

Appendix A

YES, YOU MAY
But Not Everyone Agrees

In education, we often have a tendency to restrict, reduce, or simplify in order to make the overwhelming task of teaching more manageable. Introducing young people to the chaotic world of formal language usage—reading and writing—often makes such restrictions and reductions seem unavoidable.

P. L. Thomas

The discipline of English is plagued with "rules" and prohibitions that make no grammatical or logical sense but nonetheless persist, causing millions of students to be prosecuted for crimes that don't even exist. I list below some writing strategies that good writers regularly engage in despite many English teachers' admonitions that "you can't do that."

I wish I could say that, keeping in mind the qualifications I make below, you could do these forbidden things any time you wanted to, and you could encourage your students to do the same. Unfortunately, superstitions and bad information die hard, and you may well run into a boss or a professor—yes, conceivably even an English professor—who believes in the prohibitions that make this handout necessary. (A respected business administration professor once told me that he marked things wrong on his students' papers because his fourth grade teacher had marked them on his.) And while none of these things is "wrong," you may sometimes find ways to revise when you question your use of them—"Does the sentence sound bad because I ended it with a preposition?" As is true for writing in general, you need to know your audience and be ready, for example, to stop using contractions if that's what your audience wants. When in doubt, ask your audience.

1. *You may use "I."* Writing with "I" is often more direct, lively, concise, and honest than stating something any other way. Fiction

writers, poets, and essayists have been exploring the value of the first person singular for centuries, yet often teachers ban it from their classrooms. There are times when "I" is inappropriate—when your name won't appear on a document or other names will, and in certain kinds of scientific and technical writing. But in recent years, "I" has been showing up more often even in academic articles and scientific reports. Before you reject using "I," be sure you have a good reason.

2. *You may use "you."* Sometimes—as is the case with this book—the writer has a clear sense of the audience and speaks directly to them, and "you" seems like the only natural way to go. If you're giving directions or instructions, you're almost forced to employ at least an understood "you." But you can overdo it; I usually change to "we" if I can, so I'm perceived as part of the audience, not looking down on it.

3. *You may start a sentence with anything you want.* Some teachers still say "Don't start with 'and' or 'but,'" even though thirty-five years ago, Francis Christensen showed that a significant percentage of the sentences of well-known, respected writers do. Because they fear fragments, some teachers prohibit sentences that start with "because." But that doesn't make much sense either. Students have been told "never start with a numeral," but Toni Morrison began *Beloved*, "124 was spiteful," and won a Nobel prize. I'm not sure you can legitimately start a sentence with "me," but Dylan did it: "Me, I busted out, don't even ask me how."

4. *You may use contractions.* Believe it or not, I once quit a job over this tiny issue. When I went in for my yearly discussion with the dean, he gave me back my most recent memo with three or four contractions circled in red. He proceeded to tell me that contractions weren't appropriate for business writing and would never appear in business text books, the *Journal*, the *Times*, and several similarly august publications. After an unpleasant twenty minutes, I left and went to the library, where I found contractions in each of the six publications he had mentioned, circled the contractions on photocopies, and put the copies in his box. You may use contractions almost everywhere, but you'll still run into lots of people—and perhaps some very stuffy journals—who think you can't.

5. *You may end a sentence with a preposition.* In response to the "rule" banning such prepositions, Winston Churchill is supposed to have said something like "that is the kind of arrogant pedantry up with which I shall not put," showing how awkward sentences can sound when the writer moves the preposition(s) from the end to the middle of the sentence. Some credit E.B. White with the greatest rule-breaking sentence I know: "Why did you bring that book that I was going to be read to out of up for?" Unnecessary prepositions at the ends of sentences do sometimes sound awkward: "Where did you park the car at?" But many modern grammarians consider some prepositions—like "up with" in the phrase "put up with" to be part of the verb and therefore necessary to it.

6. *You may write one-sentence paragraphs.*

   If you write lots of them, especially in a row, your writing and your thought will seem to be superficial, skimming along the surface of ideas. But a one sentence paragraph following a series of longer paragraphs can be dramatic, with an effect similar to that of an exclamation point. Used sparingly, short paragraphs can be very effective.

7. *You may split infinitives.* You may not know what an infinitive is and therefore wouldn't know how to split one, so this may not be worth thinking about. To boldly go into this territory may incur the wrath of traditionalists, who consider a split infinitive to be a sign of sloppiness or bad taste. This prohibition may have developed because you can't split an infinitive in Latin, and English grammarians liked to borrow rules from Latin, to make English seem more proper.

Appendix B

MOTIVATION THROUGH METAPHOR

Charles Woodard

Communication is survival. You and I believe that, but how do we convince composition students? We know that we *must* convince them, early on, or they won't be motivated to genuinely improve their writings. But how do we proceed, without simply repeating all of the common sense things that past English teachers have said? How do we avoid the here-we-go-again student reaction to our good advice?

I have always tried to do it through metaphor—usually through creatively vivid literary examples of the necessity of good communication. I have used characters as diverse as Hamlet, Bartleby, and J. Alfred Prufrock to argue the potential tragedy of "failure to communicate." Such examples work, but the trouble with them is that they require so much preliminary explanation that the main teaching points are too long postponed. What is needed is a metaphor that is not only creatively persuasive but also immediately accessible, and most of all *short*.

I have found it.

It is a Kiowa legend called "The Story of the Arrowmaker," by N. Scott Momaday. It appears in his *The Way to Rainy Mountain*, a collection of myths, historical events, and personal experiences which recount the Kiowa tribal experience in the vivid language of the oral tradition that has helped to preserve that experience. I pass out copies of "The Arrowmaker" to students with no explanation other than the simple statement that it is a story about language:

If an arrow is well made, it will have tooth marks upon it. That is how you know. The Kiowas made fine arrows and straightened them in their teeth. They drew them to the bow to see if they were straight. Once there was a man and his wife. They were alone at night in their tipi. By the light of the fire the man was making arrows. After a while he caught sight of something. There was a small opening in the tipi where two hides were sewn together. Someone was there on the outside, looking in. The man went on with his work, but he said to his wife:

"Someone is standing outside. Do not be afraid. Let us talk easily, as of ordinary things." He took up an arrow and straightened it in his teeth; then as it was right for him to do, he drew it to the bow and took aim, first in this direction and then in that. And all the while he was talking, as if to his wife. But this is how he spoke: "I know that you are there on the outside, for I can feel your eyes upon me. If you are a Kiowa, you will understand what I am saying, and you will speak your name." But there was no answer, and the man went on in the same way, pointing the arrow all around. At last his aim fell upon the place where his enemy stood, and he let go of the string. The arrow went straight to the enemy's heart.

I give the students plenty of time to read and re-read and consider the story, and then I ask for reactions. At first, the response is very tentative, both because the students do not know me yet and because they do not understand why I seem to think that the story is so important. It interests them, because of its mysterious dramatic action, but it is little more than a curiosity at first. Mostly they wait for me to explain, but I out-wait them—it is important not to "teach" this story in any conventional sense—and I respond to their puzzled expressions with more specific questions. Is the arrowmaker a wise man? Why does he do what he does? What risks does he take? What might have happened if he had responded differently? Such "plot" questions usually make the students more comfortable, and several of the bolder ones begin to speculate about the various consequences of the arrowmaker's choices. I let that speculation unfold for a few minutes, and then I interrupt it by suddenly asking which students I know best. Again, puzzlement. But I press the point. I did not know any of you a few minutes ago, I say. Now I know several of you better than the rest. Which ones? Why? Then the answer comes to one or more of them (again, I wait for that to happen, and rephrase the question until it does). *I now know best the ones who have spoken, the ones who, like the arrowmaker, have risked themselves in language!*

We then discuss what the risks are, and the students usually reveal their understandable fears of ridicule by others. Some even volunteer accounts of experiencing such ridicule. For example, a male student might tell of the ordeal of calling a girl for a date, and the difficulty of language in that situation. Someone else might mention the difficulty of answering questions during a job interview. Whatever the example, the group always comes back to the necessity of declaring oneself in words. And I casually observe that sooner or later each student in the room will have to do that very thing on paper to pass the course. Each student, I emphasize, will have to venture forth in language to satisfy the course requirements, and of course the implication is that all of life is like that.

At this point, if it has not come up before, I ask the students how they feel about the man standing in darkness, the man who died because he did not speak. Usually somebody is indignant about him, feeling that the arrowmaker took unfair advantage of his silence. I then readily agree that it is easy to sympathize with the man in the dark, because maybe he couldn't speak, or hear, and so perhaps he was not given a fair chance. But I also add that our sympathy doesn't alter what happened, nor can it do much for those voiceless ones among us. The tragedy remains. The man in darkness will remain anonymous because he has not been actualized in language, while the arrowmaker, the person Momaday himself refers to as "the man made of words" has a wholeness and a continuing identity, positioned as he is at the center of the circle of light.

Then I ask the students when the high point of the story's dramatic action occurs. By this time the discussion is lively (it has been obvious to me several times in the course of this part of the discussion that the students were by then consciously avoiding the destructive silence they had just observed) and we agree that in retrospect the climactic moment has to be when the arrowmaker speaks, because it is then that he risks himself (what if, I sometimes ask, the man in the dark was an enemy *who understood Kiowa?*). The actual physical event, the shooting of the arrow, we decide is anticlimactic, a foregone conclusion *once the arrowmaker has successfully risked himself in words.*

Finally, I encourage the students to talk about the particulars of the physical scene, because I want the metaphor to stick, so that I can refer to it again and again during the duration of the course. We discuss the light-dark contrast, and the fact that the man in the dark is alone while the arrowmaker has companionship, and especially that the arrowmaker is positioned in a circle, which I point out is the traditional Native American symbol for wholeness and completeness and continuation, the never-ending and ever-renewing circle of the earth. I then ask about the arrows, and what they might be symbols of, and of course the response is *words.* The arrowmaker shapes them in his *teeth*, and arrows *penetrate.* I suggest to the students that "penetrating" is a very positive word in a communications context, for it is what we mean to do when we say we want to "get through to someone." We want to *penetrate* whatever obstructions there are and *really* communicate. I conclude by pointing out that the story of the arrowmaker, with its vivid contrasting images and its simple but persuasive language, does exactly that.

Appendix C

ANOTHER OBNOXIOUS QUESTIONNAIRE

Name:
Hometown:
Local Address:
Local Telephone:
Year in College:
Major (if any):
Career goal ("Who knows?" is fine):
What are your interests, hobbies, obsessions, sports?

What do you enjoy reading? (List both general types—e.g., magazines, poetry—and specific examples—e.g., *Soldier of Fortune*, Emily Dickinson.)

What do you enjoy writing? (Poems, songs, fiction, English papers, letters, nothing?)

What music do you listen to? (Again, list both general types and specific examples.)

What other English courses are you taking or have you taken recently?

What do you hope to get out of this course?

Appendix D

IN DEFENSE OF SUBJECTIVE GRADING

What is wrong, after all, with "writing for the teacher"? As traditionally undervalued instructors of everyone's "worst subject," composition teachers become too quickly defensive when their scientific colleagues talk of the reliability of composition grades, retreat too easily into "We know the variation from teacher to teacher is bad, but we're working on it." Without denigrating the work of those who strive to find reliable composition grading methods, I think we can stop feeling guilty about what we do and admit that individuality, lack of uniformity, may be among our discipline's greatest assets.*

Our fear of our own subjectivity seems well-founded. Many composition experts would agree with E.D. Hirsch that "Until we have reliable means of rating the quality of a student's prose, we lack a sound basis for determining the teaching methods which will raise that quality most efficiently. . . . We cannot progress in other lines of pedagogical research until we solve the assessment problem" (1977, 11). How can we teach if we can't seem to agree on how and what we desire as the products of our teaching? That we don't agree on how and what we grade has been painfully demonstrated, most convincingly by Paul Diederich (1974). Any writing staff that subjects itself to grading sessions knows that this variation exists, but the traditional response to our apparent unreliability has been to hide the variation, bemoan its existence, or talk about everyone "getting tough."

Diederich has shown conclusively that the writing staff *can* be trained to grade reliably; his success with staff grading robs us of the traditional response to the grading problem: "There just isn't any better [read 'more reliable'] way." His methods yield results which are reproducible and more valid than those of objective tests, and they help students view their

---

* Throughout this paper, I will use "reliable" and "valid" in the narrow technical sense—"reliability" referring to the agreement from assessor to assessor about how a particular writer or a particular work should be evaluated; "validity" indicating that the assessing method accurately tests the skills it was designed to test.

teachers as coaches rather than judges, because teachers no longer wield the dreaded grade.

Yet despite the success of staff grading, many English departments continue to encourage teachers to grade in the traditional way, each teacher evaluating his or her students' work. It may be that these departments have examined Diederich's studies and worry about the time training sessions would take or the problems heavy staff turnover would create, or sympathize with the inconsistent student who may not work well under time pressure, with assigned topics, or on a particular day, and would therefore suffer in most staff grading programs. Some departments may resist the change to staff grading for less thoughtful reasons: the transition would be unsettling, time consuming, or politically dangerous; inertia is too strong.

Or maybe we sense that grading reliability, like any kind of enforced uniformity, would take its toll.

Most writing in educational settings continues to occur in the context of a long-standing relationship between teacher and student. The tendency, especially in recent years, has been to downplay this relationship by encouraging writers to ignore the fact that the teacher will probably be a paper's only reader, and to fight the implications of the bond between student and teacher by trying to depersonalize the grading process, removing student names from their papers, grading according to an established set of priorities, or passing final papers on to other English teachers so that the paper itself can be judged without reference to the personality of student, teacher, or class.

These approaches may have value in certain situations, but they ignore many of the benefits that can be derived from the close student-teacher relationship. A student working with a teacher is likely to write for an audience, and that sense of audience is crucial to any student's becoming a successful writer. Very few of our students will go on to write for readers as anonymous as those at Educational Testing Service, and we may find that training writers to write for unknown anyones—something that staff grading may encourage—produces writers similar to those who work in the government, writing for that great faceless "general audience." Our students will more likely be writing for a particular professor or boss or committee or group of co-workers. Students who learn to identify the quirks and desires of a particular teacher are not just "polishing the apple"; they will be ready in the future to write for the boss who loves passives and obfuscation, the professor who hates the first person, or the school board impressed with pedantry. The writer aware of his or her audience, writing for that audience, will be likely to get the job, the raise, or the "A" before another writer technically superior but unable to adjust to suit a reader.

Of course writing with the teacher in mind as audience or editor differs substantially from writing *what* the teacher is perceived to "want." Although some teachers do successfully assign subjects, only rarely can we justify judging a student's ideas as "right" or "wrong"; our subjectivity should not extend that far. We judge form and style, the presentation of ideas, the methods and logic used to reach a conclusion, but seldom the conclusion itself. We encourage students to think well and say *something*, but we should never assign that something a low grade just because we disagree with it.

When dealing with content, the teacher's most productive role may be as an elusive devil's advocate, taking the stance of a hypothetical audience for the piece of writing. Students who can discriminate between the demands of the intended audience and those of the editor can aim a paper at an imagined audience, keeping the teacher-as-editor in mind as a side concern. Less sophisticated students may not be able to write with an audience more abstract than "grade-giver" in mind, but imagining the teacher as audience is better than imagining no audience at all; it will help the student to, in Linda Flower's terms, move from writing writer-based prose to writing reader-based prose.

The problem we have traditionally faced in writing classes, then, is not that students write for the teacher, but that we have refused to admit that fact. In our desire to appear as believers in the absolute of "good writing," we have deceived students into thinking that everyone agrees with each of us. Students taught the "right" way to write by Ms. X will naturally be frustrated when Mr. Y's "right" way is different, and last year's A work gets Cs this year. No wonder students become suspicious about their English grades.

If, on the other hand, Ms. X said, "I value active sentences and smooth transitions," and Mr. Y, "You must have a clear thesis statement and a personal writing style," students would realize that they were being taught not two different "right" ways, but two different subsets of the general goal "good writing." They would understand why the same paper could be graded differently, and although they might agree more with Ms. X's or Mr. Y's emphasis, they would be able to learn from both without becoming cynical, and they would be ready for Professor Z to pay attention to something completely different. Compared to students kept in the dark about our differing standards, students able—and, indeed, encouraged—to write differently for particular teachers will not only be more flexible and aware of their audiences in the future, but will most likely learn more from their various teachers because they won't be confused trying to reconcile what appear to be contradictory dicta.

This acceptance of diverse approaches and evaluations in the writing classroom cannot be absolute, for certain emphases can harm students' writing or destroy any pleasure students may derive from it. Focusing on margin size, typographical perfection, or rigid adherence to a prescribed form would seem out of place in most courses, as would an emphasis on nothing but content, although students taught under either regimen might learn the crucial lesson about audience. But the issue of such idiosyncratic emphases is more theoretical than real. As S.W. Freedman has shown, most teachers value the same elements in a paper: content and organization (1979). Admonishing teachers to make explicit their writing values might actually reduce the differences between teachers, because teachers would become more introspective about what they do in class, and those who tend to grade spelling, punctuation, and other easily assessed features might realize, and try to eliminate, the disparity between the values they truly believe in and those that seem to inform their grading practices.

Those who worry about teacher bias for or against particular students should analyze that bias before condemning it. It would be absurd to claim that any writing grade reflects solely a writer's ability—class participation, attendance, attitude, improvement, and changes in the writer's composing process may influence a teacher, and in many cases probably should. The brilliant writer who is the class pest may suffer from the personalized grading relationship, but on occasion such "unfairness" may help both the student and class, as long as the reasons for it are made explicit. The benefits of a familiar teacher's superior ability to judge purpose and intent outweigh whatever loss of objectivity such personalization of grading may entail. And only a teacher who knows a student well can look closely at a student's writing process and help that process evolve, an evolution which may be central to a writer's improvement.

Acceptance of the subjectivity of composition grading leads to several implications for the classroom. First and most important: we must make clear to students our own sets of priorities, letting them know what we will be looking for when we grade. We can elucidate our desires both in class, as we spend time on those elements we expect to see in their writing, and when we comment to students about their papers, letting them know what we feel they should work on first and with most effort.

As a logical extension of this attitude, we should put off grading student papers for as long into the term as possible, so that students will have time to learn the system, figure out what the teacher's writing priorities are, and respond to them. A grade on the first paper might be the most effective method to let students know that they have to mend their ways quickly, but the resentment and anxiety such a quick grade may foster make such grading a pedagogical mistake.

Unsettling as it may sound, we must impress upon our students that "good writing" is at least partially relative, and to drill into them the maxim "know thy audience." We can all agree that clear, concise writing with active verbs outshines murky, passive jargon, but politicians, boards of directors, and perhaps some of our colleagues in other fields may disagree with us. Rather than send our students out as lively idealists in a world of passives and casuistry, we should prepare them to be flexible. Flexibility does not mean lowering or changing our standards; it simply means letting students know that these standards are *ours*, and that others exist, and will continue to exist, despite all efforts to eradicate them.

It should be clear from the above that I feel teachers should grade the papers of their own students. But if a department uses group grading techniques to regularize its biases and establish a uniform set of priorities, it must make every aspect of the standardization explicit, so that all composition teachers can pass the priorities on to their students. Departments which set priorities may need to train teachers specifically to teach and evaluate certain writing skills; otherwise, students' successes or failures at reaching certain uniform goals may reflect their teachers' understanding of those goals rather than their own.

Despite all attempts to objectify the teaching of writing, I don't think writing teachers need to worry about computers and teaching machines stealing their jobs in the near future. As long as there are writers, unique individuals will continue to generate unique sentences which require unique responses. None of us would want to destroy the individuality writers put into their papers, and we should be equally wary of destroying the individuality with which we read them.

REFERENCES

Diederich, Paul B. 1974. *Measuring Growth in English*. Urbana: NCTE.
Freedman, Sarah W. 1979. Why Do Teachers Give the Grades They Do? *CCC* 30: 161-64.
Hirsch, E.D., Jr. 1977. *The Philosophy of Composition*. Chicago: University of Chicago Press.

Appendix E

TEACHING ACADEMIC INTEGRITY

Susan Andersen and Brock Dethier

This appendix is an academic integrity starter kit intended to be incorporated into any course that includes academic research and writing. It consists of

1. "Oh Nothing," a Case Study in the Form of a Play
2. "Oh Nothing" Follow-up
3. Some Possible Answers
4. Five Discussion Scenarios
5. Questions About Research and Academic Integrity
6. A Sequence for Teaching Plagiarism
    Plagiarism: Levels of Paraphrasing
    Plagiarism: Paraphrasing Practice
7. Citation Exercise
8. Bibliography

Our goals: *To give students practice in thinking about ethical questions; to help students see why there are "rights" and "wrongs" in academic ethics and develop an ability to discern the difference; to discuss why doing the right thing matters.*

We want students to stop thinking about academic ethics as a game of "see what I can get away with" and start seeing their approach to academic ethics as a significant reflection of who they are, what kind of character they have, and what kind of employees they're likely to be. A student who gets involved in seriously debating these issues and takes a stand based on a moral sense of right and wrong is on the way to taking a responsible stance toward academic integrity.

Few students, and not enough teachers, are familiar with the variety of issues that come under the heading "academic integrity." Penalizing students who cross the boundaries of academic acceptability is not an efficient way to teach these issues. Researchers have found that ethical thinking and behavior can be taught (CAIRE 84; Bebeau 1-2; Rest), that adults at any age can learn to think more ethically (Bebeau 2), and that using case studies to spark student discussion about ethical issues is a more effective teaching method than focusing solely on academic and philosophical definitions of integrity issues (Pimple 1; CAIRE 90).

Medical, law, and business schools have long used real world case studies; they have been the instructional method of choice at Harvard Business School for over fifty years. The case method of teaching enables teachers to "organize and bring to life abstract and disparate concepts" that lead students to draw upon principles from different disciplines as they contemplate possible problems and resolutions ("Teaching"). Ideally, a case study helps students see the issues in a vivid, memorable way and promotes thoughtful discussion. Teachers can build on and refer back to the case throughout the semester.

The core of this appendix is a case study in the form of a play, "Oh Nothing," which can be read silently or presented to the class by three students reading the lines. We've avoided any personal pronouns so that a student of either sex can play any of the roles. (Perhaps mixing sexes in unconventional ways can shake up the stereotypical view of this scene, with Professor being male and Instructor being female.) Although the issues in this play are serious, the play itself is not, and we think the points will come across well even if students ham up their acting.

Just watching the play probably won't have any effect on students; they need to get actively involved in discussing the situation and making their own ethical judgments (Pimple 4; "Teaching"). Good discussion comes from good questions that are open-ended, exploratory, relational, and probing. Therefore, we encourage teachers to use something like our follow-up questions to help students understand the issues.

The play demonstrates that while plagiarism may be the most common and most discussed academic ethics issue, it certainly is not the only one. We don't expect students to learn any specifics about the use of human and animal subjects, but we do hope that they carry away from the play the understanding that they need to think carefully about how they're using such subjects and check with appropriate committees if they have any questions.

We made the highest-status person, Professor, the most unethical character because we wanted to undermine the idea that plagiarism is only a student issue. After discussing Professor's plagiarism, class members could volunteer instances of student plagiarism and bring the discussion closer to home.

We hope that teachers will modify the play and other materials to fit their own personality, students, and situation. To simplify and clarify some of the play's interaction, our colleague Leslie Blair rewrote the play with a narrator providing stage directions. We applaud such efforts to engage students and trust that teachers will use our materials as writing prompts to spark their own creative approaches to teaching academic ethics.

After using a class period to discuss the play, teachers will probably want to spend an additional day talking about specific examples of issues that are likely to spring up in our own classrooms—plagiarism, for instance. The final sections of this packet focus on plagiarism, each one using a different approach to engage students in making their own decisions about plagiarism.

OH NOTHING: A CASE STUDY IN THE FORM OF A PLAY

Brock Dethier & Susan Andersen

Setting: The cramped office of a college professor. Professor and Instructor are seated, facing each other.

Instructor: I read your new article in *The Journal of Hangnail Morbidity* today.

Professor: Why bother? You wrote half the thing!

Instructor: That's kind of what I was getting at. There was a paragraph on circulatory implications that seemed just like a paragraph in my thesis.

Professor: That's why I gave you a special acknowledgement in the beginning.

Instructor: But it's not in quotes, and some of my numbers have been changed . . .

[Knock on the door. Instructor pulls it open and in walks Student. Professor stands up and shakes Student's hand, then motions Student to the one free chair in the office.]

Professor: Student, why don't you begin by explaining your grievance against Instructor.

Student: I believe that Instructor has treated me unfairly on at least two occasions. First, Instructor told me I could not use animals in my project even though I had obtained permission from the Animal Rights Board.

Instructor: I just try to make sure my students stay legal.

Student: On the second occasion, Instructor stopped me from videotap-
             ing an interview with three students outside the union building.
             By the time I convinced Instructor that they were my friends
             and didn't need the Institutional Review Board's stamp of
             approval, my friends had to go off to class, and I was unable to
             reassemble the group before my presentation.

Professor: These kinds of misunderstandings are common, especially when
             you're dealing with ethical research issues. Your grievance alleges
             material harm as a result of these incidents. Could you elaborate?

Student: Having to postpone my first project meant I had an inadequate
             trial period, for which my grade dropped to a C-plus. On the
             second occasion, my inability to film my friends meant that I
             lost visual presentation points and received a B-minus on the
             assignment. As a result of those two grades, I received a C-plus
             for the course, the worst grade I've ever received.

Professor: Instructor, do you contest Student's evidence or conclusions?

Instructor: I have nothing against Student. Why would I? Once Student
             showed me the stuff was legit, I said, "fine."

Student: But I was doing everything right, and I lost points.

Professor: I'm not sure you were doing everything right. When you're
             just doing a class assignment, the Institutional Review Board
             may not care about how you treat your subjects, but if you ever
             wanted to get your work published, you'd be in trouble.

             And in the first incident, sometimes we hold our students to
             higher standards than those used by the Animal Rights Board. I
             found it surprising that the Board would approve such a project.

Student: So you're not going to raise my grade?

Professor: That's still Instructor's decision. I stand behind my staff.

Student: Is there any way I can appeal that decision?

Professor: *[standing up]* I'm sure there are a dozen ways. But first you'd
             need to talk to our Chair, Dr. Pugh. And I happen to know
             that he, at the moment, is headed to a softball game where I'm
             going to pitch.

Student: *[exiting]* I'll speak to Dr. Pugh then.

Professor: *[to Instructor]* End of that headache.

Instructor: Thanks.

             *[Instructor gets up and ruffles Professor's hair affectionately. Professor grasps
             Instructor's hand and they look into each other's eyes for a long moment. Then
             Instructor drops Professor's hand and turns to go.]*

Professor: What did you want to tell me about that silly article?

Instructor: Oh, nothing; it's great.

"OH NOTHING" FOLLOW-UP

Have students discuss and perhaps quickly research the following. Be prepared with definitions of each term and discussions of the answers.

Have students find in the play a possible example of each of the following concepts. Discuss the moral issues that each example brings up. Is there a right and a wrong in this case?

1. plagiarism

2. conflict of interest

3. violations of animal rights policy

4. violations of human subjects policy

5. data manipulation

6. use of hypothesis-and-evidence approach

Spend the rest of the period discussing other examples of the concepts, trying to make each concept as relevant to the students' lives as possible . . . and/or dig into some of the questions below.

A. In your judgment, did any of the three characters behave inappropriately or make unethical decisions? Explain.

B. Is it legitimate to hold students to higher standards than those published by the University?

C. What should Student do now? What appeal channels are likely to be open?

D. Is it a good thing that Professor "stands behind the staff"?

E. In your view, would a romantic relationship between Instructor and Professor be illegal, unethical, unwise, or not a problem?

Some Possible Answers

1. Plagiarism is the use of someone else's words or ideas without giving that person sufficient credit. Although we can't judge Professor's actions without hearing the whole story, it sounds as though Professor copied Instructor's ideas and words without using quotation marks to acknowledge the borrowing and without a formal citation. Crediting Instructor in an acknowledgment is not sufficient. What Professor did is almost certainly unethical and therefore "wrong."

2. A "conflict of interest" occurs when a person has two inconsistent loyalties or "interests" in a situation. Such conflicts are inevitable in some professions and therefore not necessarily bad—every time a teacher gives a grade, there's a conflict between the desire to make a student happy by assigning an A and the desire to communicate necessary, realistic information with a lower grade. Professor appears to have a romantic relationship with Instructor, and Professor's interest in continuing that relationship seems to conflict with Professor's responsibility to ensure that Student is treated fairly.

3 & 4. The point here is that students should know not the exact policies of their institution regarding animal and human subjects, but that every institution *has* such policies. As Professor says, most review boards will not bother with students working on class assignments, so students needn't worry about interviewing unless they're asking very private questions. While most undergraduates will never need to know the "treatment of animals" policy, linking that issue with plagiarism may help students to see plagiarism in a broader moral context. (Some students may care more about animals than about "academic integrity.")

5. Just before Student knocks, Instructor seems to be implying that Professor altered some of Instructor's data. Data manipulation is a serious and widespread problem. Students may not need coaching to see that changing a number is unethical, but it might still be valuable for them to discuss why and when such manipulation goes on and where "rounding off" or "fudging a bit" turns into "making false statements."

6. Student does an excellent job of presenting a thesis or hypothesis—that Instructor has treated Student unfairly—and backing it up with specific evidence. In fact, of the three, Student shows the most preparation, presents the best evidence, and offers the best argument. Professor is less convincing in presenting an alternative thesis—that Instructor was just following rules.

    A. Neither Instructor nor Professor treats Student's complaint with the seriousness it deserves. Instructor's interference with Student's work may well have been motivated by good intentions, to make sure no policies were broken. Instructor may not have made any ethical mistakes, but Instructor should probably do more to reduce the penalty Student seems to have paid. Professor's dismissal of Student's complaints, apparently because of Professor's relationship with Instructor, is more clearly inappropriate and perhaps unethical.

B. This is a tricky question about which reasonable people might disagree. We feel that yes, individual units of a university may set their own, more demanding standards, but they have an obligation to publicize those standards well.

C. Student has done the right thing by using the traditional "channels" of authority to try to resolve the complaint, talking first to Instructor and then to Instructor's supervisor, Professor. The next logical step would probably be for Student to take the complaint to the head of Instructor's department, presumably English. If that doesn't produce a satisfactory response, student might see if the university has an ombudsperson that handles such complaints. Student should also talk to the advisor in his/her major and, if Student thinks that Instructor was unfair because of Student's race, sexual orientation, or other personal factor, Student might talk to the university's Affirmative Action office.

D. Professor probably used the phrase "stand behind my staff" in order to deflect possible criticism. But since Professor is in the position of adjudicating student complaints as well as supporting writing staff, Professor must also "stand behind" students. So while Professor's pronouncement might sound like a good thing to the staff, it ignores a significant portion of Professor's responsibilities.

E. A roomful of ethical academics might disagree heatedly about this question. Although the relationship is almost certainly not "illegal," it would probably be considered "unethical," and against the institution's faculty code, IF Professor has supervisory power over Instructor, which seems to be the case. This difference in power is a main reason why relationships between students and professors, as well as workers and bosses, are frowned upon. The person in the position of less power—in this case, Instructor—may feel pressured to continue the relationship in order to avoid the professional wrath of the more powerful person. And that desire not to offend the more powerful person may lead the less powerful to give up some rights, as it seems to have led Instructor to give up the right to full acknowledgement of Instructor's own work. Therefore, most people would probably agree that any such relationship involving a power differential is at least risky, and probably unwise.

FIVE DISCUSSION SCENARIOS

The following scenarios provide another way to begin discussions about academic ethics. Students can read them quickly and then discuss the issues and characters involved. Each scenario raises many different ethical issues, and we have not attempted to direct readers' thinking with questions or provide our own analysis. Instead, we encourage teachers to use questions to lead the discussion of these scenarios in the most productive and relevant directions . . . or write their own.

1. Bob and many of his friends at a small residential college are taking a course in British Architectural History. They pick up their take-home exam at 9:00 on Friday morning and must turn it in by 12:00. When Bob returns to his dorm to start work, he finds that four of his friends are already sitting on the floor with his roommate, collaboratively figuring out answers to the exam. When invited to join, Bob wavers, then his pride takes over: He can do as well as all five of them put together. He completes the exam in the library and later hears that the "cool" teaching assistant for the course, Sue, stopped by his room, saw everyone working together, and said, "I see nothing." All five of Bob's friends get A's on the exam. Bob gets a B-plus.

2. Gwen, Wren, and Sven are all working frantically the night before the American Literature paper is due. Gwen put the paper off because she had a chemistry lab to complete and figured that, as an English major, she would have no trouble coming up with a good last-minute paper for American Lit. But she racks her brains for two hours and finally decides that the only way she can finish the paper AND get some sleep before her big weekend is to reprint a paper that she wrote the year before in a Critical Analysis course. She is careful to change the date and the course number on the paper, and she even adds to the works cited page some of the critical books that the American Lit professor recommended.

    Wren has a deal with Ben: she does his computer programs, and he writes her literature papers. Ben is a P.E. major, but he has produced good papers for her before, so Wren has faith . . . and doesn't ask if, as she suspects, Ben buys the papers on the Internet. Wren reasons she does the work for the literature class, she just writes programs instead of papers. She's not actually buying the papers, and the professor said it was ok to get help from peers.

Sven is on the final draft of his paper about *The Scarlet Letter* when he decides to look on the Internet for a good epigraph. After only ten minutes of searching, Sven has a dozen quotes that say what he is trying to say in his paper, but much more elegantly. Frustrated at what he considers his own weak writing, Sven rewrites a number of his sentences using the phrasings from the quotations.

3. Professor Shrek always gives the same Human Sexuality exam. Students flock to his course because it fulfills a science requirement, because of the subject matter, and because many fraternities, sororities, and dorms already own copies of previous years' exams. Graham has a friend in a fraternity who can get him a copy of the exam. He doesn't actually know anyone in the course who is planning to cheat, but he knows that Prof. Shrek grades on a bell curve, and he feels sure that all the cheating students will skew the curve. He has to get an A in the class to keep his scholarship; without it, he'll have to return to the Siberian salt mines where his ancestors have labored for generations.

4. Randy, a master's student in geology, is excited when Professor Dumble asks him to write a chapter for her book on the formation of the Wasatch mountains. She promises both pay and credit. Randy slaves on the chapter, putting everything else aside, figuring that his name on the chapter, perhaps even on the cover of the book, will be his ticket to a Ph.D. program and a big step toward career success. When the book finally comes out, Randy is devastated: he gets a check for $50, and the only place his name appears is in the acknowledgments, which include Professor Dumble's dog and forty-eight other graduate students and colleagues.

5. As part of her work/study job, Bunny does photocopying, typing, and other clerical work for Professor Snoid. Most of the work is dull, but she chuckles when she copies Snoid's Ancient Civilizations syllabus and notices that the students have to buy

Snoid's own textbook, a massive and no doubt expensive tome. Coincidentally, Bunny starts dating Ralph, who is taking Ancient Civilizations and is worried about writing the big essay on the final exam. A few days before the final, Bunny finds the final in her photocopying pile and without even meaning to, she reads the big essay question. And that night she has a date with Ralph.

QUESTIONS ABOUT RESEARCH AND ACADEMIC INTEGRITY*

Write true or false next to each statement below and be ready to discuss your answer.

1. Plagiarism is a problem only when it is intentional.

2. The safest way to make a good paper is to string together quotations from others.

3. Photocopying a page is the best way to ensure that you have all the bibliographic information you need.

4. Much bibliographic information can be found on the library's website, even when the library itself is closed.

5. When taking notes, it is crucial to use quotation marks to distinguish quotations from paraphrases.

6. Only English teachers care where you get the material for your paper.

7. The best way to use most reference books is to start at the end, with the index.

8. Sources like class texts and government documents don't need to be referenced.

9. If you paraphrase someone's ideas without quoting them directly, you can skip the citation.

10. If your paper is becoming overwhelmed with citations, you can leave some out to make it less messy.

11. If you list a person in "acknowledgements" or put a source in your bibliography, you don't need to cite the source in your paper.

---

*   May be used in conjunction with pages 1 and 2 of Ballenger's *The Curious Researcher.* Some ideas suggested by Janice Newton, "Plagiarism and the Challenge of Essay Writing: Learning from our Students." Answers: 1-F, 2-F, 3-F, 4-T, 5-T, 6-F, 7-T, 8-F, 9-F, 10-F, 11-F, 12-T, 13-F, 14-F, 15-T, 16-F, 17-T

12. Even professional writers refer often to citation reference manuals.

13. Most students learn all they need to know about source citation in high school.

14. It works fine to worry about citations as the final step in proof-reading.

15. It's possible to do great research, properly reference all sources, and still make the paper your own, with plenty of your own ideas.

16. You can assume your reader is intelligent enough to see the implications of quotations; you don't need to link them overtly to your thesis.

17. Professors (and bosses) generally want writers to think for themselves.

A SEQUENCE FOR TEACHING PLAGIARISM *

Our USU colleague Charlene Hirschi demonstrated for our staff a sequence of plagiarism activities, some of which she had learned from USU's Daren Olsen, who in turn had added on to an activity demonstrated by the late L.H. Rice of Idaho State University. We don't know if Professor Rice himself had borrowed in his turn, but the complex authorship and ownership of these pages demonstrates an important issue for teaching about plagiarism: academics, writers, and teachers at all levels borrow other peoples' words and ideas in a variety of legitimate ways. Each discipline, possibly each department, has its own not-always-well-articulated definition of what is appropriate and inappropriate sharing and borrowing. While there may be no moral or practical ambiguity about buying a paper from the Internet and turning it in as your own, much "plagiarism" is simple misunderstanding of the rules of the game and should be treated, we believe, as "ignorance" rather than "cheating."

Teachers whose students did not grow up in American school systems must constantly remind themselves that our concept of "plagiarism" is a cultural construct, and in other cultures behavior that could lead to expulsion from an American university might receive praise. We think all students getting degrees from American institutions need to learn currently accepted research writing practices, but when legitimate misunderstanding is involved, the emphasis should be on learning not punishment.

Overhead 1: A list of famous people who have been accused of plagiarism, eg. Joseph R. Biden, Jr., Merril J. Bateman, Janet Dailey, Richard

---

*   Used by permission of Daren Olsen and Charlene Hirschi.

Paul Evans, Stephen Ambrose, Doris Kearns Goodwin, Alan Dershowitz. Caption: *Who are these people, and what do they have in common?*

Overhead 2: After students have answered the first question, present the same list with each person's occupation: Biden, U.S. Senator from Delaware; Bateman, B.Y.U. President; Dailey, best-selling author of 51 books; Evans, author who has sold 8 million copies worldwide including *The Christmas Box*; Ambrose, historian; Goodwin, historian, Pulitzer Prize judge, TV talk show personality; Dershowitz, Harvard law professor. Discuss what anyone knows of their plagiarism cases and other recent high-profile cases.

Class freewrite and discussion: What is plagiarism?

Overhead 3: Definition of plagiarism. Charlene Hirschi's: "In writing, plagiarism is the intentional *or* unintentional borrowing of another person's *words, ideas,* or *structure* without giving that person proper credit."

Small group discussion: How is it possible to "steal" another person's ideas? What is the difference between an idea and its expression? Why is it important to acknowledge the source of ideas or writings that you use?

Overhead 4: The official University policy on plagiarism. *List five or more school-related activities that might be considered a form of plagiarism.*

Overhead 5: Levels of Plagiarism. Help students see the wide range of activities that might qualify as plagiarism, including different types of paraphrasing. These range from word-for-word copying to paraphrasing that uses none of the words in the original. Present examples of different reworkings of the same material, showing how as a writer uses different words and sentence structure and adds more of the writer's own ideas and voice, the passage becomes more a legitimate paraphrase, less susceptible to charges of plagiarism.

Plagiarism Practice: Give students a quotation to start with and have them write different versions of it, gradually moving away from the wording and structure of the original.

Plagiarism Identification: Give students passages from a made-up "student paper" that uses material from something the class has recently read. Each passage should be fine except for one flaw: not using necessary quotation marks or not including enough of the passage within the marks, not including the author's name or a page number in the passage, not having something in the works cited list to correspond to each in-text citation. Have students record whether they think each passage could be considered plagiarism, then discuss each one.

Charlene includes in her discussion of plagiarism a word about how she handles cases: because she cannot be objective about her own students, and because she takes student plagiarism in her class as a personal betrayal, she automatically takes plagiarism cases to the department chair. That seems like an excellent way to impress upon students both how serious and how personal plagiarism is.

Plagiarism: Levels of Paraphrasing

The Utah State University Student Code asserts that even paraphrasing another person's ideas or work can be considered plagiarism. In fact, there are many levels of paraphrasing that qualify as plagiarism—ranging from nearly word-for-word copying to heavily altered paraphrase. Here are some examples related to a famous quote by President Kennedy to help you see the different levels of plagiarism.

"My fellow Americans, ask not what your country can do for you—ask what you can do for your country."

Level 1: Outright copying word for word.

My fellow American, ask not what your country can do for you—ask what you can do for your country.

Level 2: Substituting a few words and phrases while keeping the same sentence structure.

My fellow citizens, ask not what this country can do to help you—ask what you can do to help this country.

Level 3: Substituting a few words and altering the sentence structure.

My fellow citizens, ask what you can do to help your country, instead of asking what your country can do for you.

Level 4: Light paraphrase—adding your own words and altering sentence structure so that it sounds more like you.

So, to my fellow American citizens, I would say it is important that you ask what you can do to help out this country, instead of asking what the country can do to assist you.

Level 5: Heavy paraphrase—changing almost everything you can to make it sound different, but essentially keeping the same ideas.

If, like me, you are a citizen of the United States, you shouldn't ask what this country is capable of doing for you. Instead, your duty should be to look for things you are able to do to help out this country.

Plagiarism: Paraphrasing Practice

Now see if you can take the words of someone else through all five levels of paraphrasing.

Original Phrase: "Where there is a lack of honor in government, the morals of the whole people are poisoned."   Herbert Hoover

Level 1: Outright copying word for word.

Level 2: Substituting a few words and phrases while keeping the same sentence structure.

Level 3: Substituting a few words and altering the sentence structure.

Level 4: Light paraphrase—adding your own words and altering the sentence structure so that it sounds more like you.

Level 5: Heavy paraphrase—changing almost everything you can to make it sound different, but essentially keeping the same ideas.

CITATION EXERCISE

These five short passages are from a (made-up) student paper that uses the first two pages of this document, "Teaching Academic Integrity," as a source. For the purposes of this activity, we are pretending that the document was published in the first issue of a journal called *Integrity*. Which of the following contain adequate citation information and punctuation, and which might need more?

1. According to Andersen and Dethier, not enough teachers are familiar with "academic integrity" (1). [On its Works Cited page, this paper lists: Andersen, Susan and Brock Dethier. "Teaching Academic Integrity." *Integrity* 1.1 (2004).]

2. Not a lot of students understand what academic integrity means. [no citation]

3. Andersen and Dethier suggest that "mixing sexes in unconventional ways can shake up the stereotypical view." [no citation] [On its Works Cited page, this paper lists: Andersen, Susan and Brock Dethier. "Teaching Academic Integrity." *Integrity* 1.1 (2004).]

4. Punishing students who stray outside the bounds of academic ethics does not teach students very efficiently. [no citation]

5. Ideally, a case study helps students "see the issues in a vivid, memorable way" (Andersen and Dethier 1) [On its Works Cited page, this paper lists: Andersen, Susan and Brock Dethier. "Teaching Academic Integrity." *Integrity* 1.1 (2004).]

Our Answers

1. After "Dethier," the entire sentence is taken directly from the source, so without quotation marks, it's plagiarism.

2. This could be considered "common knowledge" or just opinion and doesn't *need* any citation, but quoting from the source might give the opinion more weight.

3. Because the source is credited, this would not be considered plagiarism, but the citation is incomplete. It needs a page number.

4. Although only a word or two was taken directly from the source, this paraphrase is so close to the original in structure that most people would consider it plagiarism.

5. The entire sentence, not just the second half, should be in quotation marks.

BIBLIOGRAPHY ON ACADEMIC INTEGRITY

Bebeau, Muriel J., Kenneth D. Pimple, Karen M. T. Muskavitch, Sandra L. Borden, and David. H. Smith. *Moral Reasoning in Scientific Research: Cases for Teaching and Assessment.* Poynter Center for the Study of Ethics and American Institutions. 1995. Indiana University Bloomington. 13 January 2004 <www.indiana.edu/~poynter/mr-main.html>.

Ballenger, Bruce. *The Curious Researcher.* 4th ed. New York: Longman, 2004.

Center for Academic Integrity (CAI). *The Fundamental Values of Academic Integrity.* 1999. Duke University. 1 April 2004 <www.academicintegrity.org/pdf/FVproject.pdf>

———. "Ten Principles of Academic Integrity for Faculty." *American Association of Higher Education Bulletin.* December 1997: 12.

Cockburn, Alexander. "Alan Dershowitz, Plagiarist." *The Nation.* 13 October 2003: 9.

Committee on Science, Engineering, and Public Policy. *Responsible Science: Ensuring the Integrity of the Research Process.* National Academy of Sciences, National Academy of Engineering, Institute of Medicine. Washington D.C.: National Academy Press, 1992.

Committee on Assessing Integrity in Research Environments. (CAIRE). *Integrity in Scientific Research: Creating an Environment that Promotes Responsible Conduct.* Institute of Medicine, National Research Council. Washington, D. C.: The National Academies Press, 2002.

Cooper, Gregory, David G. Elmes, and Jeanine S. Stewart. "Issues in Teaching Ethics to Undergraduates." *Council on Undergraduate Research Quarterly.* 22.2 (2001): 55-56.

Division of Student Services. "Student code, Article VII: grievances." 2002. Utah State University. 24 July 2003 <www.usu.edu/stuserv/SCode/article7.html>.

Harris, Robert A. *The Plagiarism Handbook: Strategies for Preventing, Detecting, and Dealing with Plagiarism.* Los Angeles: Pyrczak Publishing, 2001.

Herreid, Clyde Freeman. "Case Studies in Science: A Novel Method of Science Education." 1994. University at Buffalo, State University of New York. 29 March 2004. <ublib.buffalo.edu/libraries/projects/cases/teaching/novel.html>.

Institutional Animal Care and Use Committee (IACUC). "Policies and Guidelines." 2002. Utah State University. 24 July 2003 <www.usu.edu/vpr/policies/iacuc/policies.asp>.

Institutional Review Board (IRB). "Guidelines for Research Classes." 2002. Utah State University. 23 July 2003 <www.usu.edu/vpr/policies/irb/guidelines.pdf>.

McCormick, Ginny. "Whose Idea was That?" *Stanford.* September/October 2003: 66-71.

Murray, Bridget. "Research Fraud Needn't Happen at All." *Monitor on Psychology*. February 2002: 27-28.

———. "Keeping Plagiarism at Bay in the Internet Age." *Monitor on Psychology*. February 2002: 22-24.

Newton, Janice. "Plagiarism and the challenge of essay writing: Learning from our students." 1995. York University. 1 June 2003 <www.elon.edu/sullivan/cheatpap.htm>.

Pimple, Kenneth D. *Using Case Studies in Teaching Research Ethics.* 2003. Poynter Center for the Study of Ethics. 1 June 2003 <www.poynter.indiana.edu/trecase.pdf>.

Rest, James R., Muriel J. Bebeau, and J. Volkner. "An Overview of the Psychology of Morality." *Moral Development: Advances in Research and Theory,* Ed. James R. Rest. Boston: Prager Publishers, 1986. 59-88.

Rest, James R. Foreward. *Approaches to Moral Development: New Research and Emerging Themes.* by Andrew Garrod. New York: Teachers College Press, 1993.

Taylor, Bill. "Academic Integrity: A Letter to my Students." Oakton Community College. 25 March 2004 <academicintegrity.slu.edu/letter_to_my_students.pdf>.

"Teaching with Case Studies" *Speaking of Teaching.* 5.2 (1994). *Stanford University Newsletter on Teaching.* 25 March 2004 <ctl.stanford.edu/teach/speak/stwin94.pdf>.

"Tips to Prevent Cheating." *Student Judicial Affairs.* University of California, Davis. October 1999.

Turrens, Julio F. and Elizabeth Davidson. "Data Manipulation by Undergraduates and the Risk of Future Academic Misconduct." *Council on Undergraduate Research Quarterly.* 22:2 (2001): 64-65.

REFERENCES

Abrams, M.H. 1981. *A Glossary of Literary Terms*. New York: Holt, Rinehart, Winston.

Anson, Chris M. 2002. Teaching Writing Creatively: A Summer Institute for Teachers. In Tremmel and Broz.

———— and Deanna P. Dannels. 2002. Developing Rubrics for Instruction and Evaluation. In Roen et al.

Ballenger, Bruce. 2004. *The Curious Researcher*. 4th ed. Boston: Allyn and Bacon.

————. 1990. The Importance of Writing Badly. *Christian Science Monitor*. 28 March: 18.

Belenky, Mary Field, et al. 1986. *Women's Ways of Knowing: The Development of Self, Voice, and Mind*. New York: Basic Books.

Birmingham, Elizabeth. 2000. Gender Differences in Grading Styles and TA Responses to Student Papers. In Good & Warshauer.

Bishop, Wendy and Deborah Coxwell Teague, eds. 2005. *Finding Our Way: A Writing Teacher's Sourcebook*. Boston: Houghton Mifflin.

Bleich, David. 1998. How Do the Electrons Get Across the Two Plates of the Capacitor? In McCracken and Larson.

Braddock, Richard, Richard Lloyd-Jones, Lowell Schoer. 1963. *Research in Written Composition*. Champaign: NCTE.

Breuch, Lee-Ann M. Kastman. 2002. Post-Process "Pedagogy": A Philosophical Exercise. In Villanueva.

Broz, William. 2002. Personal and Distant Mentors. In Tremmel and Broz.

Bruffee, Kenneth. 2000. Consensus Groups: A Basic Model of Classroom Collaboration. In McDonald.

Burnham, Christopher. 2001. Expressive Pedagogy: Practice/Theory, Theory/Practice. In Tate, Rupiper, and Schick.

Clark, Irene Lurkis. 1988. Preparing Future Composition Teachers in the Writing Center. *College Composition and Communication* 39: 347-50.

Collins, Billy. Introduction to Poetry. www.loc.gov/poetry/180/001.html. Accessed 11/11/04.

Corbett, Edward P.J. 2000. Mutual Friends: What Teachers Can Learn From Students and What Students Can Learn From Teachers. In McDonald.

Corbett, Edward P.J. and Robert J. Connors. 1999. *Classical Rhetoric for the Modern Student*. New York: Oxford University Press.

Corbett, Edward P.J., Nancy Myers, Gary Tate. 2000. *The Writing Teacher's Sourcebook*. 4th ed. New York: Oxford.

Council of Writing Program Administrators. 2003. "Defining and Avoiding Plagiarism: The WPA Statement of Best Practices." www.wpacouncil.org. Accessed 11/8/04.

Covino, William A. 2001. Rhetorical Pedagogy. In Tate, Rupiper, and Covino.

D'Angelo, Frank J. 1999. *Composition in the Classical Tradition*. NY: Longman.

DeGenaro, William. 2000. Challenging Ideas, Stories, and Rhetorics: Film and Politics in a Working-Class Basic Writing Classroom. In Good and Warshauer.

Dethier, Brock. 2002. Becoming a Beginner Again. *Teaching English in the Two-Year College* 29:3: 273-282.

————. 1999. *The Composition Instructor's Survival Guide*. Portsmouth: Boynton/Cook–Heinemann.

————. 2003. *From Dylan to Donne: Bridging English & Music*. Portsmouth: Boynton/Cook–Heinemann.

————. 1983. In Defense of Subjective Grading. *North Carolina English Teacher* 40:4: 3-6.

———. 2000. The Other Process Revolution. *Composition Studies* 28:1: 49-58.

Diesenhaus, Scott and Jason Leary. 2000. More Fun with Electroshock Therapy: Keeping Students Alive in English 101. In Good and Warshauer.

Duffelmeyer, Barb Blakely. 2002. New Perspectives: TA Preparation for Critical Literacy in First-Year Composition. *Composition Forum* 13.1/13.2.

Elbow, Peter. 2000. Closing My Eyes as I Speak: An Argument for Ignoring Audience. In Corbett, Myers, Tate.

———. 1986. *Embracing Contraries*. NY: Oxford.

———. 1998. Illiteracy at Oxford and Harvard: Reflections on the Inability to Write. In McCracken and Larson.

———. 1993. Ranking, Evaluating, and Liking: Sorting Out Three Forms of Judgment. In McDonald.

———. 1973. *Writing Without Teachers*. NY: Oxford.

Emig, Janet. 1971. *The Composing Processes of Twelfth Graders*. Urbana, IL: NCTE.

Farber, Jerry. 2000. "Learning How To Teach." In Corbett, Myers, Tate.

Farris, Christine. 1996. *Subject to Change: New Composition Instructors' Theory and Practice*. Cresskill, NJ: Hampton.

Farris, Christine and Chris M. Anson, eds. 1998. *Under Construction: Working at the Intersections of Composition Theory, Research, and Practice*. Logan, UT: Utah State University Press.

Flynn, Elizabeth A. 2003. Composing as a Woman. In Villanueva.

Forster, E.M. 1911. *Howard's End*. NY: G.P. Putnam's Sons.

Foster, David. 1983. *A Primer for Writing Teachers: Theories, Theorists, Issues, Problems*. Portsmouth: Boynton/Cook.

Freeland, Kate. 2002. Awakening the Writer's Identity through Conferences. In Moore and O'Neill.

Gappa, Judith M., and David W. Leslie. 1993. *The Invisible Faculty*. San Francisco: Jossey-Bass.

Gee, James Paul. 1996. *Social Linguistics and Literacies: Ideology in Discourses*. London: Falmer Press.

Gere, Anne Ruggles. 2000. Teaching Writing: The Major Theories. In McDonald.

Gilles, Roger. 2002. The Departmental Perspective. In Roen et al.

Good, Tina Lavonne and Leanne B. Warshauer. 2000. *In Our Own Voice: Graduate Students Teach Writing*. Boston: Allyn & Bacon.

Grant-Davie, Keith. Unpublished manuscript. Showing and Telling Students What We Want in a Writing Assignment. 3-4.

Harris, Joseph. 1997. *A Teaching Subject: Composition Since 1966*. Upper Saddle River, NJ: Prentice-Hall.

Harris, Muriel. 2000. Talking in the Middle: Why Writers Need Writing Tutors. In Corbett, Myers, Tate.

———. 2002. "What Would You Like to Work on Today?" The Writing Center as a Site for Teacher Training. In Pytlik and Liggett.

——— and Katherine E. Rowan. 2000. Explaining Grammatical Concepts. In McDonald.

Harris, Robert A. 2001. *The Plagiarism Handbook*. Los Angeles: Pyrczak.

Haswell, Richard H. and Min-Zhan Lu. 2000. *Comp Tales*. New York: Longman.

Hillocks, George Jr. 1999. *Ways of Thinking, Ways of Teaching*. New York: Teachers College Press.

Howard, Rebecca Moore. 2001. Collaborative Pedagogy. In Tate, Rupiper, and Schick.

Hull, Glynda and Mike Rose. 2000. Toward a Social-Cognitive Understanding of Problematic Reading and Writing. In McDonald.

Hynds, Susan. 1998. My English Education. In McCracken and Larson.

Jarratt, Susan C. 2001. Feminist Pedagogy. In Tate, Rupiper, and Schick.

Johnson, Steven. 2004. Antonio Damasio's Theory of Thinking Faster and Faster. *Discover* 25:5: 44-49.

Julier, Laura. 2001. Community-Service Pedagogy. In Tate, Rupiper, and Schick.

Kennedy, Mary. 1998. *Learning to Teach Writing: Does Teacher Education Make a Difference?* New York: Teachers College.

Kent, Thomas, ed. 1999. *Post-Process Theory: Beyond the Writing-Process Paradigm.* Carbondale, IL: Southern Illinois University Press.

Lanham, Richard. 1999. *Revising Prose.* 4th ed. New York: Longman.

McCracken, H. Thomas and Richard L. Larson with Judith Entes, eds. 1998. *Teaching College English and English Education: Reflective Stories.* Urbana: NCTE.

McDonald, James C., ed. 2000. *The Allyn and Bacon Sourcebook for College Writing Teachers.* 2nd ed. Boston: Allyn and Bacon.

McLeod, Susan H. 1997. *Notes on the Heart: Affective Issues in the Writing Classroom.* Carbondale: Southern Illinois University Press.

Meeks, Lynn Langer and Carol Jewkes Austin. 2003. *Literacy in the Secondary English Classroom.* Boston: Allyn and Bacon.

Miller, Hildy. 2002. Writing Beyond the Academy: Using Service-Learning for Professional Preparation. In Moore and O'Neill.

Milner, Joseph O'Beirne and Lucy Floyd Morcock Milner. 1999. *Bridging English.* 2nd ed. Upper Saddle River, NJ: Merrill.

Moffett, James. 1983. *Teaching the Universe of Discourse.* Portsmouth: Heinemann.

Moffett, James and Kenneth R. McElheny, eds. 1966. *Points of View: An Anthology of Stories.* NY: New American Library.

Momaday, N. Scott. 2001. *The Way to Rainy Mountain.* Albuquerque: University of New Mexico Press.

Moore, Cindy and Peggy O'Neill, eds. 2002. *Practice in Context: Situating the Work of Writing Teachers.* Urbana: NCTE.

Moran, Charles. 2001. Technology and the Teaching of Writing. In Tate, Rupiper, and Schick.

Murray, Donald M. 1982. The Listening Eye: Reflections on the Writing Conference. *Learning By Teaching.* Portsmouth: Boynton/Cook.

———. 2004. Phone interview. 16 December.

———. 1999. *Write to Learn.* 6th ed. Fort Worth: Harcourt.

Neeley, Stacia Dunn. 2000. "Only Connect . . . ": Graduate Instructors Choosing the Margin. In Good & Warshauer.

Newkirk, Thomas, ed. 1993. *Nuts and Bolts: a Practical Guide to Teaching College Composition.* Portsmouth, NH: Heinemann.

Noguchi, Rei R. 1991. *Grammar and the Teaching of Writing.* Urbana: NCTE.

Nyquist, Jody D. and Jo Sprague. 1998. Thinking Developmentally About TAs. In *The Professional Development of Graduate Teaching Assistants,* edited by Michele Marincovich, Jack Prostko, Frederic Stout. Bolton, MA: Anker Publishing.

Perry, William G., Jr. 1970. *Forms of Intellectual and Ethical Development in the College Years.* New York: Holt.

Power, Brenda Miller and Ruth Shagoury Hubbard. 1996. *Oops: What We Learn When Our Teaching Fails.* York, Maine: Stenhouse.

Pytlik, Betty P. and Sarah Liggett, eds. 2002. *Preparing College Teachers of Writing.* New York: Oxford University Press.

Ramage, John D., John C. Bean, and June Johnson. 2004. *Writing Arguments.* Concise 3rd ed. NY: Pearson.

Rankin, Elizabeth. 1994. *Seeing Yourself as a Teacher.* Urbana, IL: NCTE.

Ritchie, Joy and Kathleen Boardman. 2003. Feminism in Composition: Inclusion, Metonymy, and Disruption. In Villanueva.

Robinson, Jennifer Meta. 2000. A Question of Authority: Dealing with Disruptive Students. In Good and Warshauer.

Roen, Duane et al. 2002. *Strategies for Teaching First-Year Composition.* Urbana: NCTE.

Roseblatt, Louise M. 1996. *Literature as Exploration.* 5th ed. New York: MLA.

Rule, Rebecca. 1993. Conversations and Workshops: Conversations on Writing in Process. In Newkirk.

Schön, Donald. 1987. *Educating the Reflective Practitioner.* San Francisco: Jossey-Bass.

———. 1983. *The Reflective Practitioner: How Professionals Think in Action.* New York: Basic Books.

Shaughnessy, Mina P. 1977. *Errors and Expectations*. New York: Oxford.

Smit, David. 2002. Practice, Reflection, and Genre. In Tremmel and Broz.

Stewart, Donald C. Becoming a College English Teacher—More by Accident than Design. 1998. In McCracken and Larson.

Strong, William. 2001. *Coaching Writing: The Power of Guided Practice*. Portsmouth: Heinemann.

Stygall, Gail. 2002. Bridging Levels: Composition Theory and Practice for Preservice Teachers and TAs. In Tremmel and Broz.

Swain, Ruth Freeman. 2003. *How Sweet It Is (and Was): The History of Candy*. Holiday House: New York.

Swift, Marvin H. 1973. Clear Writing Means Clear Thinking Means . . . *Harvard Business Review* January/February.

Tchudi, Stephen. 1997. *Alternatives to Grading Student Writing*. Urbana: NCTE.

Tate, Gary, Amy Rupiper, and Kurt Schick. 2001. *A Guide to Composition Pedagogies*. New York: Oxford University Press.

Thomas, P.L. 2002. Being Honest about Writing and Individual Freedom—Or, Children, There Ain't No Rules. In Moore and O'Neill. Urbana: NCTE.

Thompson, Thomas C., ed. 2002. *Teaching Writing in High School and College*. Urbana, IL: NCTE.

Tobin, Lad. 1993. *Writing Relationships: What Really Happens in the Composition Class*. Portsmouth, NH: Heinemann.

———. 2001. Process Pedagogy. In Tate, Rupiper, and Schick.

Tompkins, Jane. 1998. Facing Yourself. In McCracken and Larson.

Tremmel, Robert and William Broz, eds. 2002. *Teaching Writing Teachers of High School English & First-Year Composition*. Portsmouth: Heinemann.

Turner, Denice. Unpublished. The Problem of Praise.

VanderStaay, Steven L. 2002. Critiquing Process: Teaching Writing Methods as Problem Solving. In Tremmel and Broz.

Villanueva, Victor, ed. 2003. *Cross-Talk in Comp Theory*. Urbana: NCTE.

———. 2002. "On Syllabi." In Roen et al.

Weaver, Constance. 1996. *Teaching Grammar in Context*. Portsmouth: Heinemann.

Wilhoit, Stephen W. 2003. *The Allyn & Bacon Teaching Assistant's Handbook*. New York: Longman.

Wilkerson, Elizabeth. 2005. First-Time Teachers. *University of Virginia Arts & Sciences* 23:1: 10-11.

Williams, Bronwyn T. 2002. *Tune In: Television & the Teaching of Writing*. Portsmouth: Boynton/Cook.

Williams, James D. 2003. *Preparing to Teach Writing: Research, Theory, and Practice*. 3rd ed. Mahwah, NJ: Lawrence Erlbaum.

Williams, Joseph. 2002. *Style—Ten Lessons in Clarity and Grace*. 7th ed. New York: Longman.

Woodard, Charles. 1985. Motivation Through Metaphor. *AWP Newsletter* 17:3: 4.

Yancey, Kathleen Blake. 1998. Theory, Practice, and the Bridge Between: The Methods Course and Reflective Rhetoric. In Farris and Anson.

Zebroski, James Thomas. 1998. Toward a Theory of Theory for Composition Studies. In Farris and Anson.

INDEX